CCCC STUDIES IN WRITING & RHETORIC

Edited by Steve Parks, University of Virginia

The aim of the CCCC Studies in Writing & Rhetoric (SWR) Series is to influence how we think about language in action and especially how writing gets taught at the college level. The methods of studies vary from the critical to historical to linguistic to ethnographic, and their authors draw on work in various fields that inform composition—including rhetoric, communication, education, discourse analysis, psychology, cultural studies, and literature. Their focuses are similarly diverse—ranging from individual writers and teachers, to work on classrooms and communities and curricula, to analyses of the social, political, and material contexts of writing and its teaching.

SWR was one of the first scholarly book series to focus on the teaching of writing. It was established in 1980 by the Conference on College Composition and Communication (CCCC) in order to promote research in the emerging field of writing studies. As our field has grown, the research sponsored by SWR has continued to articulate the commitment of CCCC to supporting the work of writing teachers as reflective practitioners and intellectuals.

We are eager to identify influential work in writing and rhetoric as it emerges. We thus ask authors to send us project proposals that clearly situate their work in the field and show how they aim to redirect our ongoing conversations about writing and its teaching. Proposals should include an overview of the project, a brief annotated table of contents, and a sample chapter. They should not exceed 10,000 words.

To submit a proposal, please register as an author at www.editorialmanager.com/nctebp. Once registered, follow the steps to submit a proposal (be sure to choose SWR Book Proposal from the drop-down list of article submission types).

Materiality and Writing Studies

Aligning Labor, Scholarship, and Teaching

Holly Hassel
North Dakota State University

Cassandra Phillips
University of Wisconsin–Milwaukee at Waukesha

Conference on College Composition and Communication

NCTE National Council of Teachers of English

National Council of Teachers of English
340 N. Neil St., Suite #104, Champaign, Illinois 61820
www.ncte.org

Tables 1.1 and 1.3 and Figure 1.3 reprinted by permission of copyright owner, the Modern Language Association of America (www.mla.org).

Staff Editor: Bonny Graham
Manuscript Editor: Leigh Scarcliff
Series Editor: Steve Parks
Interior Design: Mary Rohrer
Cover Design: Pat Mayer
Cover Image: iStock.com/Alexmia
NCTE Stock Number: 30841; eStock Number: 30858
ISBN 978-0-8141-3084-1; eISBN 978-0-8141-3085-8

Library of Congress Cataloging-in-Publication Data

Names: Hassel, Holly, author. | Phillips, Cassandra, 1971- author.
Title: Materiality and writing studies : aligning labor, scholarship, and teaching / Holly Hassel, North Dakota State University and Cassandra Phillips, University of Wisconsin Milwaukee at Waukesha.
Description: Champaign, Illinois : National Council of Teachers of English, [2022] | Series: Studies in writing & rhetoric | Includes bibliographical references and index. | Summary: "Takes an expansive look at the discipline of writing studies, arguing for centering the field's research and service on first-year writing, and offers a reimagined vision for writing studies that roots its scholarship, research, and service squarely within the changing material realities of contemporary college writing instruction"—Provided by publisher.
Identifiers: LCCN 2021047247 (print) | LCCN 2021047248 (ebook) | ISBN 9780814130841 (trade paperback) | ISBN 9780814130858 (adobe pdf)
Subjects: LCSH: English language—Rhetoric—Study and teaching (Higher)—United States. | Community college teaching—United States. | English teachers—Training of—United States. | College teachers—Training of—United States. | Academic writing—Study and teaching (Higher)—United States.
Classification: LCC PE1405.U6 H38 2022 (print) | LCC PE1405.U6 (ebook) | DDC 808/.0420711—dc23/eng/20211128
LC record available at https://lccn.loc.gov/2021047247
LC ebook record available at https://lccn.loc.gov/2021047248

CONTENTS

ACKNOWLEDGMENTS

WE WOULD LIKE TO acknowledge the many people who have contributed to the research and discussion within this book. First, to those who participated in our grant-funded study discussed in detail in Chapter 2: As we discuss throughout this book, it is no small task to completely redesign a first-year writing course at an open-access institution. These instructors participated in intensive professional development, redesigned a course, taught the course, and then prepared careful reflection and assessment of their revised courses and student work.

Second, to those who took the time to write narratives of their work at the UW Colleges that are dispersed throughout this book: these colleagues detailed important material realities of two-year-college work, and they shared their experiences dealing with the dissolution of our institution.

Finally, to all of our colleagues and peers who are doing open-access work both in Wisconsin and across the country: we learn a great deal from all of you, and we hope to continue to work together to make this environment more effective, more just, and much more visible to everyone in higher education.

1

Materiality, Labor, and Disciplinarity

English 098: Introduction to College Writing
University of Wisconsin–Waukesha
Fall 2018, the First Day

It is difficult not to be affected by the students in developmental writing[1] *from the first day. The goal of the first class is usually fairly simple—access email, student accounts, and the learning management software; write a fairly simple self-assessment; and talk about the class and its (and their) expectations. As often is the case when teaching a class such as this one, the most important goal is to have students leave the classroom thinking that they do belong in college and that it is possible to learn academic reading and writing.*

Over twenty years of working with these students doesn't diminish the humanity of their goals, the obstacles they face, and the visible emotional distress that so many of them experience. For example, even walking around the room while students are accessing their accounts and drafting an initial self-assessment reveals a wide level of disparity. After fifteen minutes of work time, one young woman has written close to a page. The rest of the students, however, are far, far short of that length, and several students cannot access their accounts, usually because of financial or clerical issues. Most eventually produce a short paragraph or two in that time, but some struggle to write more than a complete thought or sentence.

If the class goes well, students will feel comfortable raising their hands and asking for help or clarification. Because so many fight instincts to ask for help, it is important to make connections from Day 1, and to keep reminding them that they belong. Doing so is incred-

ibly difficult when they are unable to navigate their student accounts, have little to no experience with word processing, can't understand the idea of self-assessment, or struggle to draft complete thoughts in class. Some students are willing to articulate directly that they are extremely anxious about being in college, an anxiety that seems to be compounded by their furtive glances at the students who are writing freely and seem comfortable with drafting. And some will push back in different ways—a self-defense mechanism in an environment they do not trust.

Almost all of them have goals, though. When asked, they can articulate what they are hoping to do if they are successful in college: become a teacher, work for the FBI, work with computers, start a business, or fulfill a promise to someone. Hearing those goals underscores the importance of this day, and of having an understanding of the steps that must be completed to achieve these goals. For many of these students, English 098 is not the only non-degree-credit course they must take on this journey. Many of them won't pass the first time, or even the second. This journey for them is longer, has more obstacles, and is full of uncertainty. It is daunting for both the student and the instructor to think about how to achieve these goals. The needs are so broad, so encompassing, and so fraught with obstacles that it is difficult, and so very humbling, every semester, to figure out where to begin.

◈◈◈◈

We open this book with a story from one of this book's coauthors, Cassie, and her developmental writing class in order to foreground the work that animates us and that drives our research and teaching. For decades, writing studies has engaged in reflective praxis,[2] seeking to name, define, and make visible the discipline of writing studies.[3] Yet it's not often that we see students like those in Cassie's 098 class represented fully and consistently in our discipline—those who begin at our open-admissions two-year college. Whether through scholarship, research articles, learning outcomes, habits of mind, position statements, or other documents that serve as artifacts of our field, over the years we have struggled to educate our students with much of what our field has to offer. As such, we want this book to show what underrepresentation in the field's conversations looks like and feels like for two-year-college teachers and students. We want to show what it means to work in a constantly changing environment that is increasingly austere. And perhaps most important, we want to show how underrepresentation of these students and these classrooms weakens the foundation of our field through their exclusion.

Embracing the disciplinary status of writing studies as an assumption of this book, we ask the following questions: "For whom does this discipline exist? Whose interests, experiences, and values does it reflect? And what are the implications of exclusion for our most marginalized students and teachers?" We believe that asking these questions will benefit not only the students and instructors in the two-year environment, but will also benefit all instructors who teach in institutions that prioritize access over selectivity. As teachers, administrators, scholars, and members of the discipline, we argue for the value of research-based studies for a writing pedagogy and assessment that supports the important work of both access and success for students, and that provides the literacy skills required by an increasingly diverse range of students in college today. We do not see this important work sufficiently supported by our field at this moment in either the scholarship that is produced or the emphasis of graduate education. Our goal with this book is to illustrate that absence and call for the visibility, if not centering, of a changing majority of students and instructors within writing studies.

What we hope to show in this book is that the world of writing instruction in US colleges—the students, the classrooms, the instructors, the programs—is bigger, wider, and in other ways different than it is represented in research. Throughout *Materiality and Writing Studies*, we establish how writing studies has evolved such that it is centered on research-intensive institutions and tenure-line labor conditions, despite its progressive rhetoric. It is centered on students at selective universities—largely white, middle class, and traditional aged. Adapting a term from feminist scholar Audre Lorde, we call this group a "mythical norm" (116) of college students, rather than what we see as the "new majority" (Maimon) of college students. It is critical that we address that difference if we are to build sustainability between the labor, scholarship, and teaching realities of writing studies. Our foremost contention is that the new majority of students and instructors needs to be seen more clearly and described more richly within the research of our field.

We begin by demonstrating how the students at two-year colleges are reflective of an increasing majority of college students, and how because of that representativeness there is an unrecognized level of expertise about teaching and learning that two-year-college faculty have to offer in meeting their needs. Yet that knowledge has not been integrated into the discipline's knowledge base (see Toth et al. for examples). Invoking the importance of such experiences, we then suggest strategies for writing studies scholarship, teacher training, and organizational work that can move forward with an ethical, responsive agenda supporting a greater and more heterogeneous range of students' literacy development and retention in college. In doing so, we also argue for a commitment not just to students, but to more effective preparation for the work of teacher-scholar-activists (a term Patrick Sullivan has coined) to effect change around working conditions. In other words, we propose a set of priorities that build from the needs of diverse first-year writing students to priorities that are a foundation for professionalizing all instructors.

The fundamental basis for this book is a concern for how contingency as well as material realities facing instructors shape pedagogies and classrooms. As we will show, these material conditions in two-year colleges and open-access institutions shape the learning environments of students whose relationship to college is fragile and often not the highest priority in their lives. Likewise, we emphasize throughout the book the material conditions of this learning that takes place with teachers who work in precarity. We see it as a moral mandate to serve the most at-risk or structurally disadvantaged students in the country, and just as important we also see improving labor conditions as a prerequisite for a sustainable path forward for the field. Through the chapters that follow, we argue that the discipline must not only account for these students and these instructors to advance disciplinary knowledge, but must also move to center the core work of first-year writing and open-admissions institutions.

FOUNDATIONS TO REFLECT A NEW MAJORITY OF STUDENTS

We write this book based on our experiences as two-year-college English teachers who are always searching for effective, evidence-based resources to help us in our professional contexts. We are two PhD-credentialed tenured faculty who have taught for almost thirty-five years between us in two-year colleges, which inexorably affects how we view disciplinarity. Holly taught courses ranging from non-degree-credit writing to transfer-level composition for three years as an adjunct at a community college while she was working toward her PhD and for sixteen years at the University of Wisconsin Colleges (UWC), a two-year junior college. Her thinking draws deeply from her experiences as a working-class, first-generation college student and academic. Cassie did her dissertation research at a community college and then taught as an adjunct before teaching at UWC for the last twenty-plus years as a tenure-line faculty member.

We also write from a more recent position of change. We worked together for sixteen years for UWC, which was an open-access junior college with thirteen brick-and-mortar campuses and a robust online program that functioned as a single unified institution since it was first chartered by the state of Wisconsin in 1971. As a single institution, UWC had its own mission of transfer and access, statewide curriculum, faculty personnel processes, and assessment program. We saw as our focus the need to create a rigorous transfer-level curriculum that would allow students to seamlessly move to the four-year institution of their choice, or to complete a high-quality liberal arts associate's degree. Though the structure that had been established for UWC since its inception was unusual, it offered some important benefits. For example, the small sizes of our individual campuses and our locations in even the most remote corners of the state meant that a transfer-level curriculum with well-qualified instructors was accessible to many nontraditional place-committed students who would not have had the will or resources to move away for college. Our tuition and fees were also much more affordable than the residential four-year institutions. The low cost allowed students to save money by living at home. Our nontraditional student populations (who were about 25 percent to 35 percent of the student body, depending on the campus) could work in established jobs and meet their family responsibilities.

For us, then, the two-year campuses truly embodied one of the core principles of the University of Wisconsin System—the Wisconsin Idea. The Wisconsin Idea is a concept that originates from a 1905 address by former UW President Charles Van Hise, who asserted, "I shall never be content until the beneficent influence of the University reaches every family of the state" ("Wisconsin Idea"). Located in both small and large communities throughout the state, our campuses had a unique mission of access and relentlessly sought ways to distinguish our programs and classrooms. These efforts resulted in two disciplinary program awards, a Diana Hacker TYCA Award for Outstanding Programs in English for Two-Year Colleges and Teachers (2015), and a Conference on College Composition and Communication Writing Program Certificate of Excellence (2016–2017). On October 11, 2017, however, a Wisconsin newspaper leaked a story that the institution would be dissolved, and its campuses reassigned as small branch campuses—or perhaps "additional locations"[4] of nearby comprehensive campuses in the University of Wisconsin System. With the announcement of our department and institution's dissolution over the 2017–2018 year, our mission was essentially wiped out, in part because most of the four-year campuses do not invest in the mission of access in the same, mission-focused way as we did in our autonomous structure. As a result, both of us now find ourselves, differently, working in or with university contexts that have heightened our understanding of the distinct cultures of two-year- and four-year-college writing programs. We began the work on the project described in this text while we were both tenured and full-time faculty members at an autonomous two-year college; but the book has evolved in emphasis as we have each moved into different relationships with university writing programs (which we share throughout the book).

We provide this background for readers in order to contextualize how our thinking—and our literal jobs—have been shaped by both the long history of the mission of access to our campuses, as well as the subsequent abandonment of that mission by the state. We take for granted as teacher-scholars that access to education is good—it is meaningful, desirable, and central to the work of college writing instruction, particularly in two-year colleges. Though college writing courses can and historically have functioned as gatekeepers, we also know from our students how important those courses are as pathways to college because of their role in developing the critical literacy skills valued in postsecondary education. The dissolution of UWC was a threat to that mission but it also provides an object lesson to readers who also value access and critical literacy for more rather than fewer students.

Following the announcement of the institution's dissolution in 2017, our colleagues and students prepared as best as they could for the dismantling of their existing governance structures, course catalog and bulletin, transfer articulation agreements, and other institutional practices and documents (and yes, our entire award-winning writing program). We all prepared to be absorbed by what were called "receiving institutions" and sometimes "parent campuses" (or even worse, "host" campuses). This meant that all department curricular, placement, faculty evaluation, and equity work would disappear as our department was absorbed into the practices and processes of the main campus (or even eliminated, with the main campus practices to replace them).

Currently, the new arrangement purports to preserve the ability of students to start at a branch campus and move to any UW campus; however, as at most four-year campuses, transfer "out" is seen not as a success because students are pursuing their educational goals, but as an institutional loss since these campuses are losing the income from full-time student tuition and the efforts of recruitment and enrollment. UWC's original mission, like that of most two-year campuses that focus on granting certificates and associate degrees, was explicitly transfer—we always expected to prepare students to leave and go somewhere else. Our primary role was to prepare them to do so. Access, transfer, and skill-building—getting students ready to go wherever they want to go—were part of the architecture of the writing program (as in many two-year-college writing programs)—and, we think, offer a window into what the discipline of a writing studies centered on access could be. We argue that the ease with which our programs, structures, and policies were discarded in favor of those of many of the four-year host institutions is not unlike the way that writing studies scholarship overvalues the experiences of a specific echelon of students and faculty while devaluing the expertise built from years of curriculum, instruction, and assessment work in first-year composition studies. That access and transfer mission—central to the Wisconsin Idea that has governed the state's system of higher education for over a century—is now diminished.

To illustrate the specifics of this change, we include throughout the chapters the voices of our institutional colleagues reflecting on what the changes have meant, like those of Lisa Schreibersdorf, tenured faculty at what was the UW–Fond du Lac campus, and now part of University of Wisconsin–Oshkosh. We purposefully integrate these voices with those of other scholars in our field, emphasizing the recentering we champion through this book.

Lisa Schreibersdorf, UWC–Fond du Lac:
Some of the most fundamental differences relate to the access and transfer parts of our campus's mission. I've been involved in a number of conversations that took a long time to get to the moment where it clicked that we were starting from different assumptions. For example, we assume that our students will be transferring, so our system of transfer agreements, our advising processes, and the information we make available to students when they register are set up to help them see how individual courses will transfer to other institutions for future majors; we think of credit transfers proactively, while a four-year college will think of this reactively (how an advisor can help an individual student who has decided to transfer and has already taken the classes they hope to transfer). We also see being an open-access campus, without the requirement of high test scores and grades for admission, is a point of pride for our faculty and staff, not an embarrassment.

Perhaps fortuitously (even though it was incredibly difficult as an experience), the story of UWC can serve as an important reminder about the positionality of two-year-college teacher-scholar-activism in the matrix of writing studies scholarship. It can also serve as a frame for our larger arguments about writing studies, scholarship, and materiality in part because the labor of two-year-college contexts is becoming increasingly relevant to the larger higher education conversations, especially with their values of access and equity. Whether it is online and asynchronous learning, hybrid courses, flipped classrooms, distance/remote instruction, dual credit and concurrent enrollment partnerships, or success and retention interventions, two-year-college campuses have pioneered this work. Open-admissions policies mean that instruction has to be as available and flexible as possible. Instructors in these environments should become a knowledge source that is essential as we navigate the pandemic, an unanticipated event that has forced all colleges to develop accessible and flexible instruction. Likewise, if the hypothesis that more students will stay closer to home (perhaps starting at community and technical colleges nearby rather than moving to residential campuses), more campuses than ever will need to think about transfer (including reverse transfer, as students who began at their campus potentially return home—and then back again—with accumulated credits). Put another way, the knowledge about how college can look is uniquely available at two-year colleges, if only the larger academic community will ask for it.

From this context, we do not claim to speak for all two-year-college faculty (whether at a technical college, traditional community college, or junior college; whether adjunct, tenure-line, or full-time non-tenure-track). We do, however, draw from a rich foundation of decades of teaching in the two-year environment, working with hundreds of instructors both tenure-line and contingent, teaching thousands of students over that time period, and conducting research in the process. We also draw from the work we did in department, campus, and institutional governance bodies: senates; evaluation committees for faculty promotion, tenure, and retention; assessment; and curriculum. All of this work is generally less visible than teaching and research but equally important in terms of creating writing programs that work for teachers and students. We want to tell the story of teachers, scholars, and activists within this lens of political threats to our discipline's integrity. In this way, the fate of UWC can serve as a parable for broader threats to what might be our "new discipline."

We hope to make clear the voices we believe are missing from writing studies scholarship. By integrating the experiences of instructors and students like those of Lisa above and Rachel below, we aim to help them be seen (and heard) in a text like this—not just as statistics or as silent members of a large academic population, but as people who can provide firsthand knowledge of the material conditions of teaching and learning in the two-year environment. These stories told by instructors and students will underscore how the field does and does not account for their working and learning conditions.

Rachel Barger, UWC–Washington County:
As instructional academic staff, my position has always been provisional. I've essentially remained an adjunct on a semester-to-semester contract for my fourteen years for [UWC], and I had never really felt any security. But on that day [of the announcement of the dissolution], I struggled to feel anything but apprehensive. Because I'm human, I initially reacted with thoughts of how will I support my family, and should I start looking for another job? My initial selfish response was quickly replaced by my fear of what would happen to our students and community. All I could think about was the UW Colleges Mission that attracted me to my position. . . .

We questioned how joining with the University of Wisconsin–Milwaukee would affect our institutional goals. As an open-access institution located in a small community north of Milwaukee, we attract a wide variety of students with diverse backgrounds, educations, and preparation levels. Access and affordability are significant to our student population. While there is some overlap in who is attracted to both institutions, many of

> the students enrolled in our university come underprepared for college-level work. Through our strong developmental education background, we have consistently been able to meaningfully support their specific needs in ways four-year institutions hadn't needed to. And, because we give it to them at a reasonable cost, they can justify the initial risk. They get a University of Wisconsin education and a new beginning no matter where they came from or what their end goal is. Since we give opportunities to students who wouldn't otherwise have an option to go to a four-year institution, we worried about how they would survive the restructuring and how it would affect future students like them.

One way to illustrate the working environment of two-year-college faculty like Rachel is to look at the material conditions of the new majority of students, which significantly influence the two-year-college classroom. The "new discipline" of writing studies exists in part because, as Elaine Maimon notes, this new majority of students—students of color, first-generation students, and low-income students—increasingly make up our student populations, with BIPOC students significantly more likely to start their educations in two-year colleges. As College Board research shows: "44 percent of Black and 56 percent of Latinx students were in the public two-year sector in 2014, compared with 29 percent from these groups in the public four-year sector" (Ma and Baum 5). Data from the Lumina Foundation show that students are increasingly nontraditional in terms of age, are the first in their families to go to college, are financially independent, and are working significant hours while in college. Or, to be more precise:

- Thirty-seven percent of college students are twenty-five or older, and 46 percent are first-generation college-goers.
- Sixty-four percent of college students work, and 40 percent of them work full-time.
- Forty-nine percent of college students are financially independent from their parents.
- Six percent of college students serve or have served in the US armed forces.

- Twenty-four percent of college students have children or other dependents. Fifty-seven percent of students live independently—away from their parents or campus housing.
- Thirty-one percent of college students come from families at or below the Federal Poverty Guideline. The majority of college students (53 percent) come from families at or below twice the poverty level.

Data from Pew Research also demonstrate that

- In 2016, 20 percent of dependent college students were in poverty, up from 12 percent in 1996. At two-year colleges, that number has doubled from 13 percent to 27 percent between 1996 and 2016; and
- 42 percent of independent college students were in poverty in 2016, compared with 29 percent twenty years earlier.

And here UWC's story—along with the material realities of two-year colleges nationally—becomes relevant, because the discipline of writing studies should be one that responds to the needs of the students we commit to educate, and those students increasingly resemble the students that have always sought out two-year colleges as their postsecondary option. The majority of students do not experience college as a place they "go away" to, nor is it the only thing they do or even the biggest priority in their lives. These "new students" are really the "traditional students" of community-college and open-access institutions. The knowledge of writing studies should be as influenced by the diversity in our students as our students are by the knowledge of writing studies. If we are to meet the needs of our discipline's classrooms, then we need to learn from the work of teachers like those at UWC. We need to learn how to support such programs in the face of the austerity-driven restructuring of our classrooms. We require rigorous research to meet this moment, and that research has already begun in community colleges.

The existence of this research and praxis is what brings us back to the foundational role of first-year writing all across higher education. The most significant location for this kind of interactional knowledge and practice work is not just two-year colleges, but first-year writing courses, a curriculum that is a vexed, contested, and yet essential part of the field. It is also a part of the field that is underrepresented in important ways in our discipline's bodies of knowledge, even though teachers and students at two-year colleges have been doing relevant disciplinary work for decades. In this way, we build on and affirm the work of Carolyn Calhoon-Dillahunt and Chuck Bazerman, who have called for the centering of writing studies on first-year writing and writing classrooms. As Bazerman noted in his 2010 CCCC chair's address, "First-year writing remains the largest part of our work and our main site of engagement with most students. Through the efforts of our classrooms, almost every college-educated adult has come to understand more about writing" (578). Eight years later, Calhoon-Dillahunt echoed this call, citing the tagline of the show *Heroes*: "Save First-Year Comp, Save the Discipline." As an interview with Calhoon-Dillahunt in the *Council Chronicle* documents (and as we demonstrate later in this chapter), "the majority of English PhDs will likely end up teaching composition and writing in some form, either in graduate school or when they seek teaching jobs" (Ryan 28). In the context of this reality, to integrate the knowledge production in writing studies with the focus of the work people do—and in the actual places they do it—is to create the center, the core, that offers an avenue into the public discourse around writing. Yet such discourse is increasingly legislated and mandated by external stakeholders (see Adler-Kassner's CCCC chair's address, 2017). FYW instructors—whether two-year-college faculty, graduate teaching assistants, or contingent and lecturer faculty—should be acknowledged as the field's center, not its margins, particularly as they provide the foundation upon which graduate program faculty maintain their own positions with low teaching loads and hyperspecialized course assignments. The power of first-year writing instruction, either to uplift or to obstruct students, should be rooted in the experiences of students and teachers. Instead, writing programs and writing studies knowledge is often disconnected from those experiences, and (especially at research-intensive institutions with graduate programs) prioritizes staffing practices, opportunities for graduate students, and theorizing knowledge that is often imposed from above rather than emerging from the daily realities of college writing classrooms in diverse settings. We ignore this disconnect at our peril.

RECENTERING TEACHING RESEARCH TO REFLECT CURRENT LABOR CONDITIONS

Two-year-college students as a group are different from the traditional vision of an undergraduate. Faculty and instructors in two-year colleges, as well, work in significantly different conditions from those whose workload includes research and publication as an assigned component of their contracts. In addition, faculty with research expectations who research and write for the purposes of tenure might produce writing studies scholarship that represents first-year writing as a singular, and universally understood, entity—a single course or degree requirement that students fulfill in their predicted road to a major, degree, and career or graduate school. In reality, first-year writing is a complex constellation of placement processes and multiple distinct courses in reading, writing, and learning skills, and it is governed by a diverse array of department, institutional, and state expectations. Each of these features is influenced by and responds to student populations and the local academic ecology. Within this more complex understanding of what first-year writing is and does, there is an accompanying need for disciplinary scholarship that reflects the labor realities of faculty holding both contingent and full-time positions at teaching-intensive institutions (which we define as teaching twelve contact hours or more during a term—typically but not always four courses) who navigate such terrains. This is a labor reality that the majority—and increasing proportion—of those earning graduate degrees in English will occupy.

To illustrate, according to the MLA's Office of Research, "In 2016–17, the decline in the number of jobs advertised in the MLA Job Information List (JIL) continued for a fifth consecutive year. The JIL's English edition announced 851 jobs, 102 (10.7 percent) less than in 2015–16." They further report that "[t]he declines of the past five years bring the number of advertised jobs to yet another new low, below the level reached after the severe drop between 2007–08 and 2009–10. The 851 jobs in the English edition for 2016–17 are 249 (22.6 percent) below the 1,100 advertised in 2009–10, the previous low point" (1). Illustrating data (see Table 1.1) breaks these numbers down further into tenure-track positions advertised in subfields of English, which include composition and rhetoric, technical and business writing, and creative writing and journalism, put alongside literature. What the MLA data show is a fairly steady decrease in tenure-line positions across all subfields, with a slight bounce back in 2017–2018 for composition and rhetoric. The 2020 pandemic—with its upending of teaching, staffing, hiring, and budgets—is likely to have a significant negative impact on hiring of new faculty in the coming years.

Further, these figures need to be placed in the context of the number of PhDs earned in the larger field of English studies (see Table 1.2.). For the 1,232 instructors receiving terminal degrees in literature fields, creative writing, or language in 2018 or the 1,358 in 2017, a number not aligned with the available 539 tenure-track jobs advertised in that year, employment will probably mean lecturer and adjunct positions, nearly all of which will have responsibility for the teaching of college composition. Such employment will also likely be in a two-year college (TYC), teaching courses almost exclusively in the lower division. And, as Christie Toth and Patrick Sullivan note, about 25 percent of community college liberal arts faculty nationally hold doctoral degrees (253).

For quite some time, the common wisdom of the field of English has been that though literature PhDs and the accompanying job market for them has contracted to the point of unsustainability, a doctorate in writing studies would be a smart investment on the part of a graduate student seeking secure employment. The data in Table 1.2 should give us pause regarding that common wisdom. Instead, these numbers demonstrate that more and more instructors with degrees in all subfields of English, even in rhetoric and composition, can expect to work off the tenure track in less secure or part-time positions. Though an increasing amount of attention

Table 1.1. Data Drawn from MLA Office of Research Report on Advertised Tenure-Line Positions in Subfields of English

	Writing (Composition and Rhetoric)	Technical and Business Writing	Creative Writing and Journalism	Literature (all)	Total
2017–2018	112	38	65	324	539
2016–2017	94	45	80	354	573
2015–2016	135	58	91	316	600
2014–2015	161	57	96	367	681
2013–2014	164	47	79	369	659

Table 1.2. Data Drawn from National Science Foundation Data on Earned Doctorates in Letters, Historical (*Doctorate Recipients; Survey*)

	2008	2009	2010	2011	2012	2013	2014	2015	2016	2017	2018
American literature, United States and Canada	338	327	361	367	409	397	349	334	342	311	273
Comparative literature	166	179	197	192	201	218	196	165	172	166	172
Creative writing	73	76	81	84	93	79	87	97	79	84	Not listed
English language	156	104	146	179	154	92	147	153	127	159	121
English literature, British and Common-wealth	397	388	419	354	423	399	396	412	414	369	383
Rhetoric and composition	NA	NA	NA	NA	154	220	207	238	211	227	241
Speech and rhetorical studies	126	138	152	165	53	33	29	42	39	42	42
Total	1256	1212	1356	1341	1487	1438	1411	1441	1384	1358	1232

has been paid to preparing graduate students for "alt-ac" positions, and some efforts have been made to prepare students for a wider range of types of academic positions, it still seems that most doctoral programs are preparing students for a career in the academy. A 2020 *Chronicle of Higher Education* article by Leonard Cassuto and Robert A. Weisbuch makes the numbers clear, imagining the prospects of an entering class of eight graduate students in English:

> Now let's flash-forward in time. According to recent statistics, four of the eight (50 percent!) will not complete the PhD—and those are pre–Covid-19 numbers. Of the four who do finish, two will not get academic positions and will seek jobs elsewhere. The remaining pair will get full-time faculty jobs, most likely at teaching-intensive institutions. Perhaps they'll get tenure-track assistant professorships, though the chances for those positions have been shrinking. And maybe one of the two will get a tenure-track position at a research university like the one where those eight students assembled years earlier.

The solution that these authors advance is to call for "a PhD that looks outside the walls of the university, not one that turns inward," a solution we couldn't disagree more with. There is important work to do within the academy, but only if we reconceptualize what it means to work in the academy. This involves deeply investing our time and energy into preparing graduate students to be teaching-focused faculty with as much as if not more commitment than we do research faculty. Teaching-intensive positions at less-selective four-year, regional comprehensive, and especially community and technical colleges offer a rewarding and intellectually enriching professional life, and there are critical needs in such institutions for committed teacher-scholar-activists (to use Sullivan's and Darin Jensen's term). However, potential faculty preparing for the academic life of teaching-intensive schools need a different kind of graduate school experience than the ones we currently have.[5]

Those PhD recipients who make the transition to a TYC context will find a wide range of position responsibilities and types, but they can be certain that the working conditions will be markedly different from those of their senior faculty at their graduate institutions as well as from their own experiences as graduate teaching assistants. TYC institutions are diverse. They can be technical colleges that have some general education or university offerings but largely serve an applied degree program; they can be community colleges that typically have both vocational and general education/transfer curricula; or they can be junior colleges (such as UWC) that offer only a transfer-parallel liberal arts curriculum. But they do share some consistent features, as recently reported by the TYCA Workload Task Force's report, "The Profession of Teaching English in the Two-Year College: Findings from the 2019 TYCA Workload Survey." Survey data from over a thousand two-year-college faculty showed the following:

- Fifty-six percent worked off the tenure track (though of those, 20 percent had a stable position with a renewable annual contract, and another 14 percent had a permanent or multiyear contract).
- The most common teaching load identified was 28 to 35 credit hours per year (or an average of 14–17 credits, for example, on a semester schedule), though course assignments in two-year colleges can include 4-, 5-, and 6-credit corequisite courses that do not directly translate to a traditional 3-credit course structure in university settings.
- Overload teaching is common, with instructors taking on additional courses for additional compensation (more than a third of respondents do so always or regularly).
- Seventy percent of respondents spent at least one and up to six hours a week on service activities, with most identifying institutional and departmental service as the most frequent type of service performed.
- Respondents identified multiple types of disciplinary service they engage in on campus and beyond, including curriculum development (14 percent), assessment (11 percent), faculty training (10 percent) and writing program (9 percent) and developmental education program work (9 percent).

- Seventy-three percent of two-year-college faculty respondents also engage in disciplinary service, including serving as peer reviewers for conferences or journals, serving on committees or in leadership roles for professional organizations, and serving as editors or on editorial boards.
- Nearly all respondents identified participation in professional development activities—with 89 percent engaging weekly in some form of professional development. An important feature of two-year-college professional development is that PD work is not aimed toward research and writing—just 10 percent of respondents identified scholarly publication as their professional development goal. More common ongoing professional development in these contexts includes attending or presenting at conferences, participating in and facilitating training on nondisciplinary teaching topics, and facilitating disciplinary training for colleagues, among other activities.

By emphasizing research and publication over teaching (and emphasizing scholarly publication as the premier form of professional achievement), we are as a field, then, doing the opposite of what is necessary if we acknowledge that two-year colleges are an enormous, important sector of higher education employment. David Laurence's *Demography of the Faculty: A Statistical Portrait of English and Modern Languages*[6] shows that the total number of faculty members whose teaching field is postsecondary English numbers 82,400, 47.9 percent of whom teach in Carnegie associates institutions. Most striking for our purposes here, though, is his assertion that "[d]espite the extraordinarily high percentage of faculty members teaching off the tenure track in two-year colleges, the 8,704 English faculty members holding tenured and tenure-track positions in two-year colleges outnumber the tenured and tenure-track English faculty in every other sector" (2). In other words, and as we discuss throughout this book, two-year-college English teaching is an enormous site of employment for those who earn graduate credentials in the field of English (both MAs and PhDs)—one that has a crucial and distinct mission that is consistently undervalued in the academic hierarchy and prestige economy of the academy. It is undervalued even though the type of work performed by two-year-college faculty is similar in some key respects to the work that takes place in universities—with a greater proportion of it happening in the classroom.[7] We discuss the relationship between the employment conditions of two-year-college teachers and its relationship to the classroom in more depth in Chapter 3.

When thinking about how English and writing studies graduate programs prepare their graduates for work beyond the MA or PhD, these numbers must also be framed within an overall shift in employment stability and structures within higher education. And as we discuss in more detail later, the curricula of such programs are minimally aligned with the kinds of work those students will ultimately do in most teaching contexts. But it is not just a diminishing number of tenure-track positions and/or an overproduction of doctorates that is causing this labor situation. It is also the casualization of academic labor that frames the data above, a phenomenon that is particularly urgent for college composition because of the "universal requirement" of first-year writing to employ a large corps of instructors to offer sufficient sections to accommodate enrollment, while simultaneously maintaining the flexibility to cut sections (and teachers) when enrollments do not go as planned. As Marc Bousquet observed in 2003, "Since the restoration of tenure-stream lines is rarely a department-level prerogative, a department with the power to reduce graduate-student admissions will generally be driven to substitute other casual appointments (postdocs, term lectureships, single course piece workers)" (209). These are the new majority of teaching appointments that graduates from English departments will enter, whether they are earning master's degrees or doctorates, and they will need both to understand the workload expectations and the students at open-access institutions, if they choose to make a career in the academy.

Too much has changed in the last thirty years to assume that PhD overproduction is the appropriate access point for conversations about labor in our field. The casualization of labor will not be reversed anytime in the future, which is a separate but related issue in any conversation about labor realities in teaching college writing. As reported in a 2011 *Chronicle of Higher Education* article, “According to the Department of Education, in 1975, 57 percent of university faculty members were tenured or on the tenure track. By 2007 that number had dropped to 31 percent” (Ennis). A report from the AAUP confirms that “[t]he majority (70 percent) of academic positions today are not only off the tenure track but also part time, with part-time instructional staff positions making up nearly 41 percent of the academic labor force and graduate teaching assistants making up almost another 13 percent (part-time tenure-track positions make up about 1 percent of the academic labor force)” (Shulman et al. 13). Laurence’s MLA report “Demand for New Faculty Members, 1995–2016” provides a visual representation of this shift (see Figure 1.1). What this figure illustrates is that the work many graduate students are training for (or that they expect constitutes the “academic life”) will not exist when they complete their degrees. The investment of years of labor, energy, and opportunity cost will not pay off for many of them, at least not in the ways they were trained to expect.

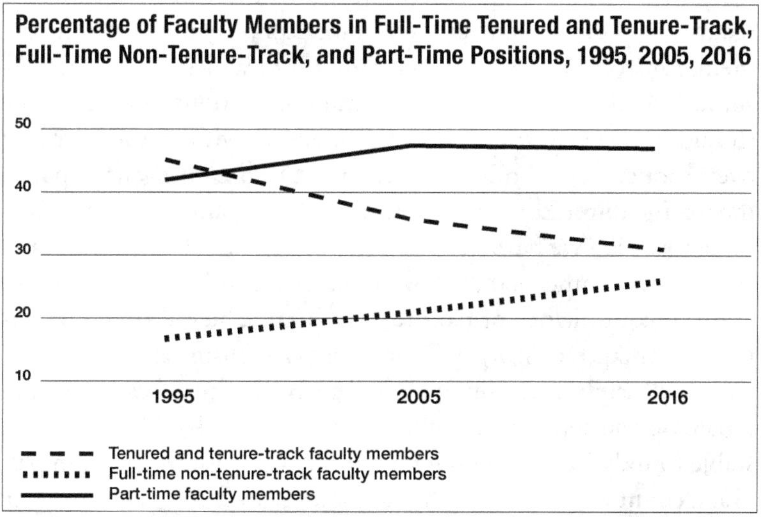

Figure 1.1. Percentage of faculty members in full-time tenured and tenure-track, full-time non-tenure-track, and part-time positions, 1995, 2005, 2016.

Efforts to change the culture of graduate programs are shown in recent professional documents like *CCCC Statement of Professional Guidance for Mentoring Graduate Students*, which offers important recommendations like "Graduate students should be encouraged and validated for career aspirations, choices, and outcomes beyond (ever fewer) conventional academic tenure-track positions," and "Graduate students and mentors should learn about the state of the academic job markets, including the casualization (i.e., the current climate of nontenure track and contingent labor) of the academic workforce."[8] Directly addressing how mentoring and program culture influence the ways that future faculty understand their professional responsibilities is one important component of the shift to this new discipline.

However, we also want to place this disciplinary conversation within the larger framework of labor activism and ideological-economic shifts in higher education that have as much of an influence on how the academic discipline of writing studies can move forward in attending to an integrated vision of labor, teaching, and scholarship. This means acknowledging that even if graduate students succeed at finding such employment, they cannot assume the security of previous generations of professors. Tenure as an employment construct has been under constant assault such that any assumptions about the stability of tenure protections into the future should be challenged (see Gardner). Along with the narrative of overproduction of PhDs and the increase in contingent appointments, the diminishment of tenure has contributed to a new discipline to which we have not adjusted. Efforts to rebuild board- and state-level documents that allow for faculty layoff in the case of program discontinuance or closure have been achieved or are underway in Arkansas, Georgia, Tennessee, Wisconsin, and Wyoming. This increasing instability within academic culture has been exacerbated by austerity measures that have substantially decreased the stable foundation of funding that public institutions could, in past years, count on to offset such fluctuations, with the result being an increasing dependence on tuition revenue to manage budgets.[9]

The cumulative effect on the ability of writing programs to ensure quality instruction, assessment, and administrative coherence is potentially devastating. Sarah Snyder notes in "Preparing to Become a Two-Year College Writing Program Administrator" that formal WPA positions in two-year colleges are rare—noting that the National Census of Writing cites just 11 percent of two-year colleges having formal WPA positions (in contrast to 51 percent of four-year programs) (107). The importance of faculty who are trained in administrative and program issues, especially specific to open-admissions and -access institutions and changing educational structures, is even more evident. Non-tenure-track (NTT) faculty are often discouraged from institutional engagement, in particular from participating in the work that is required to maintain shared governance: curricular maintenance; development of new programs; support and mentoring of new instructors, along with major and minor undergraduate students; and assessment of student learning. These are all expectations for tenure-line faculty but not a usual component of the workload of instructors working off the tenure track, meaning that the glue that holds our collective work together is weakening.

Within this context, consider data just about writing program staffing. Two sources over the last decade have attempted to track the percentage of staffing types in English departments and writing programs, the 2009 report from the CCCC Squire Office of Policy Research (Gere) and a 2014 MLA report on a staffing survey (*Data*). Table 1.3 provides a comparison across institutional types and data sources of the percentage of first-year writing courses in the surveyed departments that were taught by which types of instructors. These data demonstrate how differently configured writing programs are in terms of instructor employment status, and gesture toward why there are gaps between the ways we prepare students to become writing instructors in college (and members of a campus or program) and how the work actually looks. In institutions with PhD programs, first-year writing is essentially the province of novices—graduate teaching assistants (GTAs) whose first introduction to teaching will be the first-year writing courses that are the entry point into academic literacy development for new college students. Very few first-year writing courses are taught by tenure-line faculty in those departments that offer graduate degrees (13.4 percent and

17.6 percent, in PhD- and MA-granting campuses, respectively). The majority of the rest of the instruction is handled by part-time and full-time non-tenure-line instructors.

Put another way, first-year students at such campuses are highly likely to take a writing course with someone for whom the teaching of writing is a part-time job or an apprenticeship (63 percent of teaching staff are GTAs and part-time faculty). By contrast, 61 percent of first-year writing courses at two-year campuses are taught by full-time instructors—teachers for whom helping new college students make the transition to college literacies is their full-time work, which leads us to the question of what, exactly, professional identity in college writing programs looks like. We next want to explore the relationships between professional identity, labor, and the experience of first-year writing students alongside one another, so that we can make clear what the work of writing faculty in higher education actually does look like, and what it could look like.

Table 1.3. Percentage of Writing Program Instructors Whose Status Is Best Described by Each Employment Category

Percentage of writing program instructors whose status is best described by each of the following categories	CCCC Squire Report (2009, results not disaggregated by institution type)[10]	MLA Staffing Survey (2014, PhD-Granting Institutions)	MLA Staffing Survey (2014, MA-Granting Institutions)	MLA Staffing Survey (2014, Two-Year Colleges)
Tenure-line faculty (tenured or tenure-track)	20.93% tenured and 11.72% tenure-line (total of ~32%)	13.4%	17.6%	37%
Full-time non-tenured faculty	28.6%	23.5%	29.9%	24%
Full-time staff	7.3%	NA	NA	NA
Part-time faculty	39.44%	24.2%	37.5%	38.9%
Other (graduate teaching assistants)	33.61%	38.8%	15%	NA

MEETING THE RESEARCH NEEDS OF THE TEACHING MAJORITY

Within this higher education market labor context, we ask: What does it mean, exactly, to be a professional in the field of writing studies? A good deal of professional literature has also asked this question (for example Wardle and Scott; Larson; Del Principe). We ask it here with the purpose of advancing our queries about the relationships between labor conditions, writing studies emphases, and the needs of students—as well as how that professional identity is or is not served by the professional resources that are available. We also consider the role of the master's credential in teaching, research, and graduate education, particularly related to writing programs and curriculum.

For two-year-college tenure-line faculty who likely have primary training and backgrounds in literature, creative writing, or other related fields, and for most contingent faculty at nearly all institutional types, a different type of scholarship and research is necessary to support their work. Most teach primarily in the lower division, without the protections of tenure, with a new majority of college students. These are instructors who could benefit from, and who are looking for, research that reflects the material realities of their work. These are instructors who, along with their students, are ill-served by the gaps we describe above.

Valerie Murrenus Pilmaier, UWC Sheboygan:
I am so proud to have been a part of [UWC]. While I was offered jobs at four-year institutions, I chose to work [at UWC] because, as a first-generation student myself, I believe in the mission of access. I have witnessed, countless times, that moment of transformation when a student realizes that he/she/they do belong in college and their entire sense of self shifts. I have had the privilege to work alongside the most brilliant, dedicated instructors, all of whom are experts in their fields and believe as passionately in the mission of access as I do. I have watched our staff work twelve- to sixteen-hour days without complaint to ensure that all of the student events go off smoothly, and I have seen our

deans provide their own personal funds to pay for activities for the staff and students. If only our dedication alone could have kept it afloat. In the end, I know that we changed lives and made a difference, but I'm left with the realization of the colossal loss for our students, for our colleagues, and for our state.

Many two-year-college instructors have graduate preparation at the master's or doctoral level focused nearly exclusively on literature and creative writing. As a result, their primary research and creative work, for those whose institutions reward such efforts, falls in those related areas that are significant to their professional identities within English studies, even though writing courses make up most of their teaching responsibilities. As we have sought to differentiate writing studies as its own subfield, it's possible that more than ever before instructors who have responsibilities for teaching writing courses as well as other areas of English are discouraged from seeing relationships between those areas of their professional preparation and their daily classroom work. This is a mismatch, we argue, that calls for a shift in the scholarship we call knowledge. Annie Del Principe articulates the competing lines of thinking on this topic in her 2020 article "Cultivating a Sustainable TYC Writing Program: Collaboration, Disciplinarity, and Faculty Governance," citing Holly Larson's award-winning 2018 *TETYC* article, whose "argument seeks to elevate practitioner knowledge to scholarly, professional knowledge" (61). Larson's position, argues Del Principe, "would define being in the field of composition as teaching composition classes, reflecting on one's experiences teaching those classes, and processing those reflections and experiences reciprocally with other composition teachers" (117). Del Principe herself questions whether such a definition is fair, valid, or reflective of definitions of professional membership, concluding somewhat speculatively that "in order to have expertise and professional status in writing studies one must participate in the communal, scholarly interactions of the field—right?" (62). The different positions reflected by Larson and Del Principe expose the core questions around writing studies, professional expertise, and disciplinarity, as well as the poor alignment between the three pillars of our work: labor, teaching, and scholarship.

To further complicate these issues, we acknowledge that we've focused so far largely on the job market for the PhD in writing studies or rhetoric and composition, but that to understand the labor market for two-year colleges and for the teaching of writing, it's also important to attend to the graduate credential that most typically qualifies someone to teach in the lower-division English curriculum—the MA degree. The graduate preparation of such instructors—who make up the majority of both the two-year-college English workforce and the first-year writing instructors in most contexts[11]—gives us another way to think about the work that scholarship and research in writing studies could and should perform. If scholarship in the field is intended to advance knowledge but also establish best practices and standards, the absence of attention to systematic research on pedagogy and first-year writing (as we will demonstrate later in the book) has particular exigency for those instructors whose prior graduate preparation is not aligned with the intensive work they will do in college writing classrooms.

In the 2008 MLA/ADE report on the workforce in English, there is a special inset note remarking upon the master's degree as the standard credential for teaching in the lower division, and it should be noted that the vast majority of instructors who are teaching in two-year colleges would hold this as their highest degree. As the report authors wrote, "The data summarized in figure 14 caught the committee by surprise. We had assumed that most full-time non-tenure-track faculty members would hold the doctorate. A master's degree seems to be the qualifying degree for teaching off the tenure track (and teaching in the lower division)" (*Education*). This finding is no surprise to two-year-college faculty, or even to WPAs who regularly evaluate credentials for the teaching of first-year writing. A subsequent MLA report, the 2011 *Rethinking the Master's Degree in English for a New Century*, observed that "[i]n fact, overall in two-year institutions, about 89 percent of English faculty members do not hold a doctorate (fig. 2)" (3).[12] Most relevant from this report, though, is what it reveals about the substance of masters' programs (both MA and MFA, both of which predominate as credentials for the teaching of first-year writing) and their often inadequate inclusion of training in the teaching of writing, as well as relevant coursework on pedagogy, assessment, and composition theory.

Because the current body of writing studies scholarship is aimed largely at specialists, the graduate curricula of MA programs and the backgrounds that such instructors bring to their classrooms illustrate the ways that working conditions as well as teaching and learning conditions perform specific functions for the teaching staff of the majority of FYW courses. As the report notes,

> 62.4 percent of respondents designate the preparation of postsecondary teachers as important or very important to their missions (Table 1.4), but it is not at all clear that most programs structure course offerings and requirements that are explicitly directed to prospective teachers. Because the common curriculum for the MA degree has largely stagnated, the role of responsive and relevant scholarship is especially important. As Figure [1.2] reveals, the most common requirement is a course in research methods, required for all or most students at 63.6 percent of the programs that responded to the survey. (9)

Figure 1.3 shows what the typical required courses are for a master's degree in English, with the majority requiring research methods and literary theory, while the teaching of literature and creative writing courses was required by just a handful of programs.

In brief, then, the two courses most often required of master's students are literary theory and research methods, regardless of the area of specialization or intended employment or educational goal of the master's student. Half of programs have literary theory as a course requirement, approximately the same proportion of programs that require a course in the teaching of writing (58.1 percent), though literary theory is unlikely to be a teaching responsibility for any instructor with a master's-level credential (*Rethinking*

Fig. 5

Percentage of Departments Requiring Various Courses of All or Most Students Enrolled in Their Master's Degree Programs

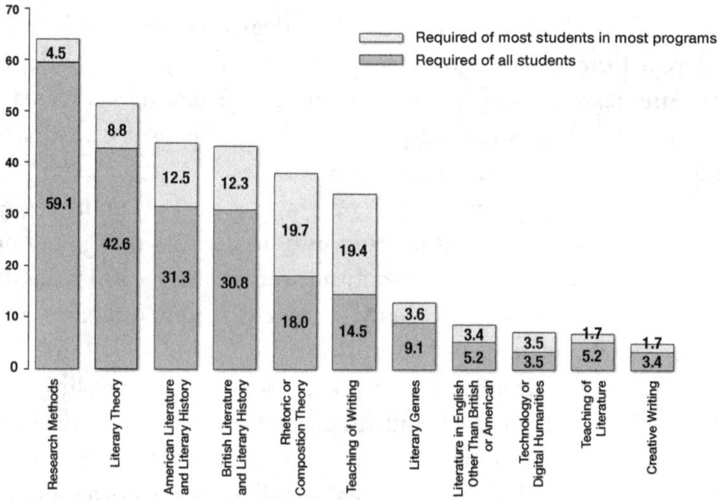

Source: 2009 ADE surveys of ADE-member departments that have master's or doctoral degree programs

Figure 1.2. Required coursework in MA programs, survey from the Associated Departments of English, 2011.

Table 5

Percentage of Departments Requiring or Not Requiring Specific Course Types

	Required of All Students	Required of Most Students in Most Programs	Required of Some Students in Some Programs	Not Required
American literature and literary history (64)	31.3	12.5	26.6	29.7
British literature and literary history (65)	30.8	12.3	24.6	32.3
Creative writing (58)	3.4	1.7	41.4	53.4
Literature in English other than British or American (58)	5.2	3.4	13.8	77.6
Literary genres (55)	9.1	3.6	9.1	78.2
Literary theory (68)	42.6	8.8	27.9	20.6
Research methods (66)	59.1	4.5	18.2	18.2
Rhetoric or composition theory (61)	18.0	19.7	36.1	26.2
Teaching of literature (58)	5.2	1.7	22.4	70.7
Teaching of writing (62)	14.5	19.4	24.2	41.9
Technology or digital humanities (57)	3.5	3.5	17.5	75.4
Other (22)	27.3	13.6	4.5	54.5

Source: 2009 ADE surveys of ADE-member departments that have master's or doctoral degree programs
Note: Response counts are given in parentheses.

Figure 1.3. Required coursework for MA degree, Associated Departments of English survey.

10).[13] Even introductory/general education literature courses informed by such coursework may be in short supply in a two-year college for instructors working off the tenure track.[14] Ultimately, the report authors conclude, the MA degree curriculum is "little different from what might have been found fifty years ago: British and American literature surveys; period course requirements; major authors; the three standard genres of fiction, poetry, and drama; and an occasional special topics course" (9).

We think it is a given that MA programs ultimately grant degrees to people who will work as instructors of first-year writing (and not literature, creative writing, or another subspecialty within English studies). It stands out that the MA credential underprepares most graduates who plan to enter a teaching position in which first-year writing courses are likely to be their primary responsibilities (or who do not plan to teach full-time but find themselves doing so for some reason or another). This is not to say that coursework in other foundational areas of English studies—such as the analysis and writing work of literary studies or the workshop and craft focus of creative writing—cannot inform the work of the first-year writing classroom or that this baseline disciplinary knowledge does not fulfill other important purposes for graduate students in English. However, being effective in the ever-changing writing classroom is most likely to occur when such creative or literary study is supported by principles and pedagogical content knowledge in composing, critical reading, rhetorical knowledge, and knowledge of processes. Perhaps with this gap in mind, professional organizations have been working to prepare guiding documents and position statements that will help writing teachers—for example, the 2016 *CCCC Statement on Preparing Teachers of College Writing* and the recently published "TYCA Guidelines for Preparing Teachers of English in the Two-Year College" (Calhoon-Dillahunt et al.). These are excellent steps toward beginning to articulate a shared understanding of what it takes to be prepared to work in a teaching-intensive position in a variety of types of institutions (see Leverenz and Goodburn; Carillo, "Beyond").

There are important implications here for graduates with MAs or PhDs who leave their degree programs with minimal or nonexistent coursework in pedagogy, composition theory, and assessment. One is that there is little opportunity for those instructors who are master's-credentialed and, increasingly, working off the tenure track, to rectify these gaps in their graduate coursework such that their knowledge is aligned with the regular work they do. As in the MLA/ADE report, the majority of writing instructors who are accounted for in the CCCC survey do not hold doctorates (51 percent MA, 13 percent MFA, 25 percent other)[15] and have no or limited opportunity for ongoing professional development either in the form of conference travel or independent research (Gere, "Initial Report"). In the MLA report, a question that sheds light on our current discussion is the sorts of professional support that non-tenure-track MA-holding faculty members (who teach the vast majority of our lower-division courses, first-year writing in particular) could expect in their departments (*Rethinking*). What we see being made clear through these data is that the professional responsibilities of writing faculty and writing program administrators, and the work that current graduate students are being prepared to do, are much different from what the work looks like at the research-intensive or research-extensive programs where they will earn their degrees. The published research, professional statements, and development opportunities must instead reflect their material realities: heavy teaching loads, diverse student populations, limited opportunities for ongoing professional development, and strapped budgets. Figure 1.4 shows the professional resources that non-tenure-track (NTT) faculty with MA credentials can expect. The vast majority of such instructors could use the library or make copies, and most have office spaces and access to computers and printers, but fewer than 15 percent of departments provided funding for independent research projects to their non-tenure-track instructors—and funds for professional development (perhaps conference attendance or workshop participation) were guaranteed available to fewer than a quarter of such instructors. Fewer than a third of instructors could count on any travel funding.

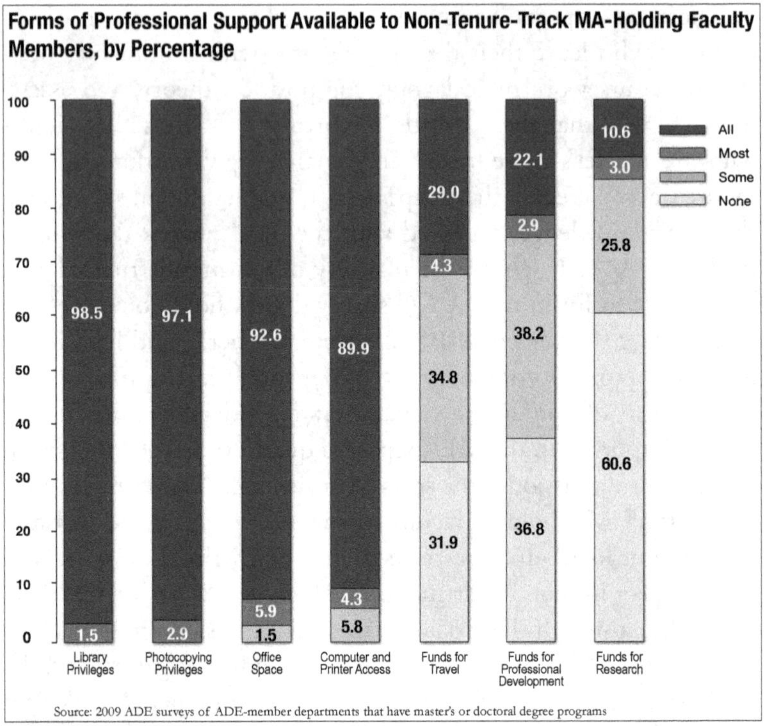

Figure 1.4. Forms of professional support available to non-tenure-track instructors

All of this is to say that whatever education, training, and professionalization most writing instructors gain in their graduate programs will—in all likelihood—not be supplemented by their employing institution (as things stand now), nor will they have resources to undertake systematic inquiry and assessment projects that can inform decision making in their own local contexts.[16] As Sarah Z. Johnson reflects in a report on her work as chair of the CCCC Task Force on Preparing Teachers of College Writing, "Professional development programs that rely solely on the altruism of full-time faculty to mentor or the desire of part-time faculty to volunteer their extra time do not work. If preparation and professional development are not built into the assigned workload of the department and into the institution's compensation structure, programs will fizzle or, worse, become a meaningless and unhelpful hoop new hires must jump through" (25). Without prior coursework or training, instructors without formal training in composition theory and practice may even find it intimidating or unwelcoming to participate in professional communities focused on composition theory and pedagogy.

The funding structures reported in these data are one way that NTT instructors are encouraged to see teaching and research as disconnected activities, but another way this disconnect is exacerbated is by the inadequate representation of the working conditions of such instructors in the body of scholarship, the lack of systematic inquiry that can inform their classroom work, and the accompanying gap in knowledge that results. Ann Penrose asks questions about membership as disciplinary practitioners and scholars in "Professional Identity in a Contingent-Labor Profession: Expertise, Autonomy, Community in Composition Teaching." She observes:

> [W]e are well aware of the factors that would make it natural for nontenure-track (NTT) faculty to wonder if they are truly members of the academic community. Despite the best efforts of WPAs and department heads, the material conditions of NTT teaching—from low pay, short-term contracts and shared offices to the lack of recognition from tenure-track "colleagues" passing in the hall—clearly create the impression that NTT faculty are not members of the professional communities in which they work. (109)

As we discuss in the next section, there are some specific ways that these gaps between preparation and employment responsibilities, and between the role of generalists and specialists, can be bridged with some strategic and intentional efforts. This alignment involves reconceiving what constitutes "membership" or how we define colleagues—and also how we define the discipline.

STABILIZING THE FIELD: ALIGNING LABOR, SCHOLARSHIP, AND TEACHING

With this changing context in mind, we argue that writing studies as a field—both the knowledge production and the material work of that field—must evolve to serve the needs of those instructors who teach writing and who need to survive in the neoliberal university, for two key reasons. First, we need research focused on such students' success, retention, and learning as an essential part of our national agenda. As the gateway course to college ways of reading, writing, and thinking, first-year writing programs serve a unique function within higher education. Engaged and quality instruction in these courses, while not serving an "inoculation function," as it has been called, does roughly map onto students' ability to proceed into more demanding reading- and writing-intensive courses (see Giordano and Hassel). It is a central component of helping students to stay in higher education and to graduate.

Second, we need to maintain the integrity of the field, by which we do not mean "rigor" or "prestige," with both of which the word *integrity* is sometimes conflated. Instead, we mean effective writing instruction that uses and responds to disciplinary knowledge in writing studies. Without engaged instructors working in relatively stable and supportive positions, the quality of instruction in writing and the accompanying gains that students can realistically make will be compromised. This lack of integrity erodes the public perception and actual quality of postsecondary writing instruction, further reinforcing the increasing effort to "take care of" or "get out of the way" those first-year writing requirements (see Hansen and Farris; *Statement on Dual Credit*). Attention to the teaching and learning conditions of college writing courses has the potential to restore public confidence in higher education and literacy development as a long-term intellectual process rather than a single experience to be eliminated as a degree requirement. In this way, *integrity* refers not to an exclusionary knowledge system or greater numbers of terminal-degree-credentialed instructors; rather, it refers to an accurate and complete picture of college writing. Such integrity reflects a reality in which the knowledge produced and disseminated matches up with those who use it, rely on it, and build upon it.

In the following pages, we tell the stories of these teachers and these students—the new majorities. We provide a road map for how the architectural components of writing studies, including our pedagogies, scholarship, and labor structures, can fit together in ways that will fulfill two goals: advancing access to higher education in the service of democratic participation and social justice and integrating the dimensions of writing studies in the service of that advancement. Without a greater, stronger foundation of work that directly relates to these teaching and learning conditions of the vast majority of writing instructors (see Hassel and Giordano, "Occupy"), it will be difficult to engage practitioners with the scholarship because it does not appear relevant to their day-to-day work of teaching first-year writing to a wide range of students. In "Rhetoric and Ideology in the Writing Class," James Berlin wrote, "It should now be apparent that a way of teaching is never innocent. Every pedagogy is imbricated in ideology, in a set of tacit assumptions about what is real, what is good, what is possible, and how power ought to be distributed" (492). This same assessment can be applied to knowledge production in the field: the scholarship that we produce reflects our values; what we publish reflects the values of the field and its gatekeepers; the material conditions that persist are, as Berlin asserts, ideologically serving a purpose. Now is an opportunity to critically reevaluate how the materiality of writing studies can be reconciled with its intellectual and symbolic substance.

◈◈◈◈

Cassie's English 098 Course: The Last Day

This particular semester was unusual in that out of the twenty-two students enrolled on the first day, sixteen attended on the last day. Around five to six of those sixteen did not attend regularly but were there to complete and submit their final portfolios and attend the last-day-of-class celebration. The last day is a mess of emotions—relief to be finished with the class, pride in completing a body of work, and fear of the final grade.

Some students will learn that they have to repeat English 098, and when one student came to this realization, he picked up his chair and threw it on the ground out of anger. His frustration was understandable—he attended class fairly regularly, and he completed many of the assignments during the semester. He was not, however, able to demon-

strate several of the key learning outcomes of English 098, mainly because two of his essays were incomplete. His outburst of anger frightened the students in the class—and me. I asked to speak to him outside in the hallway. We spoke for a few minutes and he left, and he seemed to feel a little better when he had a better understanding of the option to repeat the course with an "R" grade and realized that other students have used this option successfully each semester.

While I have not experienced a student throwing a chair before, I have experienced anger and frustration on a regular basis. Most of my colleagues have. I was shaking for at least an hour after the class and was fortunate to have a writing meeting (about this chapter) during which I could talk with Holly about what happened. We connected what happened to the material conditions we work in every day, and we tried to break down what happened on an intellectual level. I feel such an incredible sense of failure when students who risk so much to come to college do not achieve their particular goal of completing English 098—the one goal I feel as though I should be able to help them with. This feeling of failure drives a lot of us in our work, in both debilitating and productive ways.

2

Materiality and Knowledge Production

Jack and Gillian Van Treese, Instructors of English, University of Wisconsin–Milwaukee at Waukesha:
One of the unifying features of the UW Colleges was that its existence was student-driven. Each campus existed to provide access to higher education for students across the state, and the English department, especially in its focus on first-year writing and developmental education, was heavily aligned with this idea. Our department provided an array of opportunities and resources to assist in the development of curriculum and teaching practices, making sure they were easily accessible to ensure participation across the campuses. Mentors, beyond our home campus, were available for answering questions and providing feedback on teaching materials. The English department website was a vast resource, containing sample syllabi, course texts, learning activities, and suggested background reading. And, every year, there were a variety of instructional professional development opportunities led by our developmental English program coordinator and our writing program administrator. These coordinators visited each campus, holding workshops focused on topics like placement, developmental reading and writing, and studio classes. There were also workshops offered online. Our semesterly department meetings included breakout sessions focused on pedagogical issues. And we both participated in a yearlong grant-funded project to redesign a course to better align with learning outcomes, receiving professional development funding as compensation. Needless to say, we felt continually energized and supported by our department and its commitment to teaching.

As discussed in Chapter 1, our interest in writing this book stems from years of working to develop programs and writing curricula in the two-year-college environment, coupled with our awareness of the increasingly dire circumstances for stable employment in college English. These working experiences led us to inquire about the lack of a specific kind of research focusing on the teaching of writing to a wide range of learners in an environment similar to ours. We also looked for resources and training to undertake and publish that research, so we could then use it for program and classroom improvement. In short, we needed research and scholarship that could help us do our jobs better and we had difficulty finding it. We are not unlike Jack and Gillian, and their comments above speak to the need for the teaching majority to have professional resources that meet their needs as classroom instructors. Though these two teachers both had a strong background in writing studies as graduate students, like many of us they needed to adapt to the context of a two-year college when they arrived. In this chapter, we explore whether the current scholarship meets such needs and whether the current scholarship in writing studies benefits from the insights they have to share in the field.

Over the last decade, for example, in our work with the UW System two-year colleges, we had to build a writing program from scratch. The national standards and position statements set forth by CCCC, NCTE, and CWPA were invaluable for providing the disciplinary foundation for the program. However, one area where we struggled to locate relevant research and evidence-based best practices was in curricular adaptation and pedagogical implementation of these learning outcomes and standards with two-year-college student populations. This was particularly the case for research that reflected student literacy development from basic writing[1] to more advanced writing classes as well as longitudinal research from the point of placement to fulfilling the core class required for an associate degree. Before we included practices, assignments, or learning activities in our classrooms, before we made recommendations to our department, we wanted to understand how these practices were assessed across an entire classroom or program. For us, studies that focus on one or two students (or even a small group) weren't applicable to our student population. We would always wonder, "What about the other students, those not addressed in the classroom study?" Because many of those "other" students are *most* of our students—the ones who don't volunteer for research projects, or the ones who don't attend class regularly. Our students are the ones who work forty hours a week or the ones who have gaps in their education that affect classroom engagement and success. They are the writers whose confidence has often been battered by negative educational experiences and who have little faith in the educational system—or teachers—to support them.

In addition, the work that takes place in university settings differs not just in the student populations but in the very material and labor contexts from those in which two-year-college instructors teach. Unlike their university counterparts, two-year-college instructors teach at least four and sometimes up to seven or eight classes a semester, all of them lower-division. As the recent TYCA Workload Survey documents, the typical teaching load for two-year-college faculty is between 28 and 35 credit hours per year, with 41 percent of the 804 respondents identifying this as the standard load for tenure-line faculty. This workload translates into five or six sections per semester as the most common teaching load. Similarly, another 13 percent of respondents identified standard loads as high as 53 credit hours each year, though workload varies by whether instructors are full-time, tenure-line, or adjunct, and by whether they are on quarters or semesters. In this way, the material realities of our own work did not reflect many of the national standards that are built around workloads that include working with students who are majors in the field of English or writing and rhetoric studies or students who are admitted through a selective review process. Our material realities do not include instructors who work with graduate students or who have teaching loads closer to two or three classes a semester for different reasons.

Clearly, the priorities and needs of two-year-college writing programs are different from those at comprehensive or research-intensive campuses, especially when considering the differences in workload and focus on first-year writing. Finding the kind of work that accounted for these material realities in program-building and development work was challenging, confirming what Doug Hesse observes in his recent review of composition journals: "The gap between the worlds of our scholarship, our practice, and the worlds of others' practices has, if anything, increased over the years. . . . Composition itself is divided between those who focus on classrooms and teaching and those who focus on managing and theorizing the enterprise" ("Journals" 393). Writing studies needs to take seriously this misalignment because not to do so is to continue an unsustainable enterprise. In practically every institution, first-year writing is the foundation on which curriculum, budgets, and hiring are built. FYW programs fund minors, majors, and graduate programs; they serve as "apprenticeships" and labs within which new teachers learn the craft of writing instruction. Even if the moral imperative to support and improve quality first-year writing programs did not exist, the budget realities themselves should make clear that, in terms of sustainability, it is FYW that keeps this discipline afloat.

With these issues in mind, in this chapter we report on our analysis of multiple scholarly journals in the field, calling attention to the proportion of scholarship available that uses a systematic research design, is assessment-oriented, and addresses the majority of teachers and students in the field of writing studies: two-year-college students, instructors, and contingent faculty. In doing this analysis, we focus specifically on journals and journal articles rather than on scholarly monographs or edited collections because of the accessibility and timeliness of articles. For two-year-college instructors and contingent faculty with heavy teaching loads and few professional development resources, finding the time to purchase and read entire scholarly monographs is challenging; articles not only provide regular access to new scholarship in the form of a journal that appears four or six times a year; there's also the reassurance that they are peer-reviewed, and often, that access to them is provided by a library or department subscription. In our analysis of the major journals in writing studies, we argue that pedagogy-focused research providing materially situated best practices, particularly longitudinally across courses (for students whose first-year writing experience is multiple semesters or years) is challenging to find, and we demonstrate how critically necessary that missing research is to resource-strapped writing programs.[2] Finally, we introduce readers to the work in two-year-college writing studies as a way of highlighting not just what such programs need but also what they offer to the discipline.

THE RESEARCH WE NEED

Understanding knowledge production in the field means examining the sources of research and scholarship that create that foundation of what we know as a discipline. In particular, the place and space for first-year writing (or introduction to college writing) occupies a kind of "everywhere and nowhere" role because of its central role in our institutions and our discipline. This role presents challenges that result in college composition sitting at both the center and the fringes of the discipline.[3] Writing teachers often take fragmented avenues to locate scholarship relevant to their work, particularly scholarship that takes a systematic approach to teaching and learning in first-year writing. In this chapter, we are interested in mapping out how and where that research is published and with what frequency. In particular, we focus on work that uses systematic inquiry (a term we do not see as necessarily synonymous with quantitative and empirical methods), work that is assessment-oriented, and work that pays attention to the wide range of teaching and learning spaces that writing teachers occupy. Like Rich Haswell, who defined and documented the need for more RAD (replicable, aggregable, and data-supported) work in the field (as well as McClure and Goldstein in 2012), we call for more work that is an assessment of teaching and learning, not just work that is "about" teaching or that considers teaching implications as a kind of addendum to its primary focus.

One important feature we also see as critical to systematic inquiry is whether subjects of study are "picked randomly or through an explicit and transferable system of selection" in contrast to non-RAD work, which Haswell defines as a "study of texts or human participants selected by the authors as isolated examples, points of clarification, or demonstration of an argument" ("NCTE/CCCC's Recent War" 208). We agree with Haswell that systematic inquiry overlaps with RAD research in that it has "assessment orientation": a consideration of the comprehensive set of data/human subjects with clear boundaries; in other words, the full set of participants, the full corpus of texts, or the full range of student materials. In defining RAD research, Haswell suggests that RAD is not synonymous with *empirical* in part because it is also not necessarily theoretical or quantitative. In essence, as he notes, "RAD scholarship may be feminist, empirical, ethnomethodological, contextual, action, liberatory, or critical" (202). Many writing studies scholars (see Haswell, "NCTE/CCCC's Recent War" and *Academically Adrift*; McClure and Goldstein; Hesse, "Nation" and "Journals"; Anson; Hassel, "Research Gaps") have also written about the need for generalizable, systematically gathered evidence.

As other scholars have traced the explanation for a decline in what we'll call systematic inquiry (using a wide range of methodologies), we will not repeat that here. Instead, like Hesse, we believe the field has a "need for us to produce strategic research that bridges the high school and college years. By strategic, I mean research that can be made meaningful to policymakers in a climate smitten and smirched by benchmarking" ("Nation" W422). Like Haswell, and from our position doing professional work within a sector that is underresourced and regularly under legislative assault (two-year colleges, developmental education), we believe in "a best effort inquiry into the actualities of a situation, inquiry that is explicitly enough systematized in sampling, execution, and analysis to be replicated; exactly enough circumscribed to be extended; and factually enough supported to be verified" ("NCTE/CCCC's Recent War" 201). And finally, like Chris Anson, we see the need for "a more robust plan for building on the strong base of existing research into our assumptions about how students best learn to write" (12). We use this existing line of scholarly conversation as a foundation for integrating the labor and pedagogical realities of writing studies. We use it to show that we cannot, as Anson states, "continue to rely on our belief in our pedagogies and administrative decisions, whether theorized or not, whether argued from logic or anecdote, experience or conviction," in part because "we do no better to support a case for those decisions than what most detractors do to support cases against them" (11–12). Certainly, like Hesse's and Anson's policy- and politically situated calls, our own thinking is informed by the ways that the systematic study of the teaching of writing and of writers—when integrated with the material conditions of writing instruction in postsecondary contexts and the increasingly diverse student populations served by those writing classrooms—is of great interest to the practical work of the field.

Indeed, one key reason such practical research is important is the degree to which compositionists are called upon with increasing urgency to support—or defend—their program's values, choices, and priorities. Whether these arguments are about securing professional development funding, establishing and supporting a writing program administrator position, providing resources for students, facilitating support for the training of instructors, raising the course caps for writing and developmental courses (Kalish et al.), or establishing credit hours and time with students (Jaschik, "Retaliation"), *data* is the day's watchword. For example, we fought (unsuccessfully) to keep our composition class sizes at twenty-two, even with disciplinary statements that recommend numbers well below that as well as our own research on class size at our institution (see Phillips and Ahrenhoerster). The impact of increased class sizes is significant for instructors who regularly teach between eighty and a hundred first-year writing students a semester (or more), and the ripple effect of forced curricular and pedagogical changes as a result of those increases disproportionately falls on our most marginalized students (see Queen for a complex discussion of class size). Much of the research decontextualizes issues such as these in ways that are not helpful to make specific arguments to administrators or other relevant parties and in ways that ignore the disproportionate impact on instructors and writing programs with a primary focus on first-year and developmental writing.

In the increasing environment of austerity—most often affecting the lowest-resourced and most at-risk students and institutions—these needs will only become more pressing. As we discuss throughout this book, for vulnerable institutions and marginalized instructors the weight of disciplinary position statements or standards is not sufficient to support particular kinds of professional and institutional work. Research that uses systematic inquiry, however, can be used for the following pragmatic and crucial purposes:

- *To support classroom- and program-level decision making*: both individual instructors and program directors (or department chairs and committee chairs with responsibility for curriculum or learning outcomes) need substantive scholarship and research that uses systematic inquiry with a focused research question and across a range of student types to make decisions. This evidence should be not solely quantitative or qualitative, but mixed methodologically so that numerical data can be used for big-picture thinking—for example, what proportion of students did or did not succeed using a particular pedagogical approach—and accompanied by qualitative analysis that can pinpoint the how and why of success and failure at a specific learning task.
- *To ground departments' discussions about their values and choices*: Most writing courses in the United States are housed within English departments, not freestanding writing or rhetoric programs (67 percent in Ann Ruggles Gere's data; 82 percent in Emily Isaacs's study of regional comprehensives; 54 percent in the National Census of Writing's 2013 surveys of first-year writing—though the percentage for two-year colleges in the survey is 96 percent). This typically means that conversations around curricular work (whether the topic is standards for evaluation, model curricular sequences or shared book assignments for writing courses, or development of learning outcomes and course goals required by most accrediting bodies) are taking place among department members with a wide range of levels of exposure to scholarship and research in writing studies and a lot of autonomy about how or whether they

adopt any kind of regularized curriculum (see Hancock and Reid and Del Principe for articles describing the departmental dynamics in two-year-college English/humanities departments). Systematic inquiry into teaching and learning—composition as a "teaching subject"—is the sturdiest foundation upon which to fix such discussions, because it reflects the relationship between pedagogy, disciplinary content knowledge, and assessment

- *To anchor professional development workshops or activities tied to mentoring, instructional support, and evaluation of instructors*: for those instructors, particularly those working in NTT positions and who have minimal access to professional development resources (as we showed in Chapter 1), internal workshops and trainings serve particularly important functions to develop their pedagogical and assessment approaches. Such instructors may be teaching at multiple institutions and are especially in need of ongoing support to cultivate pedagogical adaptability so they can apply the most appropriate approaches to these various student populations, programs, and classroom spaces. Research using systematic inquiry both provides a foundation and knowledge and serves as a model for instructors to implement their own effective assessment practices that can help them identify and respond to the differing needs of different student populations and instructional environments, particularly when employing institutions can struggle to consistently offer instructors such support.
- *To marshal support for institutional processes involving departmental or institutional colleagues and administrators*: For many program coordinators, WPAs, and chairs who are managing a writing program in institutions of whatever size, invariably there are ongoing challenges to maintaining program quality in the face of austerity pressures. These might be about class sizes/course maxima; oversight of programs like developmental education or ESL; online courses and programs, writing centers or other tutoring models like writing studio; placement assessment; competency-based course options or prior

> learning assessments; or dual credit/concurrent enrollment course options, to name a few. We have to come to these conversations armed with systematically collected, peer-reviewed data in the field that uses epistemological models that resonate with the administrative class that has the responsibility for authorizing and allocating resources. Without unassailable information, the easiest, most efficient, or most cost-saving option will be the chosen one, and these are often incompatible with the resources required for quality writing program work.

For these reasons, systematic inquiry focused on the teaching and learning connected to first-year writing is particularly important. In addition, instructors need a wide variety of such research to reflect their specific local contexts. Research that supports the work we describe above becomes even more compelling and persuasive when it demonstrates rich connections to the environments and students with which these instructors work.

THE RESEARCH WE HAVE

We analyzed journal articles in *College Composition and Communication* (*CCC*), *College English*, *Writing Program Administration* (*WPA*), and *Composition Studies* from 2000 to 2018 (see Appendix A). We selected these journals for their presence in the field, as we see them as four of the primary periodical resources for teachers of writing. In addition, these journals include within their purview research and scholarship on teaching first-year writing. *CCC*'s mission includes supporting "college teachers in reflecting on and improving their practices in teaching writing." *College English* is targeted at scholar-teachers and includes among its foci rhetoric-composition, reading theory, literary studies, and pedagogy. *WPA*, while focusing on program administration, includes among its "topics of interest" faculty professional development, classroom research studies, application of national learning outcomes, program assessment, and labor conditions. Finally, in addition to focusing on rhetoric and composition, *Composition Studies* includes within its mission "teaching college writing" and "preparing the field's future teacher-scholars." Overall, then, we selected these journals because of their explicit attention to writing pedagogy and instructor and classroom research. We specifically did not include *Teaching English in the Two-Year College* in part because one coauthor previously published an analysis of articles in that journal (Hassel, "Research Gaps"). Further, we were interested in examining how and where two-year-college writing programs (students and instructors) are part of writing studies writ large, since such journals are about college writing and should account for the work taking place in the two-year-college part of their mission as comprehensively serving the needs of compositionists.

Our primary goal with our analysis was to provide a data-driven picture of the alignment of labor, pedagogy, and scholarship. As such, our analysis was influenced by Lynn Bloom, Donald Daiker, and Edward White's *Composition in the Twenty-First Century: Crisis and Change*. John Trimbur estimated in that volume that "rhetoric and composition resembles other academic fields in which a fairly small percentage of professionals—10 percent or so—produce around half of the publications" (140). While we were not interested so much in *who* was doing the publishing, we were interested in *what* was being published within a limited set of data that were of particular (but not exclusive) importance for our two-year-college working environment. And as noted in Chapter 1, the kind of scholarship and research that most graduate degree holders in English need has to be pedagogically practical. Because we are focused on instructors who work in the kind of environment we do, we designed these categories to parse out issues particularly relevant for the two-year-college environment and contingent faculty. Given the stakes of the first-year writing classroom in such an environment, identifying systematic research that can ethically inform program development and be integrated into classrooms with undergraduate students was a critical part of our methodology. Because of our focus, however, we did not include in our categories (unless it was directly related to first-year writing or pedagogy) research or scholarship on graduate students or graduate education, literature or rhetoric, or multidisciplinary studies.

To do this work, we developed categories of analysis—writing classrooms, writing pedagogy, and research features. In this section, we describe and unpack each of the categories we used for our journal analysis. We also detail some of the roadblocks we faced with our methodology and how we worked through them (see Appendix B for an example). In analyzing the articles published from the year 2000 to 2018 (when we began writing and revising this manuscript), we identified three categories that speak to the pressing needs in teaching-intensive institutions (see Table 2.1).

Category 1: Writing Classrooms

For this category, we focused on general themes faced by writing instructors in the classroom.

Table 2.1. Overview of Categories of Analysis

Categories of Analysis: Materiality and Scholarship Relationships	Subtopics
Category 1: Writing Classrooms	• Teaching writing and workload management • Negotiating academic and classroom communities • Aligning pedagogical practices with philosophy • Adapting pedagogical practices and philosophies to institutional and other contexts • Locations of teaching and the role of context • Variation in student preparation for college or classroom expectations • Specific classroom practices
Category 2: Writing Pedagogy	• Composing and processes • Critical reading and thinking • Developing rhetorical knowledge • Conducting effective research • Conventions/practices of academic writing
Category 3: Research Features	• Methodology • Systematic assessment • Research subject(s) • Research site(s)

1. Teaching Writing and Workload Management: Articles placed in this category address workload in a variety of ways, ranging from labor discussions about a particular activity or teaching philosophy to the addressing of pedagogical relationships between labor and working conditions. Those working conditions might include number or kind of writing courses taught or working with a particular student population.
2. Negotiating Academic and Classroom Communities: Articles in this category address classroom issues and student learning behaviors including noncognitive factors. Articles in this category dealt with the ways that students perceive or interpret classroom pedagogy.
3. Aligning Pedagogical Practices with Philosophy: In this category we included articles that discussed how instructors or programs implement specific teaching practices, learning activities, and assignments in support of a pedagogical philosophy or approach.
4. Adapting Pedagogical Practices and Philosophies to Institutional and Other Contexts: Building on the previous category, articles that met this criterion addressed how a teaching philosophy or practice was affected by the location of the institution or the context of a classroom. These contexts could include a specific student population, a specific kind of institution, or a pedagogical approach focused on localized contexts or needs.
5. Locations of Teaching and the Role of Context: By "locations of teaching" we mean material conditions and employment status of instructors, including faculty status, tenure track, non-tenure-track, part-time, contingent, etc. Articles in this category could also include those that discussed instructors focused on ESL or basic writing. For the most part, articles we placed in this category were easy to categorize. They addressed a specific population of instructors or type of institution. The only difficulty we had placing articles in this category arose when the institution or instructor type was not clearly identified, and we would have to go back and look

more closely. We were surprised at how many articles did not identify the type of institution or employment status of instructors.

6. Variation in Student Preparation for College or Classroom Expectations: Articles in this category dealt with issues of academic preparation, gaps in education, issues related to transfer, and retention. We also identified articles in this category that presented a particular teaching and learning or classroom challenge that required new learning (or unlearning) on the part of students in order to adjust to the present expectations or demands.
7. Specific Classroom Practices: In this final category, we included articles that developed or implemented a specific classroom practice and then discussed that implementation. This category had the highest rate of placement of all of the categories in our analysis—around 57 percent of all the articles in these journals from 2000 to 2018 addressed a specific classroom practice in some way.

Category 2: Writing Pedagogy

In our second category, we tagged articles as one or more of five pedagogical subcategories based on the WPA Outcomes (with the exception of composing in electronic environments, in part because this is strongly reflected in the other five categories). Our interest in this category stemmed from many requests we received from instructors (and each other) for research on student learning under each of the major disciplinary outcomes, which were the basis for the writing program curriculum and program research we conducted (and discuss in Chapter 4). These subcategories included

1. Composing and Processes: articles that addressed writing processes (invention, drafting, revision) and strategies for composing and giving feedback for example.
2. Critical Reading and Thinking: articles that addressed pedagogical strategies for helping students use critical reading strategies, understand complex texts, and develop nuanced perspectives.

3. Developing Rhetorical Knowledge: articles that addressed helping students increase their awareness of rhetorical choices, genre conventions, and the way texts work.
4. Conducting Effective Research: articles that addressed preparing for, managing, and conducting research.
5. Conventions/practices of Academic Writing: articles that addressed conventions for documenting and integrating sources, as well as conventions of academic language and style.

These categories align in a general way with what we call *disciplinary learning domains* in Chapter 3 of this book.

Category 3: Research Features

Last, we looked specifically at the features of each of the research studies in order to develop a sense not just of the focus or subject of the study, but also whether it had an explicit methodology, whether it used systematic inquiry, and who the primary subjects or sites of study were in the article.

- Methodology: For each article, we examined and noted the author's research approach and methods used. We identified the type of evidence collected, including interviews, surveys, student writing, institutional documents, archives, field notes, and other relevant textual evidence. The methodologies we encountered included historical, theoretical, classroom-based, case study, narrative, and rhetorical analysis. If we could not identify a particular methodology, and if the author(s) did not identify a particular methodology within the article, we noted "none" in that field.
- Systematic Inquiry: In this category we identified the articles that used a systematic approach, resembling the RAD method of Haswell, to support the claims about writing classrooms and pedagogy (see discussion of systematic research earlier in this chapter). Our goal was to identify research articles that did not use "purposeful sampling," as Albert Rouzie discusses in his 2001 *CCCC* article, "Conversation and Carrying-On: Play, Conflict, and Serio-Ludic Discourse in Synchronous

Computer Conferencing," rather, those articles that systematically assessed student learning across all research subjects.

- Research Subject(s): We included this category simply to get an understanding of the population being discussed, researched, or analyzed. The research subject could include the author, an instructor, a student, or a group of people in a course or community (for example, first-year writing, undergraduate, graduate, community member, instructor, administrator, etc.). As with the Locations of Teaching category, we were surprised by how many articles did not include what we see as important information about the research subject. For example, when discussing instructors, many articles did not identify employment status.
- Research Site(s): When identified by the author(s) in some way, we noted where the research (if applicable) took place. While we noted all sites, we looked specifically for research sites in two-year colleges (we did not include basic writing classes at four-years because those are different student populations, for the most part). We also tagged articles in this category if, for example, authors specifically mentioned that a student in their study or research project had transferred from a community college, typically referred to by a student participant in the article as part of reflective writing or interview transcripts.

These categories are organized around the traditional features of an academic research article from the subject of study to the method of inquiry.

In our process of analyzing and coding the articles, we used a variation of content analysis (see Huckin; Boettger and Palmer) to identify the categories described above in each article. After an extensive set of norming sessions, one reader made an initial assessment in each of the categories; this assessment was followed by a discussion between the two coauthors, and then a finalizing of the category assignment in each of the areas outlined above. There were many times where journal articles we read fit fairly neatly into the categories we describe. However, with some articles the categorization process was not as clear-cut and required a second reading, further discussion, and deeper analysis. For example, there were common article structures that caused us to flag and extend our analysis. The first was multitopic articles. Multitopic articles addressed more than one category, but often in a briefer or more indirect way. The second structure was what we referred to as "add-on articles," or articles that briefly addressed practical applications or classroom strategies at the end of the article. While these articles did address teaching and pedagogy, they required further analysis before we could designate them as fitting fully within a category. For articles that fell into these categories, we added an asterisk to our tables. Finally, there were articles that did not have a traditional journal article structure, such as interviews with scholars, symposia, or shorter vignettes about topics in a themed issue. For these articles, depending on their length and complexity, we sometimes excluded them from our analysis (such was the case for many of the shorter vignettes) or we analyzed them further to discuss their inclusion and categorization. At the point of tabulating final assessments, some minor adjustments were made, particularly as we conducted a second review of the *WPA* journal as a site of much of the research on writing classrooms and pedagogies that fell into an "indirect" category, by virtue of the nature of its editorial focus. We reviewed and tagged additional articles from our first round of analysis more precisely as "indirectly" addressing writing classrooms and pedagogies. This evolving category referred to research about writing classrooms and pedagogies that were typically filtered through the lens of a WPA or WPA administrator paradigm, often presented specifically with the purpose of implementing within a program, not a specific classroom or instructor.

Analysis of Research on Writing Classrooms and Writing Teachers

The tables in this section break down each of the three categories: writing classrooms, writing pedagogy, and research features. What the analysis reveals is that between one-quarter and one-half, depending on the journal, of scholarship published in the four journals actually focuses on the daily realities of writing classrooms and on writing pedagogy. However, a very small percentage of research articles addresses two-year colleges or labor conditions directly in their studies. As we discuss in more detail in this section, there is also an extremely wide range of research that uses a systematic research design, again depending on the journal, from nearly half in *WPA* to just 13 percent in *College English*. Last, in looking across the journals and how they addressed teaching contexts, labor conditions, and student populations, the topical emphasis of the majority of articles focused on writing classrooms and writing pedagogy nearly always focused on presenting a new, innovative, or experimental class design or practice. Overall, the key findings of our analysis show that

1. The labor and workload conditions of writing instructors are rarely part of research studies.
2. Two-year-college students and teachers are extraordinarily underrepresented.
3. Much of the scholarship published on writing classrooms and pedagogy does not use an approach that could be considered systematic inquiry or display an assessment orientation (a comprehensive look at a complete group of participants).

What this means is that such work can rarely be used in any convincing way for the purposes we identified at the outset of this chapter—supporting classroom and program-level decision making, grounding departmental discussions about values and choices, anchoring professional development workshops tied to mentoring, instructional support, and evaluation of instructors, and marshaling support for institutional processes.

Categories 1 and 2: Writing Classrooms and Writing Pedagogy

As noted in the previous chapter, we know that the majority of those earning graduate degrees in English, regardless of specialization, are likely to work off the tenure track, likely to teach at open-access campuses or two-year campuses, and, given the demographics of higher education in the twenty-first century, likely to teach in classrooms with a diversity of student populations (see Chapters 1 and 4). To set this material reality alongside knowledge in the field,

Table 2.2 reflects the number and percentage of the total articles that focused on writing classrooms and writing pedagogy, broken down by journal and also aggregated. We treat these two categories together in this section because they are interconnected and there are points at which it becomes useful to separate out the classroom material realities for pedagogical approaches, as we will do later in this analysis.

As Table 2.2 demonstrates, 35 percent of the articles in all four journals met the criteria for Categories 1 and 2, with *Composition Studies* having the most classroom- and pedagogy-focused articles at 54 percent, and *College English* having the least at 24 percent. While these numbers were lower than we expected, they provide an important baseline for further analysis of writing pedagogy and classroom-based research. For example, we were interested in looking at how labor realities and classroom diversity are reflected in the scholarship. In particular, we wanted to gain an understanding of how the labor conditions of a specific group of teachers, undergraduate writing faculty,[4] are part of the knowledge foundation for writing classrooms and pedagogy. First, we identified in our coding (in this case, Categories 1 and 2) when articles addressed

Table 2.2. Total Number of Articles That Explicitly Address Undergraduate Writing Classrooms and/or Writing Pedagogy

N=1130	Total Research or Feature Articles	Category 1 (Writing Classrooms) and Category 2 (Writing Pedagogy) (n=)	Category 1 (Writing Classrooms) and Category 2 (Writing Pedagogy) Focused (%)
CE	419	102	24
CCC	334	143	43
WPA	206	59	29
CS	171	92	54
Aggregate	1130	396	35

contingency—in either a specific, explicit, and contextualized way, or in a way that at least acknowledged contingency and its role in the classroom or in terms of the author or study participants' experiences (whatever the article topic). Table 2.3 shows the results of that analysis. Within those articles that centered on writing pedagogy and writing classrooms, few extended the analysis to consider the employment status of participating instructors or its implications for the study. By tracking which of the writing-program-focused articles addressed employment status (contingent/noncontingent) we could observe trends in how or whether these material realities became part of the conclusions drawn by the writers. Frankly, it was so unusual to see it addressed that the times participating instructors' employment conditions were made part of the study discussion were quite noticeable. For example, one piece described the implementation of a service-learning component into first-year writing courses, and identified participating instructors in the project as all working off the tenure track, either as graduate teaching assistants or contingent instructors; however, it was not acknowledged in the article how those respective employment positions are highly influential contexts that might shape whether, how, and with what consequences teachers might take on what is often a substantial increase in emotional, social, and logistical work that

Table 2.3. Total Number of Articles (Aggregate and by Journal) That Address Non-Tenure-Track Faculty Positions as an Explicit Part of the Article[5]

	Writing Classroom and Writing Programs Focused (N)	Non-tenure Track (n)	Non-tenure Track (%)
CE	102	4	4
CCC	143	5	3
WPA	59	8	14
CS	92	2	2
Aggregate	396	19	5

accompanies service-learning pedagogies.[6] In this way, the subfield of labor or contingency studies within English studies is largely segmented off from other areas.

In addition (and as stated earlier), the vast majority of instructors earning degrees in English will teach multiple sections of first-year writing. Contingent-appointment instructors might teach anywhere from three to six sections of writing in a semester. With just 5 percent of articles on writing classrooms addressing contingent working conditions—including how to effectively respond to student writing, or how to structure curriculum in a way that is manageable and effective—the issues that are often most immediate and pressing to writing teachers are underaddressed in the available knowledge foundation. Yet such research would provide the kind of evidence-based and data-driven recommendations that could be directly useful to both programs and instructors who must balance their material working conditions with pedagogical best practices. We see this issue also reflected in the misalignment with articles that address student needs or student preparation, in that emotional labor, on the part of both instructors and students, in two-year colleges and basic and degree-credit composition courses is an invisible component of the work that writing instructors often do (see Massé and Hogan; Dunbar and Baker; Shayne; Biswas). When working with struggling, underprepared, marginalized, and underserved student populations, this labor is intensified.

A second finding in Category 1 and 2 was that in the total body of scholarship over this period that addressed writing classrooms and writing pedagogy, no journal had a greater than single-digit representation of students and/or instructors in two-year colleges, which is a nearly complete lack of representation of the largest segment of writing teachers working in the field. *WPA* had the greatest representation of two-year-college students and teachers, at 8 percent, with just 2 of the 92 articles in *Composition Studies* addressing two-year colleges, as illustrated in Table 2.4. Our previous chapter discusses labor conditions and highlights how students and material conditions within two-year colleges are distinct from those in traditional four-year and research-intensive/doctoral-granting in-

Table 2.4. Total Number of Articles (Aggregate and by Journal) That Address, Are Located in, or Include Two-Year-College Students and Instructors

	Writing Classroom and Writing Pedagogy Focused (N)	Two-Year Colleges (N)	Two-Year Colleges (%)
CE	102	6	6
CCC	143	8	6
WPA	59	5	8
CS	92	2	2
Aggregate	396	21	5

stitutions. The work at two-years and many open-admissions four years is distinct in that online writing, basic writing, developmental writing and reading coursework, writing studies, accelerated learning programs, and many other unique features of work with diverse student populations predominate. These institutional realities are considered by many in the field to be specific disciplinary areas of study. What this means is that instructor and student needs in these kinds of institutions go in some cases almost entirely unrepresented in the published scholarship available as a resource for instructors—either for ongoing professional development or even during their graduate education. Further, the topics that are relevant to instructors in such settings (though we did not track this in our analysis) would presumably also be underrepresented. This means that the kinds of program, assessment, and curricular work required for operational functioning on two-year-college campuses must be learned "on the job," which then delays the ability of new instructors to adjust to the teaching duties and institutional culture. This gap also has negative consequences for students in those classrooms, whose needs may go unmet while program work goes undone or unassessed and instructors work to develop the needed knowledge foundation.

Finally, within Categories 1 and 2, we did some further subcategorizing to dive deeper into the specific emphases within classrooms and pedagogy articles. We categorized each piece (some were assigned more than one category) with a focus, including working conditions, classroom pedagogical choices, aligning philosophy and practice, developing pedagogies and practices that respond to specific students and institutional contexts, or trying out/advocating for a specific pedagogical approach (Table 2.5). Though there are a number of possible interesting findings of Table 2.5, we want to point to the largest category of research articles within Category 2: writing pedagogy and writing outcomes, the articles identifying a specific pedagogical practice. The "experimental pedagogy" article made up the majority of articles about writing classrooms. Typically, such articles proposed a new approach, pedagogical strategy, or theme for a course, and then either reported on a systematic study of that practice or described the practice narratively.

This focus on experimental pedagogies intersects with the earlier point that the majority of articles focused on writing classrooms are not systematic—about three-quarters at 76 percent (see Table 2.6 on page 63). We see this as creating limitations for writing teachers because the largest category of pedagogical articles is experimental pedagogy, as reflected in our categories of analysis as "advocat-

Table 2.5. Topical Emphasis of Writing Classroom and Pedagogy Articles

N	1 Materiality	2 Classroom	3 Philosophy and Practice	4 Inst. Context	5 Locations	6 Student Preparation and Needs	7 Specific Practice
CE	1	17	37	26	18	21	60
CCC	5	34	49	38	32	40	65
WPA	3	8	11	5	12	15	21
CS	3	12	27	5	7	1	80
Aggregate	12	71	124	74	69	77	226
%	3%	18%	31%	19%	17%	19%	57%

ing for a specific classroom practice." Over 50 percent of those articles offered a description of an innovative practice, typically situated within a theoretical rationale, but only a small percentage include a comprehensive assessment of whether that pedagogical idea achieved its specific goals across a complete section or sections. That is, often such articles' selected examples are used to illustrate the effectiveness of the practice, but without an accompanying discussion of students who struggled or did not achieve the goals of the practice.

We want to note that there are articles that push back against this type of research narrative. Matthew Vetter's May 2018 article in *College English,* "Teaching Wikipedia: Appalachian Rhetoric and the Encyclopedic Politics of Representation," describes in detail the methodology of samples collected and the evidence from student writing or interviews supporting the claims, as well as including a section that demonstrates that some students did not experience success with or were challenged by the curricular approach. Vetter explains in a section headed "Student Access":

> The majority of students in this study learned about Wikipedia's cultural politics through a successful engagement with the encyclopedia—noticing gaps in coverage and working to fill those gaps through their own research and writing. However, highlighting only those stories would misrepresent other students, whose planned edits weren't as successful: 18 percent (3 of 17) of students reported some level of access difficulty, noting their own struggles to enter and contribute to the Wikipedia community. (418)

Vetter then goes on to unpack and explain the challenges students faced with logistical or rhetorical access to the pedagogical goals of the curriculum described. This discussion is especially important because the study takes place at a midsize public institution—but also in a "junior level general education course" (399). Deploying or applying this approach, which is engaging and supported by the writer's inquiry practice, would require significant adjustment to use for a different type of program, course, or student population.

The connections between the material conditions of labor in

teaching-intensive writing-studies jobs and pedagogical experimentation are such that the costs of curricular revision for students and instructors are high, an issue we will address in more detail in Chapter 3. For instructors like those in our study, teaching four to five sections of multiple courses (often in different media or geographical locations), implementing an experimental pedagogy is a risky and labor-intensive process. The TYCA Workload Survey reported in "TYCA Working Paper #2, Two-Year College English Faculty Teaching Adjustments Related to Workload," as the working paper summary of qualitative responses reports:

> [I]ssues like learning activities, readings, or assignments were framed as recycled, despite a desire for the ability to update materials or approaches. Examples of language indicating compromises to creativity in teaching include "Innovation often takes a backseat—I tend to do the same things (that I know work) to save me prep time" and "limits innovation and trying new things." Most comments about compromises to creativity focused on saving course preparation time. (6)

Managing multiple sections means that introducing a new curriculum or instructional approach needs to be the same across sections, for the sake of workload management. This could be a risky proposition if the pedagogy or curriculum ends up being unworkable or even damaging in some way, perhaps poorly preparing basic writing students for the next course or being so difficult to implement that students drop out or fail. For structurally disadvantaged students, such an outcome in one course can mean the difference between being retained in college or not. Instructors in such contexts are also potentially hamstrung by writing program guidelines or curricular approaches that may be dictated by a WPA, by a state-level set of course objectives and outcomes, or by some other external constraint, such as teaching at and designing courses for multiple institutions or programs. John Raucci's February 2021 "Replication Agenda for Composition Studies" speaks to this issue indirectly; Raucci argues that replication "demands close attention to the social and material conditions of the original research site," and that "foregrounding replication as collaboration, sharing, and reciprocity instead of merely attacking or overturning results aligns with the disciplinary values of composition scholars" (450). We see Raucci's call as highly relevant to the results of our analysis. If an academic value system calls for continual innovation rather than *verification of what we know across multiple contexts*, it is challenging to develop a firm foundation of knowledge in the field; this is a particular problem for fields like ours where labor is increasingly precarious and the institutional spaces in which writing is taught are so diverse.

Though we understand the attractiveness of the experimental practice or pedagogy article, it is concerning from the standpoint of aligning labor, teaching, and scholarship that so many of the articles about writing classrooms and pedagogies have this focus, in part because there is no real way for the average writing instructor or writing program to actualize that scholarship without specific high-stakes risks to their students or programs.

Category 3: Research Features

Our last, more nuanced, breakdown of the corpus of articles specifically focused on writing program and writing classroom are articles that fulfilled a model of systematic inquiry along the lines of (but not synonymous with) the RAD model proposed by Haswell. We very loosely defined this (within our designated undergraduate writing classrooms and pedagogy-focused articles) as having three features. Those features included documenting and explaining a method of investigation as well as the evidence collected to support that investigation (methodology), demonstrating directly or indirectly a line of investigation that starts from a research question (systematic inquiry), and drawing from a comprehensive or close-to-comprehensive representation of the body of students' work or classroom results (such that the results of the inquiry could be said to be both reflective of the range of writing and writers included in the study, and/or be generalizable to other classrooms).[7] Table 2.6, below, shows the breakdown of those Category 1 and 2 articles focused on classrooms and pedagogies that used systematic inquiry.

WPA and *CCC* are the journals most likely to publish writing-classroom research using a systematic design during this period, with *Composition Studies* and *College English* the least likely (Table 2.6, at 13 percent and 14 percent respectively). That being said, just a quarter of those articles that had writing classrooms or pedagogy as their site and subject of study used a systematic approach that could be considered generalizable research about the teaching of writing. And as we noted in Table 2.5, there was very little overlap between the experimental pedagogy category and systematic inquiry (just 25 percent of those articles used a systematic inquiry approach). What we see as an important implication for writing studies teacher-scholars, then, is the misalignment between the ways and purposes for publishing articles about writing pedagogy and the importance of considering the needs and material realities of the new majority of teachers and students.

We see, then, a relationship between the important work of writing courses, the need for research that serves the professional needs of the new majority of college writing teachers, and the value/relevance of systematic inquiry to help instructors know what approaches, pedagogies, and practices will help students best achieve the desired learning outcomes. Research, citation, and information literacy are just some examples (source-based writing and research techniques) for which writing instructors need multiple and varied

Table 2.6. Total Number of Articles (Aggregate and by Journal) That Use a Systematic Research Design

	Writing Classroom and Writing Pedagogy Focused (N)	Systematic Inquiry (n)	Systematic Inquiry (%)
CE	102	14	14
CCC	143	39	27
WPA	59	29	49
CS	92	12	13
Aggregate	396	94	28

ways of implementing the outcomes into different classroom sites. Information literacy seems especially critical as a transferable skill, especially given its focus as the core requirement of most writing programs.

Ultimately, research should be driven by the critical needs of the field. If we believe that all teachers of writing are members of the field, as we make clear earlier, then the results of the analysis in this chapter suggest that not only is there a gap between teaching and scholarship, but the vast majority of scholarship itself is not emerging from the exciting—and important—laboratories of the field of writing studies—first-year writing classrooms.

WHAT TWO-YEAR-COLLEGE WRITING STUDIES OFFERS

—Jennifer Heinert, UW–Waukesha, –Washington, and Online

As I began to participate in and understand the English department of which I was a new member, it was clear to me that despite how strikingly different the workloads and institutions were, the department values were very similar to the one I had observed as a graduate student in many ways: literary research and courses were the main subject of discussion and debate; enrollment in literature courses was the central concern of most department meetings. The unstated assumption was that as a professor who wanted to earn tenure I would be expected to publish work in literary studies, and I undertook this role immediately and successfully.

However, there was a disjuncture between what I was asked to do in the research part of my job and the 4-4 teaching load that was 3-3 teaching first-year writing. And while I made progress publishing and presenting about the novels of Toni Morrison, I was rarely teaching novels in anything but a survey course—there were no opportunities for me to teach students in major courses, nor graduate students, and no resources for undergraduate research partners in literary study. My peers and department colleagues might occasionally ask about research projects informally, but our individual specialized fields from graduate training were not a source of common ground or collaboration. We staked out territories in the course catalog that reflected our interests but were largely isolated when it came to research, conferences, and publication.

As the semesters passed, I began to shift my research attention to the majority of my teaching load out of necessity. While I had been well prepared to teach writing, I was not well prepared to teach the structurally disadvantaged students at a rural commuter campus in a geographically disparate institution. I was overwhelmed by the workload, and my department had no resources in the form of a cohesive writing program to help support me as I transitioned and adjusted—no curriculum, learning outcomes, placement process, or assessment program. While it was clear to me that the department retention and promotion committee wanted to make sure I was doing an effective job teaching writing, there was nothing that articulated what that meant. I found myself reaching out to colleagues to discuss and workshop the problems and solutions I had created intuitively and independently, and started to build relationships with faculty and instructors who not only valued the teaching of writing but also pointed me to professional resources and publications that helped introduce me to the concept of writing studies as a discipline. I began to understand how my training had been a solid foundation, but it was not a substitute for disciplinary expertise.

In flagship residential universities, comprehensive regional universities, or private liberal arts colleges, first-year writing is a small part of the overall language study students do and given less attention than minor and major courses, at least by the swath of full-time/tenure-line faculty who are often focused on upper-division instruction in their areas of specialty. And in the first two settings, first-year writing is largely the province of graduate students in MA or PhD programs and non-tenure-track faculty. Two-year colleges, by contrast, focus exclusively on developmental reading and writing, on first-year writing courses, and on introducing students to college-level literacy work. That is the singular area of attention for English instructors who teach both academic transfer programs and writing courses that fulfill vocational course requirements. As a result, there is extensive knowledge production emerging from these contexts that is undervalued in the field at large—even those programs that do not identify as "academic transfer" are important teaching and learning contexts for literacy inquiry exactly *because* they offer writing studies a different kind of writing development and emphasis than the traditional FYW course. As Holly Larson asked in 2018, calling on the work of Gloria Anzaldúa and Cherrie Moraga, "Why cannot my colleagues' and my kitchen-table conversations on critical writing or pedagogical issues be valuable scholarly work in itself?" (122). Teacher-scholar-activists like Darin Jensen, Howard Tinberg, and Jeff Andelora have similarly called for greater attention to the TYCs as a site of writing studies research as well as the gap that opens in the production of knowledge by the field's inattention to them.

One specific illustration of this gap is the issue of online writing instruction as an area of scholarly inquiry, which we have touched on previously. Online, hybrid, and alternative-delivery models of instruction have been the bread and butter of two-year colleges for decades. However, the National Census of Writing housed at Swarthmore—whose mission is to "provide a data-based landscape of writing instruction at two- and four-year public and not-for-profit institutions of higher education in the United States," even in the time of COVID (at least, at the time of this writing) does not include a survey response box for respondents to indicate whether they have online course offerings in their curricula. This exclusion is important because two-year campuses, with their call to serve local students and working adults, are more likely than four-year universities to offer online courses.

The online writing instruction gap is also illustrated by the Postsecondary Writing Course Caps (PWCC) managed by Hassel and crowdsourced through various listservs. At the original time of this writing prepandemic (October 2019), 86 of 382 respondents identified as two-year institutions. Of the two-year campuses, 35 indicated they offered online sections, or 40.70 percent. By contrast, of the 296 respondents from four-year institutions, just 49 indicated they offered online sections of writing courses (16.55 percent). In other words, before COVID-19, two-year English departments were two and a half times as likely to offer writing courses online. This is something new instructors are perhaps less likely to have had experience doing prior to starting a two-year-college teaching position, given that universities seem to be less frequently offering online courses. Matt Reed, a regular commentator on higher education issues facing two-year colleges, states, "Online instruction is not new in the community college world. Many have been doing it for 20 years," observing that "community college students are often older and are balancing external obligations with college. The students need the option." In particular, Reed critiques a series of *Chronicle of Higher Ed* essays that were published in June of 2020, where he notes that even the title, "The Great Reopening Debate," belies the reality that students at two-year colleges have—for twenty years—"long built de facto 'hybrid' schedules by combining on-site and online classes [that allow] them to work around paid jobs and family obligations," and observes that the hot take in the *Chronicle* fails to recognize that the "great reopening debate" is "not either-or, just as it hasn't been either-or for the last 20 years."

Our experience in the two-year environment reflects this argument. Almost ten years ago, we were tasked, along with our colleagues, to revise the entire first-year writing online program as well as to create writing courses for the Flexible Option program (what could be described as a competency-based writing program; see Trader et al.). During this process, we had very few resources to help us with this work (see Giordano and Phillips). And ten years later, there is still little to no research about designing online writing programs in an access institution. Perhaps COVID-19 will increase the attention given to online teaching, but even if it does it is likely to repeat the structural hierarchies of face-to-face education. As Reed says, conversations about opening colleges during COVID across the country are completely shutting out two-year campuses.

He further argues that in "The Great Reopening Debate," "Out of 23 essays, four are from the Ivy League (Yale, Harvard, Columbia and Brown). At least five are from public flagships (UNC, U of Maryland, UC Santa Barbara, Rutgers and the U of Washington, with a possible sixth from [a] large research university in the Midwest). Community colleges? Zero. Completely skunked." Similarly, in a *New York Times Magazine* article, "What Will College Be Like in the Fall?" (Bazelon), community colleges are barely mentioned.

We emphasize online writing instruction (OWI) as a kind of "mini-case study" of research gaps because we think it is emblematic of the misalignment that is the emphasis of this book largely and of this chapter specifically. Research interests in two-year-college writing studies are often driven by need, and the needs and demands of our programs are different from those in traditional universities. It is true that online writing instruction has not been ignored by writing studies. Disciplinarily, online writing instruction is an area of professional interest signified by the Online Writing Instruction standing group in CCCC, the Global Society of Online Literacy Educators, and other resources. However, limited attention has been paid by university-dominated professional organizations to either the needs of two-year-college writing teachers and students or the expertise that such instructors have developed over their years of dedicating their professional labor to adaptable, responsive, and innovative pedagogies.

Simply put, university-initiated disciplinary projects, without careful attention to the work that takes place in TYCs, will be missing crucial components of the college student experience in the United States and will produce knowledge about the field that is simply inaccurate or incomplete. If we are willing to alter the view that the work done by the teaching majority, with the most structurally disadvantaged, underrepresented, and marginalized students is not real college or not of interest to writing studies scholars, then the call we make here is urgent. Seth Kahn's 2020 essay in *College English*, "We Value Teaching Too Much to Keep Devaluing It," gets at an explanation for why this inattention persists. As Kahn writes, the reason that writing studies ignores the work at two-year colleges, which is focused on teaching, is the field's overall devaluing of teaching:

> It's impossible to quantify the impact that the discourse of teaching devaluation has, but at least recognizing it helps to explain why so many people have worked so hard to argue so well about how to improve labor conditions in the field and have produced such hit-and-miss results. Right alongside all that hard work to do right is a discourse that denigrates the value of the exact same labor for which we demand labor justice. At best, these two sets of arguments combine to produce a mixed message: Yes, teaching matters, but no, we'd prefer not to pay people very well to do it. So, we don't. (595)

We appreciate Kahn's careful read of how research and teaching are often framed as separate activities, one of which has greater value attached to it than the other, and how the ways that symbolic and financial capital are attached to the faculty work that has the least contact with students shapes the values of higher education more broadly. As Kahn writes, consequences of this hierarchy are significant: "The most direct damage happens to graduate students and job seekers who are actively dissuaded from pursuing teaching positions because they aren't prestigious enough or don't afford enough research time and to faculty in NTT positions who suffer profound professional disrespect of various kinds, ranging from accusations of personal failure to blame for the collapse of the job market—if not the whole institution of tenure" (592). We would add to this assessment that not only does devaluing teaching-intensive work (of which there is no more significant site than two-year colleges, as labor conditions outlined above show), but we also exclude important sites of knowledge from disciplinary scholarship that can offer fresh insights about writers and writing.

TYC WRITING STUDIES RESEARCH: A BRIEF INTRODUCTION

As our discussion of OWI illustrates, two-year-college writing programs are exciting sites for research into writing and writers—and offer distinct lines of inquiry that are often not present or not high-priority in university environments. We describe some of those innovations in this section. But just as the material realities and working conditions in two-year colleges differ in important ways from those of the four-year institutions we describe above, so too do the research environments that limit the ability of two-year-college teacher-scholars to undertake research projects with the same frequency and support as university colleagues. While two-year scholars have contributed valuable research to the field (as we cite in this chapter), most two-year instructors will face a variety of obstacles to accessing and conducting systematic research. Perhaps most significant, the workload and working conditions described earlier in this chapter make it very difficult if not impossible to devote adequate time to conduct research. Teaching multiple and varied preps for up to six sections or more a semester means that, both by definition and by necessity, the instructor's primary responsibility is teaching, purely from a labor standpoint.

But even beyond institutional designators, two-year colleges are not set up to be research institutions in terms of budgetary allocations, professional expectations, and institutional culture in a way that fosters (consistent) research activity. When an instructor is on the tenure track at a two-year institution, research expectations are rarely as high as at other types of institutions, thereby deprioritizing access and resources when figuring out budget allocations and stipends. And not unlike many other types of institutions, research on basic, developmental, or even first-year writers is often at the bottom of the hierarchy and receives less privilege than more traditional research, or than areas that focus on high-performing students such as those in undergraduate research or honors programs. Developmental reading and writing programs are often areas of contention for institutions who have them; they are often assessed for elimination rather than researched for data on retention and literacy development. We have not seen any articles appear in *CCC* that report on or address basic/developmental writing, which gives writing studies scholars further permission to ignore this part of college writing transition work. This is illustrated by one of Cassie's experiences working on a research project.

◈◈◈◈

During one of the last days of class, a student approached me about a research project I was working on that was focused on developmental readers and writers. He asked me, "Can you tell me more about what you are doing with the student work you collect?" During the previous class, a fellow instructor had read the IRB script and asked for participation in the collection of data. During that class, the research protocol was distributed and in my class of twenty-two students only two gave permission to use their work. This was, unfortunately, normal. After two years of collecting data, I have learned that about 10 percent participation is all I can count on.

This student and I talked a bit about my research, but I could tell he was anxious. After I assured him repeatedly that he did not have to participate, and that I really wouldn't know which students had given permission until after the semester ended, he left. That number of participants (two) did not change, and I later thought about how much I was asking for these students to sign away access to their work. Not only might they be anxious to share their work outside of our classroom, but they might be mistrustful of how it could be used against them or how it might portray them. They know where they are in the hierarchy.

◈◈◈◈

As the above vignette from Cassie's experience shows, there are other obstacles instructors face when conducting systematic and/or longitudinal research in two-year environments, and again, many of those obstacles are connected to the data described earlier in this chapter. In addition to the amount of time instructors do (or do not) have to conduct research, they also face the limitations of students' time—the time students spend in the institution, the time students spend on campus, and even the amount of time students spend in the classroom. As we've noted, most campuses are commuter campuses with students attending classes and returning home or going to work for most of their day. Most students are part-time. Most students will not attend classes for more than two years, if that. The National Center for Education Statistics data tracking students who began their educations at public two-year colleges in 2009 shows the complex educational pathways for two-year-college students completing *any credential at their enrolling institution*:

> The 8-year completion rates for the cohort were higher among full-time students (30 percent for first-time students and 38 percent for non-first-time students) than among part-time students (16 percent for first-time students and 21 percent for non-first-time students). Two percent or less of students in the four groups remained enrolled 8 years after entry. Transfer rates 8 years after entry were higher among non-first-time students (37 percent for part-time students and 30 percent for full-time students) than among first-time students (24 percent for both full-time and part-time students). The percentage of students whose enrollment status was unknown 8 years after entry, however, varied widely among the four groups, from 30 percent for non-first-time, full-time students to 58 percent for first-time, part-time students. (*Postsecondary Outcomes*)

All of these factors—transfer, inconsistent enrollment status, and poor cross-institutional data tracking—make continued access to students and their participation in this work difficult (Woodworth).

In addition, most students have not been exposed to a research environment in the same way that those at four-year campuses have. At those institutions, students generally have some exposure to classroom research conducted by professors or may be aware of the research component of faculty professional responsibilities. In the two-year environment, not only is that exposure rare, but students' backgrounds with education and academia in general are often complex. That is, higher education has not served them well, whether through cost to attend, admissions standards, or placement procedures. Many students have consistently received negative messages about their writing, reading, and general abilities as students or their commitment to higher education.

Despite these challenging contexts for participating in scholarly conversations in writing studies, a strong body of scholarly work exists on two-year-college writing studies, some of which has informed broader disciplinary conversations and shaped the praxis-focused work of TYC faculty. Christie Toth, Patrick Sullivan, and Carolyn Calhoon-Dillahunt make several important observations in their *CCC* article, "Two-Year College Teacher-Scholar-Activism: Reconstructing the Disciplinary Matrix of Writing Studies." Two-year-college scholarship is transdisciplinary (reflecting the different subfields of English and allied fields within which TYC faculty are trained); it has an established record of building and marshaling disciplinary evidence to inform public policy; and it is committed to building equity and access for the broadest range of students seeking a postsecondary education. In this section, we sketch a picture of the published TYC writing studies work for those readers less familiar with its accomplishments. Likewise, we offer some hypotheses about how and why this body of work has failed to gain traction within the larger field of writing studies. In doing so, we hope to make clear what TYC scholarship in writing studies has to offer the field at large, and how—in key ways—the areas of the field most linked to practice are those that are taken up earliest by TYC teacher-scholar-activists. In this way, the larger field can and should look to TYC scholarship not as less valuable because of its practitioner emphasis but as at the vanguard of the discipline because TYC writing studies scholarship quickly recognizes and responds to practice-focused areas of the field before they become exigent to the broader community.

Though basic writing and writers as a construct for making curricular decisions is shifting, the open-admissions work in two-year colleges in the early 1960s played a significant role in expanding college access and the accompanying development of academic literacy to a broader swath of potential students than ever before (see Anderst et al.). The work taking place on the ground currently around improving that access and success has happened at two-year colleges, including the accelerated learning program (Adams et al.), integrated reading and writing (Bickerstaff and Raufman; Doran), multiple-measures placement (Hassel and Giordano, "Blurry Borders"), and writing studio (Grego and Thompson; Sutton and Chandler) as a form of corequisite support for students.

Though these teaching and learning issues rarely make it into the mainstream writing-studies journal conversations, they are critical to the work of making higher education accessible and possible for the new majority of college students.

In part this is because of the challenges we describe above—formal studies that look closely at the transition of students whose prior literacy and educational experiences are not aligned with college are less likely to participate in the kind of formal research work that writing-studies scholarship publishes. Small but notable studies, however, that engage systematically with questions of interest to open-access writing programs offer us knowledge that would otherwise not be available. For example, Howard Tinberg and Jean-Paul Nadeau's *Community College Writer: Exceeding Expectations* offers a yearlong look at two-year-college writing students. Likewise, Marilyn Sternglass's landmark longitudinal look at students progressing from basic writing courses in a community college to college-level work, *Time to Know Them*, earned both the 1998 Mina P. Shaughnessy Award from the Modern Language Association and the 1999 Outstanding Book Award from the Conference on College Composition and Communication, in part because, as a review of her work notes, "Sternglass's study illustrates that students supposedly doomed to fail can succeed given the right opportunities, and student success has immeasurable 'social and economic benefits' (296) to society" (Liese 24).

Sternglass's project began with fifty-three volunteers "who agreed to fill out an initial demographic questionnaire, to be interviewed twice a semester about their writing, to provide copies of all writing (papers and examinations) in all of their classes and, later, to allow a research assistant to sit in on one of their classes each semester." By the end of the project, six years later, however, just nine student participants remained. Annie Del Principe and Rachel Ihara's 2017 article, "A Long Look at Reading in the Community College: A Longitudinal Analysis of Student Reading Experiences" offers important findings about college reading practices and tasks, but the authors faced challenges similar to those facing Tinberg and Nadeau and Sternglass, noting that despite recruiting across developmental writing and first-year writing courses, the study focused on "[t]en students [who] participated in the project on some level" (186). But as they describe in their methods section, the results include complete records from just five of those students, just one of whom was placed into the lowest level developmental writing courses (though the project began with six). As Del Principe and Ihara explain:

> Although we do not know precisely why the other five students chose to discontinue the study, we do know that two transferred shortly after joining the study, and two left CC in poor academic standing with GPAs of 1.5 and 1.0. It is worth noting that these two, and a third student who stopped taking part in the study, were all developmental students. Thus, despite our efforts to secure a number of developmental students proportional to the population at large, these were precisely the students who were unable or unwilling, for whatever reasons, to continue meeting with us for interviews. (186–87)

Tinberg and Nadeau's book, as well, shows the struggle to recruit and engage TYC students in this kind of project; multiple recruitment efforts and phases resulted in sixteen students participating in their yearlong project (of nearly a thousand students eligible as first-semester students at their Massachusetts campus, Bristol Community College), and just four students were able to complete all dimensions of the project culminating in an end-of-spring-semester interview with the researchers.

We think these efforts to reflect TYC students (specifically those beginning in developmental coursework) in writing studies are necessary, but we must acknowledge how challenging it is. And yet, there is a moral imperative to do it. The work of TYC writing studies allows for an understanding of the literacy experiences of students whom university programs *will simply never see* and who deserve to see themselves represented in scholarship. And in doing that work, we learn more about the obstacles these students face as writers—and can reveal the barriers that institutions of higher education and writing programs may create and reinforce, barriers that prevent many of the most marginalized and minoritized students from being retained in college. Furthermore, our students know how important access to literacy education is. Joan, one of the students in Sternglass's study, wrote, "[O]ne can conclude [that] education was, and still remains, the key element involved in overcoming oppression. One should never forget that knowledge is the one tool that can be used to overpower the white man" (68).

GAPS IN COMPOSED KNOWLEDGE

We are certainly not the first to draw attention to the labor and working conditions of writing studies as well as writing programs in higher education. However, with this chapter, we aim to continue the work of painting the larger picture or adjusted view of writing studies that we began in Chapter 1 when we analyzed the misalignment of knowledge production with workload and labor in postsecondary writing instruction. With this analysis we show the ways that the published research in our flagship peer-reviewed journals in the field can be mapped out in relation to the first two pillars in our larger project—labor and pedagogy. We are interested in providing this kind of big-picture analysis because, so often, the lived conditions of graduate education and scholarly production encourage "new" and "original" investigations and suggest that the primary and most valuable research is that which breaks new ground or revises settled assumptions. We know this has to be balanced against the doctoral and master's degree expectation of creating "new knowledge," but we think sometimes verified or updated knowledge is as useful as new knowledge for the purposes of building a disciplinary foundation.

Scholarship serves both to reflect who we are and what we do, and is a record of how we will look back in the field's future. It is a critical resource for teacher-scholars of writing to help us do our jobs better throughout our careers, and it can be a critical resource to help us reach a variety of students across shifting populations. Therefore it is not enough to say that our classrooms should be informed by the growing body of knowledge in the field; rather, the body of knowledge in the field must also be informed by our classrooms and the material realities instructors face every day. There are clear relationships, we think, between the reality that just 11 percent of two-year-college writing programs have a stable, expertise-based WPA—and, as Steven Accardi and Jillian Grauman observe, "These resilient academic leadership roles, common at universities and four-year colleges, are critically needed at the two-year college to assemble, develop, and produce writing program knowledge" (80). In other words, there is a mutual responsibility for labor conditions in two-year colleges that make it possible for faculty to conduct the kinds of inquiry, assessment, and writing that will become durable professional knowledge; and it is incumbent upon journals to find ways to expand the definition of what constitutes professional knowledge to include praxis-oriented scholarship.

We turn again here to comments from Jack and Gillian, reflecting on the transition from an autonomous program with support for instructors to a branch campus, separated off from a larger supportive academic unit.

Jack and Gillian Van Treese, UWC–Milwaukee at Waukesha: After our first year of no longer being a part of this institution and instead part of UW–Milwaukee, much has changed, and we find ourselves missing what used to be. The English faculty and staff do not have a relationship with UWM's English department, but instead are part of a multidiscipline department within our own college. This new department has, understandably, spent much of the year on developing policy and procedure, so there have been no disciplinary workshops focused on teaching, we've lost many of the resources that our old department website provided, and there is little communication on issues related to developing or maintaining our writing program. Although requested, at this point there is no WPA or developmental English coordinator position; instead, the department chair is expected to oversee our writing and developmental programs as part of leading all disciplines falling under humanities and arts. Although it has been good to engage with colleagues from other disciplines in our new department structure, we find ourselves feeling more isolated in our teaching, unsure of whom to turn to with programmatic questions, and afraid that our discipline might lose its voice within our new institution.

If at first the COVID-19 pandemic required us to "reimagine" our classrooms for an online environment, we have now gained less-immediate insights—that teaching and learning in a pandemic require more work not just to put teaching in a new modality but to teach in and of itself. Just showing up in a room with students—and marking their absence/presence—can no longer be a "placeholder" or a proxy for either teaching or learning. Professional organizations such as CCCC and CWPA have sought to synthesize and fill the gap for what is missing and how to "rebuild" our programs in responsive and adaptable ways (see the *CCCC and CWPA Joint Statement in Response to the COVID-19 Pandemic*). However, our analysis of published scholarship shows how ill-prepared we are to support teachers and students when traditional structures change—or fail.

3

Materiality, Teaching, and Disciplinary Learning

◈◈◈◈

Fall 2019—Midterm Conferences

Holly

My life is different now, but what is most different is how I spend my time. At a position where I work with tenure, with a 40 percent assignment to teaching, a 40 percent assignment to research, and a 20 percent to service, Week 6 of the semester includes conferences with students. In my first year, I never saw a first-year writing student; this year I asked to teach the two-course sequence, English 110 and English 120. Most students start in 120 but we offer an increasing number of 110 sections; placement is exclusively based on ACT score, and the students who enroll fulfill many of the unstated assumptions when we use the term good students*—they come to class, they submit the work, they try hard, they do the reading. Even teaching students who by their standardized test scores would be categorized as "at-risk," at least in the area of writing and reading, the differences are stark between working in an open-admissions two-year institution and working in a four-year university with a graduate program such as this one. I am one of two tenured faculty teaching first-year writing; the other is the WPA. We offer 98 sections of first-year writing.*

My conference week looks much different. I can fit all the conferences in by canceling a week of class and using my office hours. All the students attend; most bring writing. All of the students, who by many measures are underprepared for college writing, express anxiety or frustration with writing, saying "English is my worst subject" or "I'm not a strong writer" or "I struggle with reading and writing." Several describe what I would call "literacy interventions" in elementary school like intensive reading courses for students reading below grade level, and supplemental private tutoring supported by their parents.

I have enough time to give every student feedback on two different essay drafts, and also to ask, "How is your first semester going?," and really listen to the answer. One student cries, but it's because writing is hard for her and she struggles to navigate the ambiguity of the drafting, editing, feedback process, experiencing it as a failure. I have time to reassure her and talk about strategies for moving her projects forward. A student who emails me to say he is canceling because he doesn't have any writing is coaxed into showing up for his conference anyway, and when I realize he is failing all his classes, I can stage an intervention that involves a lot of coaching and follow-up meetings as well as references to multiple on-campus resources.

Cassie

Conference week for me is, in many ways, absolute chaos. This semester, for example, I have two sections of developmental writing (one online), a section of a variation of an ALP model first-semester writing course with a combined workshop credit, and a section of business writing mainly taken by second-year students. The business writing conferences are straightforward. Students come, they are usually prepared, they have questions, and they want feedback. The conferences are time-consuming, but they generally go as planned.

The conferences for the other three sections of writing involve a great deal of work to arrange, and even then rarely go as planned. For the face-to-face classes, the students cannot meet outside of class time because of other classes, work, and family commitments. This means I have to try and schedule all of the conferences within the confines of class hours—which does not work, logistically. Even if I schedule twenty-minute conferences for developmental writers, they almost always go over. Also, if I were to cancel more than two classes of developmental writing, it would seriously set back the most underprepared students as they would not have structured in-class writing time for over a week. But every semester I try. I know most of my colleagues do as well.

Many of these students are not prepared for conferences and we spend time getting ready to discuss writing they have not yet completed or talking about assignments they do not understand. Some of them do not show and have to be rescheduled to a time the following week or other arrangements have to be made, neither of which is optimal for their development as writers. The unfortunate truth is that I do not end up conferring with all students, and the ones who do not show up or reschedule are impacted, sometimes seriously. That impact has me questioning the whole process, over and over. Like so many things with struggling students—when something works, students are able to continue to the next level. When it doesn't work, they drop back multiple levels and sometimes out of college entirely.

◈◈◈◈

The world of writing-studies scholarship, particularly that which defines best practices in writing programs, emerges almost from an ideal reality. Even as professionals in the field have worked hard to create sets of evidence and research-informed recommendations that build on what we know about writing and writers (through research, position statements, resolutions, etc.), the material conditions of the two-year environment are often so far from that ideal reality that it makes operationalizing those guidelines nearly impossible. Likewise, some of those practices have implications for open-access students that are not only unhelpful, but in some cases even harmful to student success in the classroom.

As we write this, COVID-19 has caused many instructors across the country to make dramatic changes to their teaching. For example, there is a Facebook group called "Pandemic Pedagogy," and it has 37,712 members as of August 2020. As group members geared up for fall semester, one instructor posted a request for help, noting that they were moving from a 1-1 graduate teaching assistant position at a four-year campus to a 6-6 load at a technical college. They wondered how to translate the best practices that they had learned in graduate school (feedback on student work, conferences), in this new context. This new TYC teacher may find suggestions for strategies from willing peers, but as we show in Chapter 2, they will find limited, if any, research and scholarship in the major journals that address these teaching and learning conditions. As we show in that chapter, fewer than 10 percent of all articles published between 2000 and 2018 in *College English, Composition Studies, College Composition and Communication*, and *WPA* address this context. Certainly, this instructor will find *Teaching English in the Two-Year College* for instructors who teach primarily first-year writing and literature or other lower-division courses. For instructors whose teaching load includes non-degree-credit courses, corequisite, writing studio, or integrated reading and writing courses (now mandated as replacements for "remedial" coursework), *The Journal of Basic Writing* is an essential publication. However, these relatively recently developed curricular interventions are underaddressed even in those publications. Even less available are systematically gathered studies of writing classrooms or programs that address best practices in this context.

In this chapter, we examine this environment from a classroom perspective. We start by distilling some of the "core composed knowledge" in writing studies and set it alongside the reality of two-year-college writing students and teachers. Our intention is not to say that disciplinary knowledge is wrong—in fact, we value this knowledge for much of our professional work. Rather, our intention is to show that there are gaps in what much of this disciplinary knowledge accounts for in terms of what college writers need to learn and what the materiality of college writing classrooms is. When we ignore these gaps, student learning is affected. Our goal is to show the material realities of two-year-college writing studies from a classroom perspective, including instructor workload and material conditions, and then to offer some ways to account for those realities in the broader disciplinary conversations. We make this argument by (1) Providing a detailed overview of two-year-college workload, (2) describing our research project and the teachers and students who participated, (3) contextualizing our use of *disciplinary learning domains* (defined below) and explaining and grounding our methodology, and (4) offering an in-depth analysis of student learning and instructional perspectives, sorted by each disciplinary learning domain.

TEACHING AND LEARNING IN THE TWO-YEAR ENVIRONMENT

The two-year-college sector serves approximately 43 percent of undergraduate students. It also disproportionately enrolls students of color, with 44 percent of Black and 56 percent of Latinx students enrolled in the two-year sector, compared with 29 percent of each of these groups in public four-years (Ma and Baum). Nontraditional students are also concentrated in two-year colleges, with 58 percent of students in two-year colleges starting their college coursework under age twenty compared with 80 percent on traditional four-year campuses. Though low-income students also disproportionately enroll in two-year colleges, they are less likely to apply for financial aid—61 percent apply for federal aid compared with 70 percent in four-years. Additional data from the US Department of Education shows that the students who were most likely to be eligible for federal student aid are also the least likely to complete the application, with parental level of education as a major predictor in completing the FAFSA: 60 percent of students whose parents have a high school diploma or GED compared with 73 percent of students whose parents held a bachelor's degree completed the FAFSA. Income level, as well, has an influence: 53.9 percent of students from the lowest fifth of the income quintile completed the FAFSA compared with 72.8 percent of students in the highest fifth and 66.7 percent in the middle three-fifths (Bahr et al.).

Though the report does not break out FAFSA completion rates by postsecondary sector (two-year versus four-year), our own experience with majority first-generation and working-class students (see also Smith, "First-Generation College Students"), is that many students at community colleges are either not aware of or are highly resistant to the FAFSA. There are negative perceptions of going into debt for college, and the Department of Education suggests that the reasons offered by students for not applying for financial aid are that they do not want to take on debt by (28 percent of students) and they do not have enough information to complete it at (23 percent of students). In addition, 33 percent of students responded that they didn't need the aid to afford college or thought they might not want to qualify for it (32 percent) (Bahr et al.). Two-year-college students, as well, are more likely to be working full- or part-time, often to pay for their college education as they go. About two-thirds of TYC students work, one-third full-time, compared to about 20 percent of students in other contexts working full-time. Twenty-one percent of students have dependents in TYC compared with 11 percent on four-year campuses (Ma and Baum).

In other words, the huge difference in graduation and success rates for two-year-college students (in our experience) is often much less about academic potential or talent and much more about what can be the punishing demands of an inflexible institution—higher education—as well as the lack of material resources for their work. While two-year-college students are managing multiple demands on their time and energy, two-year-college writing instructors are managing intense teaching loads. They are also helping students work against some significant challenges, and often, prior failure. We think the data show that two-year-college students are highly resilient, but that their relationship to college is fragile. As such, for instructors, work includes not just assigning reading and teaching writing. Their work also often requires acculturating students to the demands of postsecondary learning and the unwritten rules of college (an understanding of which university students are more likely to bring with them to their studies) and helping them draw on the resources that are available in the academic environment to stay engaged with their studies.

To illustrate, we return to the Two-Year College English Association (TYCA) Workload Task Force data, emerging from a national survey on two-year-college faculty workload in Fall 2019. Working papers and a white paper resulting from that survey focused on issues related to labor, assessment, student readiness, developmental education reform, and adjustments to teaching, as well as a report documenting the workload realities of two-year-college English faculty. We introduced some of this data in Chapter 1, but the numbers bear repeating here as we place them alongside the real teachers and students who are discussed in this chapter.

The survey results show that 42 percent of 1,062 respondents teach twenty-eight to thirty-five credit hours annually as part of their contractual teaching loads (see Figure 3.1). Though credit hours do not translate directly into number of courses, five courses per term (or fifteen credits) seems to be typical for faculty at community colleges.[1] Further, more than one-third of respondents reported that they always or frequently teach overloads beyond their contractual obligations (see Figure 3.2). Data from the survey show that 57 percent of faculty sometimes, frequently, or always take on overloads on top of their typical loads (which, as noted, seem to hover around fifteen credits). We saw this firsthand in a research project conducted by Holly Hassel and Joanne Giordano, whose recent study of new two-year-college faculty included a participant who began her first semester at a community college with a 5/5 course load by taking on the maximum number of additional overloads allowed by the contact—three courses per term. This means that she began her first term with a load of eight writing courses,

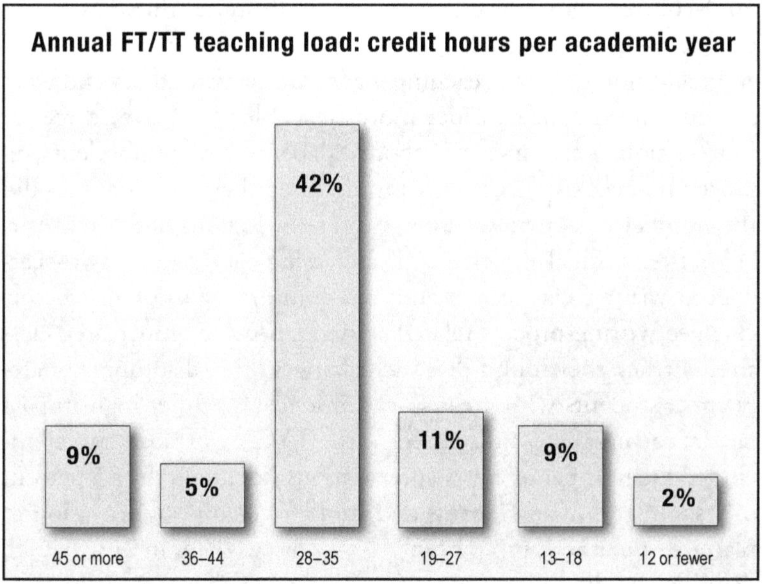

Figure 3.1. Annual full-time/tenure-line teaching load in two-year-college English: credit hours per academic year.

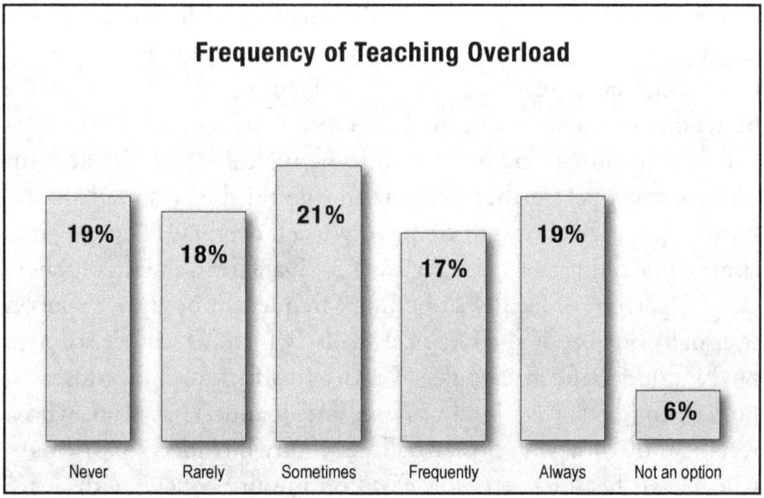

Figure 3.2. Frequency of teaching courses beyond one's contractual obligation in two-year-college English programs.

a mix of first-semester (English 101) and second-semester (English 102) courses. As the survey data above illustrate, this instructor's experience is not unusual.

In addition to heavy teaching loads (for many, well beyond what some faculty might consider more typical loads of two, three, or four sections per semester), about 80 percent of respondents reported that class sizes/course-caps increased their workloads, as did the number of course sections. Cassandra Phillips and Greg Ahrenhoerster studied the effects of increasing class sizes in two-year-college writing classrooms and also found that most instructors changed writing-process-related activities because of increased class size. Further, they found that such changes often disproportionately affect students with greater academic needs. Other high-impact factors for instructors discussed in the TYCA workload survey included the number of course preparations (identified by 55 percent of respondents as significant) and students' readiness in relation to placement methods (53 percent). As we discuss later in this chapter, defining the disciplinary knowledge needs of the new majority of teachers and students means fully grasping their contexts—which include varying levels of time, energy, and agency, as well as understanding that first-year writing is not a monolithic concept with a shared meaning and structure across higher ed sectors or employment statuses.

As the TYCA workload survey illustrates, the degree to which different material components of respondents' work influence their teaching conditions varies. Table 3.1 shows the responses to the question, "How much autonomy do you have over the following aspects of your teaching?" Autonomy and academic freedom—historically, cornerstones of academic work—have potentially very different inflections in the two-year-college context. The survey data above suggest that TYC instructors can expect to have a lot of flexibility in the areas of course content, as is consistent with AAUP recommendations. Yet the TYCA Working Paper #1 confirms that those instructors who are most satisfied with their work also have "positions that had autonomy regarding taking overloads, had class caps that are consonant with recommendations by professional organizations, and had differentials or adjustments when teaching

Table 3.1. Degree of Autonomy That Survey Respondents Indicated They Have over the Various Components of Their Workload

	A Lot	Some	None
Number of Sections	15%	39%	45%
Types of Courses	20%	65%	14%
Course Content	75%	23%	2%
Mode of Delivery	9%	45%	45%
Schedule	12%	60%	27%
Overload	15%	46%	39%
Summer Teaching	10%	38%	52%
Schedule for Office Hours	74%	21%	4%
Structure of Office Hours	22%	39%	39%

writing courses versus other kinds of courses" (Klausman, Roberts, and Snyder 7).

That being said, most instructors who come to TYC contexts from graduate school actually have had very limited autonomy even in the area of course content, at least in many graduate programs where teaching assistants are expected to adhere to a particular curriculum that is typically developed by a WPA or faculty committee. This level of autonomy in an area where new instructors have had very limited prior experience can be a struggle. One instructor who participated in a research study in 2019–2020 of new two-year-college instructors moving from graduate school to TYC positions illustrates this problematic structure. In a reflective journal, the faculty member wrote:

> While I was an adjunct, I taught a themed course on monsters at my four-year university. The last time I taught the class, the students struggled because I had a *lot* of game mechanics in the course and they found that confusing. Since I would be starting my new teaching job with only a week to prepare seven courses, I decided to use that course since it was mostly already complete. I sometimes regret that decision just because my students have struggled with the course theme almost the entire semester, something that wasn't an issue at the institution where I taught previously. My previous students, while cautious about the subject at first, always eventually embraced the class theme and thought deeply about it, and it showed in their writing. This semester, I've practically had to drag the students along and more than once I wished I could just get a redo on the entire semester. It really made me question my pedagogy and why I chose the theme.

By contrast, the area that instructors can expect to have the least autonomy in includes the number of sections they teach, the delivery mode, and whether they teach an overload or summer section. This could mean, for full-time faculty, that they are expected to teach overloads with little room to refuse, or for adjunct faculty, that they have limited ability to influence what their courseload will be each term. Small or satellite campus locations, as well, can limit the flexibility that faculty at larger four-year campuses enjoy, as TYCA Working Paper #3 explains:

> Course offerings and scheduling also need to reflect when students take courses, the number of online sections that meet the needs of a campus population, and courses that students need for degree completion and transfer. Additional institutional constraints can limit the choices that a program or instructor has in creating a flexible and sustainable teaching load—for example, room availability, number of campuses and the distance between them, the size of the student population, availability of ESL and developmental coursework, numbers and types of non-composition courses required for degree completion and transfer within a state system, and fluctuations in the writing program enrollments between fall and spring. (Giordano and Wegner 11)

In summary, these distinct teaching and learning features of the new teaching majority and the new student majority can help readers understand more clearly the consequences of devaluing teaching work—what most people who earn graduate degrees in English will spend the most time on—by emphasizing research as a separate, more important, and disconnected part of the daily work of writing studies. These consequences do not just affect writing teachers in two-year colleges or in contingent positions who want to do more professional development but find themselves with few resources. Such instructors will go to the published research through the usual avenues and perhaps find something that they can map on to their students and classroom needs. But the other consequence is that writing studies as a field misses grounded, praxis-developed knowledge that goes beyond experience and anecdote (though those are also useful forms of knowing). With values that emerge from the situated exigencies of two-year-college contexts, there is much that the broader writing studies scholarly community can and should learn.

OUR PROJECT: CORE LITERACY SKILLS ACROSS THE TWO-YEAR-COLLEGE WRITING CURRICULUM

Our work toward this recentering of first-year writing is rooted in projects we undertook with colleagues between 2009 and 2018. As we will show, our former institution (now dissolved) was reflective of the demographics and staffing practices of many two-year colleges, while also distinct in some ways we will describe. In this section, we provide an overview of the material realities in both the labor and the learning of the instructors and students who participated in a grant-funded research project. Doing so we hope will further our goal of establishing the connections between labor, scholarship, and teaching, as we've laid out in the first two chapters of this book.

From 2013 to 2015, we collaborated with colleagues to create a faculty development opportunity focused on supporting instructors in a state-wide institution (see Hassel et al., "Imperative"). The University of Wisconsin System invested resources in supporting what they called (then) the "growth agenda," intended to build enrollment across the system. Our project, "Professional Development for Core English Skills Instructors: Using Research-Based Teaching Strategies to Improve Student Retention and Academic Success," was intended to be both a professional development opportunity for instructors and also an opportunity to gather empirical evidence about effective strategies for helping open-admissions students make a successful transition to college. Through a series of workshops, online activities, and conversations about course materials, our research team facilitated course revision and simultaneously collected student writing and assignments from thirty-seven instructors across our thirteen campuses, and thus from hundreds of students.

For this chapter, we draw from this body of student work and instructor reflections to create, somewhat deductively, a way of tracking students' progress across the writing courses they enrolled in during the project duration. Because the project included a "model" curriculum that we developed to work across multiple modalities (f2f, online, and the "flex" or competency-based assessment project launched under Governor Scott Walker),[2] we were able to gather a set of instructor materials and student writing that was produced under similar curricular and pedagogical conditions across multiple campuses. For the purposes of the analysis and results we describe here, we attached each of the writing tasks or assessments used in the model course designed for the grant period to a group of what we call *disciplinary learning domains* (detailed in the next section of this chapter) to allow for a more flexible categorization and assessment of students' progress in these areas.[3] Ultimately, our goal was to set a large corpus of student writing against disciplinary outcomes. For each participating student, we looked at three to six pieces of formal writing, from either a midterm portfolio (typically eight to ten pages), or final portfolio (between eighteen and twenty-two pages). The writing usually included cover letters, rhetorical analyses, arguments, syntheses, and literacy narratives, which were among the recommended assignments in the model curriculum created for the project.

We selected a diverse array of sections of student writing from the instructors who participated and contributed portfolios of student writing. These selections included students and instructors from across the writing sequence in our institution (English 098: a non-degree-credit writing course; English 101: the first-semester writing course that students receive elective credit for but that does not fulfill the degree requirement at most four-year institutions or for our Associates of Arts and Sciences degree; and English 102: the research-intensive second semester course that fulfills the degree requirement). Of the seven participating instructors, two were on the tenure track and five worked in non-tenure-line positions. They represented five of our thirteen campuses. Of the seventy-eight students who contributed their writing to the repository, fifteen were taking English 098; forty-six were enrolled in English 101, and seventeen were enrolled in English 102. Our selection rationale included a desire to reflect a range of the campuses across our geographically disparate and multisite statewide institution, a range of employment statuses, and our varied student populations (see Appendix B).

Before we discuss the details of our analysis of student work, we want to offer an overview of the material realities in both labor and learning of the instructors and students who participated in the grant-funded research project. Table 3.2 shows the demographics and background of UWC students, and how or whether they are representative of two-year-college students nationally. As Table 3.2 shows, our student population is mostly reflective of the national

Table 3.2. Demographic and Statistical Data about Two-Year-College Students, UW Colleges Compared with National Data

	UW Colleges Students	National Students
Admission Rates	100 percent of applicants who completed the application admitted ("The New Freshman Class: Fall 2017," Appendix B)	Most community colleges are open-admission
Pell Recipients	For reasons we can only speculate about, during the last few years of the institution's existence, the numbers dropped steadily: 2013–2014: 38% 2014–2015: 34% 2015–2016: 31% 2016–2017: 26% ("Student Financial Aid" memoranda)	Rate of Pell receipt for community-college students 38 percent in 2011–2012, the same as four-years, though eligible TYC students apply in lower numbers
Start in Developmental English	24 percent of students placed into non-degree-credit course, English 098 ("The New Freshman Class: Fall 2017, Table 21, p. 14)	Data vary. According to the CCRC, 33 percent were referred to developmental reading (Bailey et al.); the US Department of Education reports that 28 percent of students are placed into developmental writing or reading "within six years of entering college" (*Developmental Education* 5).

Continued on next page

Table 3.2. Continued

Tuition and Fees	$5,126 ("UW System Tuition Chart")	According to the College Board, in 2017–2018, the average published tuition and fees for full-time students at public two-year institutions nationally were $3,560 (*Trends*, Table 1).
Degree Attainment	Associate's degree: • Between 21 and 23 percent within 3 years (150 percent of the normal time for required for the completion of a program) (Kalish et al. 265) Bachelor's degree: • 7.1 percent within four years (typical completion time) • 24.6 percent within six years (150 percent of the normal time required) ("Retention")	37.5 percent earned a credential from a two- or four-year institution within six years. (Shapiro et al.).

two-year-college data, where we could locate it, with the exception that on average our student population is whiter than the national average because of the majority-white upper midwestern location.[4]

An overview of the teaching assignments and employment status of the instructors whose students contributed writing to our analysis provides more context to the material conditions of our project participants. The instructor breakdown in Table 3.3 reflects both our institutional proportion of tenure- to non-tenure-line instructors, which is aligned with the national percentages cited in Chapter 1. A report from the AAUP confirms: "The majority (70 percent) of academic positions today are not only off the tenure track but also part time, with part-time instructional staff positions making up nearly 41 percent of the academic labor force and graduate teaching assistants making up almost another 13 percent (part-time tenure-track positions make up about 1 percent of the academic labor force)" (Shulman et al. 13). We highlight these instructors' workloads and employment statuses as part of demonstrating how their material circumstances (number of course preps, course caps, instructor background and preparation, physical or virtual location of course) influence the degree to which students and instructors in

Table 3.3. Employment Status and Course Load for Participating Instructors

Instructor[5]	Employment Status (Non-tenure-line instructors receive a one-semester or one-year contract but are eligible for benefits at a 50 percent appointment.)	Fall 2014 Courseload[6]
Ann (PhD in literature)	Tenure-line faculty (second year)	• Writing Studio tutorial (8 hours of tutoring), 1 section • English 101: College Writing and Critical Reading, 2 sections • English 250: Introduction to Literary Studies, 1 section
Carrie (PhD in creative writing)	Tenure-line faculty (third year)	• English 101: College Writing and Critical Reading, 1 section • English 102: Critical Writing, Reading, and Research, 2 sections • English 203: Creative Writing 1, 1 section
Erica (PhD)	Benefits-eligible lecturer with a 100 percent appointment	• English 098: Introduction to College Writing (non-degree-credit), 1 section • Writing Studio Tutorial (8 hours of tutoring), 1 section • English 101: College Writing and Critical Reading, 1 section • English 102: Critical Writing, Reading, and Research, 2 sections

Table 3.3. Continued

Morgan (PhD in literature)	Benefits-eligible lecturer with a 100 percent appointment	• English 098: Introduction to College Writing (non-degree-credit), 1 section • English 101: College Writing and Critical Reading and • English 102: Critical Writing, Reading, and Research (dual-credit course taught in a local rural high school), 1 section • LEA 101: Academic Reading (non-degree-credit), 2 sections
Jack (Master's)	Benefits-eligible lecturer with a 100 percent appointment	• English 098: Introduction to College Writing (non-degree-credit), 1 section • Writing Studio Tutorial (8 hours of tutoring in writing center, equivalent to a one-course appointment) • English 101: College Writing and Critical Reading, 2 sections (one dual-credit taught onsite at a local military academy) • English 102: Critical Writing, Reading, and Research, 1 section (taught onsite at a local military academy)
Kristen (PhD in rhetoric and composition)	Benefits-eligible lecturer with 60 percent appointment	• Business Writing, 1 section • Writing Studio (8 hours of tutorial time), 1 section • English 102: Critical Writing, Reading and Research, 1 section
Rachel (Master's)	Benefits-eligible lecturer with 80 percent appointment	• English 101: College Writing and Critical Reading, 3 sections • English 102: Critical Writing, Reading, and Research, 1 section

open-access classrooms can both inform the production of generalizable research and make use of it as part of their work.

For example, one participating instructor (not included in the above group) completed the online workshop and f2f seminar in the professional development project, with the intention of revising her English 098 course to teach in the subsequent spring semester.

However, fluctuations in enrollment and the precarity of contingent employment meant that though her course materials demonstrated proficient and effective revisions aligned with the project goals, she was not able to assess their effectiveness because her assigned section was canceled because of low enrollments (see Daniel for discussion of the precariat enterprise of first-year writing). Another participating instructor teaching a section of the non-degree-credit writing course reflected on the challenge of assessing the effectiveness of her curricular revisions:

> For English 098, I see many barriers to achieving the learning outcomes and competencies. Every semester, a significant portion of the class does not complete the course requirements because of barriers of time management, homework completion, understanding and acting on course requirements, class participation, and life stressors such as housing insecurity, childcare issues, or health issues. Certainly, the skills needed to address those barriers must be learned and developed over time. They also likely relate in complex ways to academic preparation.

Two-year instructors not only manage unstable appointments and heavy teaching loads, but they also work with students who have significant needs for academic and nonacademic support if they are to be able to stay in college. Even in a project like our current one, there were instructors who would have participated, but the realities of open-access programs prevented them from doing so.

Disciplinary Learning Domains: Understanding Student Experiences in FYW

To anchor our analysis of student writing and student learning, we started by identifying works of scholarship and professional statements that collectively make explicit a case for "core knowledge" in writing studies. We took this approach in order to have a basis for setting two-year-college writing instruction alongside what would reasonably be considered a "disciplinary center." The scholarship and professional statements we ultimately focused on include

- the threshold concepts approach defined in *Naming What We Know: Threshold Concepts of Writing Studies (NWWK)* (Adler-Kassner and Wardle, eds.), which began to emerge concurrent with the Writing about Writing movement in the first decade of the 2000s
- the *WPA Outcomes Statement for First-Year Composition* (published in 1999, with multiple subsequent updates)

We see *NWWK*'s threshold concepts as attempting to define central writing-studies knowledge in a broad way, while the WPA outcomes statement focuses on central writing studies knowledge in the nearly universal postsecondary writing course. The prevailing methodology for defining these two knowledge centers in writing studies has largely been focused on small-scale groups of experts seeking professional consensus (versus other methods—for example an empirical study or systematic study of student learning such as those we outline in Chapter 2). In establishing what could be called agreed-upon knowledge and outcomes, taken together these documents serve as disciplinary learning domains (DLDs). We use these DLDs to map students' FYW experiences during the year we conducted the research project that guides this chapter.

The first effort to define threshold concepts in writing studies is reflected in the title of Linda Adler-Kassner and Elizabeth Wardle's 2015 *Naming What We Know: Threshold Concepts of Writing Studies*. With its professional-consensus model, the editors "invited forty-five . . . teacher-scholars to participate on a wiki . . . proposing ideas, phenomena, knowledge, or orientations they considered to be threshold concepts." This process was followed by further guided refining that resulted in "a total of thirty-seven threshold concepts as 'what we know'—from research in writing studies and aligned fields (i.e., linguistics, learning theory, and psychology" (4). Adler-Kassner and Wardle's book, and its follow-up, *(Re)Considering What We Know*, each took steps to build a knowledge foundation that continues to distill what counts as "known."

The *WPA Outcomes Statement for First-Year Composition*, including the most recent revision in 2014, used a similar professional-consensus model. As Dylan Dryer et al. articulate in "Revising

FYC Outcomes for a Multimodal, Digitally Composed World: The WPA Outcomes Statement for First-Year Composition (Version 3.0)," "Statement 3.0 remains the realization of a set of beliefs about what writing is and can be and how it should and shouldn't be taught in the first year(s) of US postsecondary education" (136). As Dryer and his colleagues recount, "[t]he group, which came to be known as the Outcomes Collective, had a loose steering committee and encouraged the participation of any interested writing teacher," while a second revision included an online survey distributed through listservs, which received 223 responses.[7] Emily Isaacs reports that of the four-year institutions in her study, *Writing at the State U: Instruction and Administration at 106 Comprehensive Universities,* 22.6 percent that require FYC have adopted or adapted the WPA outcomes statement. We imagine the number would be different (likely lower) if two-year-college writing programs were surveyed. The WPA outcomes statement development appears to us to be the most inclusive and expansive method of creating a "center" for first-year writing, in terms of the process by which it was created, and reflective of a broad range of students and instructors.

Each of these approaches, though valid methodologically and research-based, has limitations in its ability to create an intellectual center for first-year writing, specifically one that includes the complete range of college writers as well as a complete representation of college teacher-scholars. In this way, attempts to establish disciplinary benchmarks ultimately show how the values embedded in them are shaped by the process of creating them. Expertise is by definition specialized—and yet specialization can lead to a kind of tunnel vision.

To make what we think is a mis-centering more visible, we propose alternative ways to think about outcomes, habits of mind, and threshold concepts that reflect the students who attend access institutions. By merging them into the DLD framework, we reimagine disciplinary learning in order to account for the schooling experiences of the structurally disadvantaged and marginalized students who make up the majority of the two-year-college student population. Drawing from our research project, we highlight how the material conditions of our instructors and students show gaps in the DLDs—gaps which must be addressed in writing classrooms to better serve the needs of students. What we see as being neglected in the schema is attention to understanding how college writers develop—across time and within the murky, complex, and individuated space between secondary and postsecondary contexts, a space that is more complex for two-year-college students than it is for what has been the typical profile of a traditional college student. We ask: What pedagogical approaches, expertise, and material conditions help writers develop their rhetorical and composing tool kits, and what does that look like for the very, very wide range of the new majority of college students?

In our subsequent analysis, we aim to use the DLDs that are reflective of current disciplinary thinking about students' learning needs and goals as a starting point for analyzing the student experience in multiple writing courses in our institution. We focus on the work of identifying roadblocks, misconceptions, and pathways into DLDs in order to encompass threshold concepts, outcomes, and knowledge domains, or "how they are experienced by students" (Entwistle 32). In particular, we use the existing DLDs to imagine what disciplinary knowledge could look like in first-year writing if . . .

- marginalized students are centered as the source of knowledge, including students who would be considered traditionally "underprepared" for college-level writing, which would shift the student population typically reflected in composition research studies, in other words a "backward design" approach;
- the naming of these domains derived from a careful study of student writing, as well as students' and teachers' reflections, as an alternative to an expert consensus model; and
- a systematic, assessment-oriented approach was used, one that draws from multiple sources of data including student formal writing, student reflective writing, and teacher reflections as the basis for identifying DLDs for new learners to the discipline.

Naming these domains, then, becomes as much a pedagogical project as a scholarly one. If threshold concepts, outcomes, and habits of mind can be used to help students learn to write more effectively and cross this portal as writers, then unpacking how they are applicable to students and teachers in two-year-college contexts provides an important source of data for writing studies.

Methodology: Mapping Student Learning across Disciplinary Domains

We had a rich and robust body of student work from multiple campuses, multiple instructors, and different courses to work with, so our goal was to use that body of work to help us understand how and whether it aligns with the "composed knowledge" of writing studies. In particular, we were interested in trying to understand how the experiences of the student writers in two-year colleges could add to the body of knowledge in the discipline of writing studies. Rather than try to separately assess or compare multiple different kinds of statements and scholarship (many of which have claims to a central role to writing studies or first-year writing),[8] we synthesized them and developed a map for assessing students' growth holistically over the course of the semester. Table 3.4 offers an overview of the ways we integrate these two sets of statements of disciplinary knowledge (either outcomes or concepts) in order to assess students' writing. We also identify in Column 4 the sorts of evidence that showed achievement in each of the three areas.[9] As we did with the published scholarship in Chapter 2, we collaborated to review and discuss each student's work completed throughout the term, assessing and categorizing the level at which their materials showed progress toward or achievement in each of the DLDs. We derived our categories of analysis from the existing literature, developed a set of criteria by which the student samples would be assessed, and systematically analyzed each portfolio of work against the criteria. In this way our approach was less one of coding and more one of assessment of student work against predefined criteria established by disciplinary standards or expectations.

Like those of Kathleen Blake Yancey (1998) and Michele Eodice et al. (2017), our process was iterative and inter-reader-validated.

The curricular redesign project was structured around helping instructors redesign sections of our three-course sequence, the model curriculum for which was drawn from disciplinary best practices, organizational outcomes statements and position statements, and the CWPA's *Framework for Success in Postsecondary Writing* (see Appendix C for our learning outcomes for the three courses). The

Table 3.4. Types of Evidence Showing Students' Achievement of or Progress toward Each of the Learning Domains

<table>
<tr><th></th><th>Threshold Concepts</th><th>Relevant WPA Outcome Statement Categories (Types of Results)</th><th>Types of Evidence Demonstrating Achievement of or Progress in DLD</th></tr>
<tr><td>DLD 1: Rhetorical and Genre Knowledge</td><td>Concept 1: Writing is a social and rhetorical activity.

Concept 2: Writing speaks to situations through recognizable forms.</td><td>Rhetorical Knowledge</td><td>• Student can successfully complete a rhetorical analysis of a text.
• Student can successfully identify rhetorical strategies used in a text and connect them to the author's purpose and audience.
• Student can identify different rhetorical situations and corresponding writing strategies/processes.
• Students' formal writing to assignments align with the assigned genre conventions or rhetorical purpose (researched argument, research proposal, rhetorical analysis, research review, cover letter, etc.).
• In reflective writing, student explained new knowledge or experience gained by writing in multiple genres.</td></tr>
</table>

Continued on next page

Table 3.4. Continued

DLD 2: Critical Literacy	Concept 3: Writing enacts and creates identities and ideologies.	Critical Thinking, Reading, and Composing Rhetorical Knowledge Knowledge of Conventions	• When asked to read and discuss texts that specifically address questions of literacy and power, student can accurately write about those ideas and demonstrate understanding. • Students can articulate how their prior experience shaped their current skills or challenges. • Students can successfully critically analyze texts (published, their peers', or their own) focusing on literacy and power.
DLD 3: Process Skills and Knowledge	Concept 4: All writers have more to learn. Concept 5: Writing is (also always) a cognitive activity.	Processes Critical Thinking, Reading, and Composing	• Student participated in/demonstrated a multistage writing process. • Student stated a commitment to using a multistage and iterative writing process in their reflective writing. • Student articulated use of peer or instructor feedback to inform revision. • Student accurately identified strengths and areas for future improvement (self-assessment aligned with formal writing features). • Student expressed in reflective writing the learning achieved through writing-process activities. • Student expressed in reflective writing the value of learning new writing skills, including writing for different purposes and audiences previously.

student work we examined predates the threshold concepts published in 2015 in *Naming What We Know*, but, at the same time, the work students produced emerged from a curriculum built from the foundation of the "gold standard" *WPA Outcomes Statement for First-Year Composition*, which outlines first-year writing learning outcomes for students. Our analysis, then, focused on a comparison intending to surface how disciplinary outcomes, benchmarks, and concepts might look through a different process, an inductive rather than deductive process: what were the barriers to students' progress? What misconceptions did they bring to their work? What learning roadblocks made it challenging for them to "cross the threshold" in the enrolled course's outcomes? What does assessing this work against the stated composed knowledge and benchmarks of writing studies reveal?

After an initial review of the seventy-eight participating students' materials in which the two coauthors each independently read each student's portfolio, we went through together and tagged evidence in the writing on a spreadsheet, noting where we identified evidence that the DLD was "achieved," "developing," or "not evident." We also noted where we returned to our notes and categorizations in order to surface themes. Our focus was on finding answers to the following questions:

1. Does the student writing demonstrate progress toward or achievement of the DLD?
2. What can we learn about the challenges, barriers, or roadblocks toward achieving the DLD from students' formal writing, reflective writing, and instructor assessments?
3. What disciplinary knowledge is challenged, unreflected, or differently understood by centering our conclusions about student writing and writers on two-year-college writing students?

To determine the responses to questions 1 and 3, we looked for the presence or absence of evidence in students' writing at any point in the semester, identifying whether the student was showing development (or progress) or whether the students' writing suggested achievement in that DLD. (An overview of each of the three areas and an example of what achievement, development, or absence of that feature might look like is provided in detail in Appendix B). To determine the answer to Question 2, we tracked emerging themes as we analyzed student work, observing what, if any, cognitive, metacognitive, or material factors appeared to be constraining that student's ability to demonstrate progress in the learning domain. Again, our ultimate goal was to sketch out how a systematic examination of a corpus of student writing from open-access writers (many of whom started as underprepared for college-level writing and reading tasks by standard measures for college readiness)[10] helped us see gaps, trends, or new insights about the work of teaching and learning in two-year-college writing classrooms. As we read and categorized student work, we looked for cognitive and metacognitive evidence in both formal writing and reflective writing as shown in Table 3.5, which defines the criteria by which students' writing was assessed as having met, not met, or be making progress toward the DLD.

Analysis: What Student Learning Tells Us about Disciplinary Concepts

Our analysis shows how the DLDs connect to the various first-year writing standards that have been established in the recent decades as writing studies has crystallized as a discipline. Each DLD has its own subsection, and each includes multiple examples of student writing and reflection for analysis. This is, of course the continued tension in knowledge making—to what extent are we creating an ideal that is theoretically grounded, and to what extent are these ideals derived from the grounded experience of those who enact them? In considering the experiences and texts of the participating students and instructors in our study, we aim to illustrate how DLDs could and should evolve to reflect the lived practices of diverse first-year writers who do not bring with them the privilege and assumptions of middle-class and continuing-generation students, particularly those who pursue postsecondary college immediately after high school and do so full-time and on a campus.

Table 3.5. Analysis Rubric for Categorizing Student Progress in Each of the Disciplinary Learning Domains

	Multiple pieces of evidence of DLD (Accomplished)	At least one piece of evidence of DLD (Developing)	No evidence of DLD (No)	Not assessed/ not assessable (missing student writing, no relevant assignment) (NA)
Criteria for evaluating students' progress in the disciplinary learning domain	Understanding of this learning domain articulated in reflective writing Demonstration of this learning domain in formal writing assignments	Either of the two (cognitive or metacognitive demonstration) Understanding articulated in reflective writing Demonstration of this learning domain in formal writing assignments	Student does not demonstrate either evidence of the learning domain in reflective/ metacognitive work or formal writing assignments	Student did not complete the assignment. No course assignment addressed

DLD 1: Rhetorical and Genre Knowledge: Writer Compliance and the Values of First-Year Writing

Nancy Sommers has said all along, "Too often as composition teachers we conclude that students do not willingly revise . . . it is not that students are unwilling to revise, but rather that they do what they have been taught to do in a consistently narrow and predictable way" (383). As Sommers and Laura Saltz and scholars like

Tom Fox (1999) and Mike Rose (1985) have previously confirmed, we saw that students in our project, particularly the struggling writers in the basic writing course, were most likely to focus in their reflective writing on lower-order concerns, or those issues that are most tangible and regulated by rules.

In their writing, participating students discussed their writing in terms of compliance with sentence-level correctness, and primarily revised their writing to conform with their perception of instructor expectations around reducing and eliminating error. Rose articulated this worldview—which many students in our project have internalized—as "Writing ability is judged in terms of the presence of error and can thus be quantified. Writing is a skill or a tool rather than a discipline" ("Language" 341). When framed in the context of the first learning domain—understanding the social and rhetorical aspects of writing, as well as the ways genre and purpose shape writer's choices—the majority of the students in our project sample were showing growth or progress, which is shown in Table 3.6, where we identified evidence in student writing that 63 percent of them were increasing their ability to focus on the social and rhetorical aspects of writing.

What the results of this analysis suggested to us was that like many college students our two-year-college writers were engaging in and showing progress in the development of rhetorical and genre awareness. However, they were particularly likely to be starting from a basis of a focus on compliance with teacher expectations

Table 3.6. Student Writer Achievement of DLD 1, Rhetorical and Genre Knowledge

All sections aggregated (78=n)	DLD 1: Rhetorical and Genre Knowledge
Developing	27% (21)
Accomplished	36% (28)
No evidence	29% (23)
NA	8% (6)

and on sentence-level correctness (as Sommers's classic 1980 article on revision strategies established). What we add through student examples in this section is (a) how this emphasis on sentence-level correctness as a writing goal limited students' ability to make progress in other global areas, (b) how negative prior experiences with writing undergird this emphasis, and (c) how widespread this compliance focus with authority and correctness was throughout the group of student participants, whether they were in English 098 or 102. We offer some theoretical framing later in this section on how class, authority, and power strongly influence student attitudes in this area, as well as the pedagogical implications that come with understanding these dispositions.

Examples from students' reflective writing can illustrate how students grappled with the disciplinary language of thinking about audience and purposes and their understanding of writing that was more typical of the focus Rose and Sommers described. Participating students focused more intensively in their reflective writing on the calculable and formulaic dimensions of their writing tasks. Students like Lance, reflecting on his learning in the English 098: Introduction to College Writing course, described his goals as:

> Some of the subjects I wanted to focus on my grammar, my thesis, and my variety in word choice.[11] Going through High School I never had great grammar within my papers. I would always get marked points off because of it, so I thought I would challenge myself to become better at it during college. My weakest part of grammar is punctuation. After handed in the completed essays and seeing my graded essay, I've seen a huge improvement in my grammar. I barley if ever, have gotten points taken off.

This attention to grammar and punctuation was echoed by Lor, also an 098 student, who writes, "I've learned a lot about sentence structure, grammar, vocabulary, and other key items that build an excellent essay. While I struggled with building an essay." This emphasis is shown with an even greater level of exigency by another student, Josiah, reflecting on English 098:

> The first thing I have been working on this year is my punctuation. This is something I have lacked most of my life and was one of my biggest goals when I started school. When I would write I would basically ramble on with my thoughts forget to put in any punctuation. I would focus so much on getting my thoughts on paper I would forget how to translate those thoughts correctly on paper. It was one of the biggest things holding me back most of my life.

Later in the course, Josiah was able to expand his understanding of the kinds of writing goals that would help him progress through the curriculum, noting "The one thing I believe I can take away from this year is If I keep working on my punctuation and my organization and using my own thoughts I am on the way to becoming a good writer." Josiah's insight reflects Sommers and Saltz's observation that "Students who continue to see writing as a matter of mechanics or a series of isolated exercises tend never to see the ways writing can serve them as a medium in which to explore their own interests" (Sommers and Saltz 140; Perl; Sommers). To an extent, then, DLD 1 is an area that two-year-college students need support in developing, and as a learning outcome is certainly essential to the two-year-college writing curriculum.

Achieving this shift from correctness to rhetorical thinking certainly was not limited to the students in our project who began in English 098; English 101 and 102 students also demonstrated some of this preoccupation with sentence-level and formatting issues in their reflection. Jackie, an English 101 student, also identified punctuation as a primary writer's goal, writing in an early informal letter to the instructor, "Punctuation is going to be one of my largest challenges because, again like I stated earlier, I have not been using these skills since I graduated from high school 5 years ago," a concern that is then repeated in a later reflection. Sometimes even high-skilled students who had started in the core degree requirement course (102) demonstrated this tendency, such as Immanuel:

> While there are plenty of nit-picky questions I could ask, the only one I'm truly concerned with is the use of the italicised

> "should" in the first paragraph. Is it okay to have? Or is it too "snarky"? Also, are my transitions good enough between each paragraph or do they need to be more specific? Are the intro and conclusion paragraphs decent enough? Would the intro need more summary (as they are integrated)? Should the conclusion take a little longer to go from specific back to broad? Do I really need a title for a RA [rhetorical analysis]?

Like Immanuel, his classmate, Dean, linked grammar, formatting, and sentence structure to his growth as a writer: "What I took away from this semester is how to analyze article better, well as all of the grammar, format and sentence structure I learned to find and correct in my drafts. But I really do believe that I made a lot of progress in my writing skills." Rather than working toward an understanding of rhetorical and genre knowledge, novice college writers like Tim focus on technical and surface features, particularly with a view toward complying with perceived (or actual) instructor expectations for error-free prose. For example, Tim writes that the emphasis of his prior coursework was on "proper grammar, at least two pages, and double spaced," mirrored by Warren, who reflects these exact values in his prior writing assignments but in more detail:

> The biggest difference between high school essays and college essays is the time between each essay. In high school, we waited at least a couple weeks before we even started the next essay, in college we wait maybe a week before we move on to a new topic and start the next essay. Another difference is the actual length of the essays. When in high school the required length was generally two or three pages, in college that required length went up to a bigger range in length, anywhere from two pages to sometimes ten or more pages. The third biggest difference is editing because college is way more in depth when it comes to editing than high school ever was.

In other words, even in the third class in the sequence, which some students placed into and others were taking in their third or fourth semester if they had started in English 098, students were working toward but not yet demonstrating consistently their awareness of the ways writing is audience- and purpose-based.

As writers who (for diverse reasons) recognized that their own literacy practices and participation in academic writing was misaligned with the expectations of school writing, students emphasized correctness, numerical points, and compliance over rhetorical and genre knowledge. To some extent this shows that students were hyperaware of audience, but that audience was quite narrowly defined as the instructor. We see this positioning illustrated really clearly in comments from an English 101 student, Ellen, whose author's note for a course paper read "I know this is a bit short but I will be sending you some paragraphs so that you can re-edit them to make sure I will get a good grade." In our experience, students focused intensely on earning high grades are less prevalent in the two-year-college environment than in more selective contexts. What strikes us here about Ellen's emphasis is less the desire for a good grade and more the writer-compliance values. In this case, the authoritative judgment of the instructor is reinforced by the student, whether the teacher accepts that identity or not.

The focus that many of our participating students placed on surface-level correctness is, we think, deeply connected with the ethos and ideology of schooling as focused on compliance with hegemonic discourse expectations, expectations that are rooted in white, middle-class language standards (see Royster; Canagarajah). As Mya Poe et al. observe, "validation tools that help us understand the local effects of writing assessment can be critically important: use of these tools may mean the difference between college success and failure for many students" ("Legal" 589). Like Poe, Inoue, and Elliot, we agree that "[w]riting assessment must also include classroom assessment" (4).[12] We are deeply interested in the ways that assessment values within the context of the classroom can and do reflect four key variables: larger assessment stages in the overall college-writing sorting and ranking process; students' prior experience of writing assessment; the intersections of labor conditions, pedagogy, and scholarship that influence assessment at all levels; and the disparate consequences of assessment practices in open-admissions and two-year colleges.

This compliance and correctness emphasis—despite not being an emphasis in either of the English 102 sections that we included as part of our project—seems to support two possible explanations. First, there is Sommers's classic observation above that "they do what they have been taught to do in a consistently narrow and predictable way" (383); "students understand the revision process as a rewording activity" (381). Second, the hidden curriculum of what is taught versus what students actually learn (or a gap between the stated and unstated curriculum) can also illustrate what we learned from these open-access student writers. The vocabulary for talking about writing that is used by the field of writing studies is not available to many students who start at open-admissions campuses, and/or does not reflect the realities of their experience (see Kareem). The component parts of writing and the values that many of these student writers identified as shaping how they were assessed in prior writing courses may on their surface reflect an emphasis on formatting and sentence-level issues. We think, instead, it may actually signal their ongoing development and understanding of the vocabulary of writing studies that supports metacognitive growth and allows for a more sophisticated discussion of their progress.

It's true that many university students also struggle with the concept of audience. However, our contention is that the preoccupation with adhering to white, middle-class standards of academic English created barriers for students in moving past that learning roadblock in really disproportionate ways for two-year-college students, in part because the rightness of their own assumptions had been reinforced over and over in their prior schooling. As John Warner, Jess Calarco, and others have observed, the differences in the schooling experiences of marginalized students and students with race, gender, and class privilege vary in important ways—the latter experience more opportunities to engage in independent and critical-thinking tasks, while the former are coached to defer and conform to defined standards. The jump to college-level-writing expectations that emphasize learning independently, thinking critically, making arguments, conducting analysis, and interacting with complex sources is particularly large for students whose prior schooling has perhaps deemphasized or even excluded these kinds of literacy experiences. As such, it is that much more challenging to achieve a move to critical thinking and rhetorical independence in the context of the writing classroom.

Pierre Bourdieu and Annette Lareau influence us here through their theories of orientation and habitus in relation to structures of power. Students who are marginalized, whether through class, race, ability, or other minoritized identities, are more likely to experience both externally imposed and internally imposed orientations toward compliance with structures of power than are middle-class and continuing-generation students. In other words, they are more likely to have educational experiences that emphasize writer compliance (see work by Mike Rose; Lisa Delpit; Lareau; and Matthew Taylor). Students whose prior learning has emphasized formatting, correctness, length, and other features of writer compliance are doubly punished by the values of first-year writing courses that are inattentive to process or that do not actively work to equip students for a focus on global issues, rhetorical knowledge, and critical reading. It may be that the field of writing studies has been wrestling with what Lisa Ede calls the "floating signifier" of the terms *writing process*, *post-process theory*, and *writing as a social process* for decades now (85). But what is learned by most students in secondary English courses, especially those without access to advanced, honors, or college-credit coursework, is still built on assumptions about correctness, compliance, and to a lesser extent current-traditional pedagogical assumptions.[13] Such assumptions are evident in the reflective writing of the students in this project group, who echoed writer compliance as values they brought with them to college writing. Tim and Warren (previously quoted), for example, offer descriptions of their perception of the classroom values endorsed in their prior English course that are eerily similar.

In addition to considering the disparate impact that specific pedagogical approaches, curricula, and assessment criteria have on marginalized and at-risk students, we also see evidence of the ways that close examination and empirically grounded research into this corpus of work by first-year writers might inform the continued defining and redefining of what constitutes disciplinary knowledge. That is, if we conceive of threshold concepts, first-year writing outcomes, or habits of mind as foundational disciplinary knowledge, then they must be grounded in the language of learning (and the language of learning must be grounded in them) and in the work that takes place to become an expert in the field. For example, we can't help but notice how much more important the threshold concept "Writing can be taught and learned" is for students who have largely had experiences of failure as writers, just as "Failure can be an important part of writing development" has potentially harmful implications for struggling writers who are often beaten down by the feedback they've received in the past about the inadequacies of their writing.

We also want to note that while many of these reflections demonstrate the ways that these developing writers must unlearn preconceived notions about writing, writing process, and assessment, they also must learn to do so in an (academic) environment that has not necessarily served them well in the past. We are asking a lot of these students to trust people who tell them to change many of the ways they have learned or been previously assessed. Similarly, if writing studies intends to continue to invest not just in setting outcomes or benchmarks but also in analyzing the kinds of barriers that new college writers face to achieving them, then tracing the challenges encountered by the complete range of student writers seeking to earn a postsecondary credential is the next task for the field of writing studies. The cultivation of critical literacy skills rather than compliance with authority is thus of key importance for two-year-college writing students.

DLD 2: Critical Literacy, Language, Knowledge, and Power

Two-year-college students and instructors have a complex relationship with critical literacy, particularly because of their situatedness within the institutional hierarchy and their orientation to education. Much of what we explore in this section is something we ourselves have struggled to articulate and analyze. We know that critical literacy as Ira Shor defined it is essential for students to learn in college: "Critical literacy can be thought of as a social practice in itself and as a tool for the study of other social practices. That is, critical literacy is reflective and reflexive: Language use and education are social practices used to critically study all social practices including the social practices of language use and education" (11). But we also know that critical literacy is not emphasized in the first-year writing documents produced by professional organizations. For the purposes of this analysis, we analyzed students' opportunities to make and success at making progress toward critical literacy (as defined above). We defined DLD 2 as a key idea within Threshold Concept 3 (in *NWWK*), "Writing enacts and creates identities and ideologies" (48) and the related outcome that used to be a component of the *WPA Outcomes Statement for First-Year Composition*, "Understand the relationships among language, knowledge, and power" (*WPA Outcomes Statement for First-Year Composition*, version 2.0 [2008]). We cite Shor's definition above, as well, because we think it offers a somewhat more focused understanding of what critical literacy looks like and what it does. Though "enacting and creating identities and ideologies" and "understand[ing] the relationships among language, knowledge, and power" do get, in a theoretical way, at the gist of what critical literacy is, we see direct treatment of "critical literacy" as a curricular and pedagogical goal often absent from the literacy goals of postsecondary first-year writing. In our assessment of student work, the interesting and possibly troubling finding from the analysis is shown in Table 3.7. As our numerical breakdown shows, the vast majority of students across all sections

Table 3.7. Percentage of Assessed Students' Progress toward DLD 2, Critical Literacy

All sections aggregated (78=n)	DLD 2: Critical Literacy
Developing	8% (6)
Accomplished	3% (2)
No evidence	3% (2)
NA	87% (68)

of the courses could not be assessed on critical literacy as we defined it in DLD 3, even though, we would argue, it is an unstated assumption of nearly all college instruction.

To unpack this result, we reflected on the curricular approach in the model assignment sequence, derived from the WPA outcomes statement and our own research. This gap was notable in some ways because the curriculum revision project that was the foundation of this analysis was reflective of the pedagogical approaches valued by the field (see Eodice et al. 125). Likewise, the model curriculum that became the foundation of the departmental program was purposefully aligned with the WPA outcomes for first-year writing (version 3.0 [2014]). While this table appears quite simple—87 percent of students could not be assessed in terms of progress toward critical literacy—we think it represents just the complexity of the act of translating critical literacy into the first-year writing classroom. Teaching about the relationships between literacy and power is a process—one that is difficult to assess across reflective pieces or single essays. Therefore, in this section we explore (a) the minimal attention to critical literacy in either of the two professional resources that make up DLD 2, and (b) the limited discussion among faculty of how to make critical literacy (not critical pedagogy) part of the FYW curriculum in a meaningful way, particularly for marginalized and minoritized students.

Our first theorizing about this gap is derived from the documents themselves. For example, a potential factor in this missing piece is the evolution of the WPA outcomes statement. As Dylan Dryer et al. recount in "Revising FYC Outcomes for a Multimodal, Digitally Composed World: The WPA Outcomes Statement for First-Year Composition (Version 3.0)," "Statement 3.0 remains the realization of a set of beliefs about what writing is and can be and how it should and shouldn't be taught in the first year(s) of US postsecondary education" (136). The article documents the revision process and invites readers to use the revised statement in specific ways—for curricular, faculty development, research, documentation, and outreach purposes, for example. We will be the first to agree with the WPA Outcomes Statement Revision Task

Force/Revising FYC Outcomes researchers "that neither they nor students were likely ever to fully 'understand the collaborative and social aspects of writing processes' or entirely 'understand the relationships among language, knowledge, and power (version 2.0)'" (Dryer et al. 137). We also see how the elimination of the broad—but pointed—outcome that language and culture and power are interconnected can potentially influence what it is that instructors (or programs) emphasize in their curriculum. Recall that in Isaacs's study, 22.6 percent of programs had adopted the WPA outcomes for their program (xvi). Eliminating the reference to power and how it works from the formal document may signal a tacit recognition that this need not be a priority for writing studies or writing teachers. Anne Ruggles Gere et al., on the other hand, in their February 2021 article "Communal Justicing: Writing Assessment, Disciplinary Infrastructure, and the Case for Critical Language Awareness," propose a revised outcome focused on "conventions" in the well-used *Framework for Success in Postsecondary Writing* that moves from standard language ideology to one that directly aims to help writers cultivate critical awareness of language variety and how asymmetrical power structures privilege narrow and hierarchical notions of correctness to the detriment of student writers (397).

At the time we created the model curriculum, the results of the elimination of this outcome certainly did not stand out to us. However, what our subsequent analysis of the student work produced as a part of the project then showed us was that the development of critical literacy skills did not automatically become a priority of instructors. Though the participating instructors were not specifically directed or required to use any specific theme or set of readings in their course revisions, the notable observation we made was that only instructors who directly asked students through content to discuss power and language—in this instance, Gwen's English 098 section that focused on social class and work—had the opportunities to demonstrate progress in this DLD.

The second explanation that emerged from this post-project analysis is how in the material circumstances faced by two-year-college writing teachers and students—without an explicit curricular emphasis on critical literacy—they struggled to make it a priority. In our own experience with teaching critical literacy in first-year writing, we have struggled as well. We have found, especially in developmental writing courses, that many of these students are struggling to find a way to belong to college, or even to the idea that they belong in college. For the marginalized students in the two-year-college classroom, so much of the focus of the course is helping to equip them with an array of strategies and tools to navigate college writing that to step back and critique literacy and its structures is almost an opposite motion that could be counterproductive within their initial exposure to college reading and writing.

As a point of illustration, then, we focus on Gwen's section of English 098 as well as a section of English 101 taught by Ann, where many of the assigned readings addressed topics related to critical literacy. The reading and writing in these sections focused on questions about knowledge and the value of different types of work. They revealed with regularity how students called into question the value of critical literacy altogether as well as the ways that students in these courses made epistemological assumptions about knowledge itself. Though this focus invited students to engage in complex thinking about what constitutes a credible perspective, or how one distinguishes between competing viewpoints, it also provides a window into what critical literacy means for students who are newcomers to ways of academic thinking and how it can even be indistinguishable from a position of general skepticism.

Specifically, evidence from student writing demonstrated the way that suspicion about "knowing" and who has the ability to know or do things was a distinct thread in student texts. This seems particularly important given the urgency that many academics are feeling to help students more accurately assess the quality and validity of sources and the increasing need for information literacy in an era of "fake news" and greater levels of distrust of information sources. For example, an English 101 student, Bethany, who was analyzing a critical essay by Henry Giroux, characterized rhetorical strategies used by the author as "manipulating his audience's emotions and opinions on his subject and him as an author," a view reflected in assertions by other student writers who saw rhetorical analysis as uncovering what was ultimately a manipulation of facts. As Lor writes in an English 098 analysis of an article on multiple intelligences, "McGreal uses an outside source of Visser, Ashton, and Vernon's quote mentioning that 'multiple independent kinds of intelligence implies that anyone can be intelligent'. . . (2). This phrase doesn't prove that Gardner's Multiple Intelligence Theory is incorrect or that they favored IQ and EQ but shows a biased view and also only states a narrow-minded comment about a type of general intelligence." A similar example of concern with bias is shown in Anthony's analysis of an article about parenting by Anna Quindlen, when he also identifies rhetorical strategies as a form of bias. As Anthony writes,

> She states in the article, "Children are overscheduled and are deprived of the gift of boredom" (Quindlen). I am here to analyze her thoughts and ideas to obtain a clearer understanding. She is clearly biased about children being overscheduled and trying to persuade parents to let them do essentially "nothing." She states her own opinion as well as others, such as a study done. All in all, the essay serves adequate to readers for she provides strong support for her claim on a monumental complex issue from her own experiences, to a study that was done.

This concern with "bias" becomes a teaching and learning challenge of particular relevance within two-year-college contexts because two-year-college students are often the least likely to have backgrounds rich in the kinds of literacy practices that are most directly relevant to what they are called to do in college courses. In 2020, as we write this book in the midst of a global pandemic, the ramifications of not understanding the difference between critical literacy and conspiracy theorizing are not just important but matters of life and death. As a result, the responsibilities of writing teachers to help students overcome distrust of evidence and a mistrust of judgment-making are a critical component of what we do—but also a laborious intellectual and curricular challenge.

Lance, for example, in his analysis of the readings in his 098 course that focus on types of intelligence, writes:

> This essay I will describe how I think the authors proof of intelligence, their audience, and how their attitude toward the blue color workers can influence their article. Scott McGreal believe in the IQ as an intelligence scale. Scott tries to persuade his argument by attempting to appear smart/reliable, tries to make Gar[d]ner look bad, and uses evidence in his defense. Scott tries to appear smart/reliable by acting like he knows everything. For example, he said "the few studies that have been done do not actually support the idea that there are many different kinds of 'intelligence' operating separately from each other." This sentence argues his statement because it seems like he knows all the facts about intelligence.

This skeptical stance toward "knowing" and certainty can be a significant barrier to real critical literacy, particularly in the current political and cultural moment. Kneejerk critique of anyone with claims to knowledge is, however, distinct from an ability to analyze sources, let alone the social practices Shor defines as related to systems and structures. If the conclusion students come to is that "no one knows anything," then that prevents more critically literate assessments that might look more like "lots of people know lots of things, and we can distinguish between qualities of knowledges." Further, blanket rejection of knowability can be difficult to move past, and indeed become a barrier to actual critical literacy.

This stance of anti–epistemological certainty is shown by Angela, who discussed restaurant reviews as a part of an assignment asking her to synthesize reviews and take a position on the restaurant: "Well when it comes down to the reviewers of Yelp.com, The Linkery has many unsatisfied customers and also many satisfied customers. It could be about a 50-50 for both sides. The real question is, what side are you going to take? Also would you try the Linkery experience for yourself?" Though this reflects an effort at reader engagement, it also suggests a kind of intellectual relativism that culminates in Angela's conclusion:

> I personally would try the restaurant for myself before making any decisions off of someone else's great experience to someone's terrible experience. I do this because my expectations of service may different to Sarah A.'s and Lana R.'s. . . . So it comes down to whatever side you want to take. I'm still in the middle of all of this because I don't like to make my decision until I've tried The Linkery experience.

This distrust of evidence and position-taking can also extend to students' own assessment of their work, and to the evaluative rhetorical tasks that ask them to make such judgments. This relativist approach is demonstrated by Mel, who writes,

> I did only mention two positive associations with the learning outcomes along with one weakness, which might seem lacking of quantity, but I did this for a strict reason: I'm still learning. I could have mentioned a specific example for each learning outcome, but I believe that would have the opposite result of what you are looking for in this cover letter. I have mentioned what I consider my strongest learning outcomes, and where I seek improvement; if I would have given those details for each learning outcome, the quality would diminish, and it would not really characterize what my individual strengths and weaknesses are. I am taking a very large risk writing this cover letter in this fashion, as this portfolio is 50 percent of my final grade, but I think this shows what the learning outcomes have taught ME, and how I should not be characterized like every other English student that takes this course.

The quantitative breakdown of our assessment and the qualitative analysis of student writing leads us to some speculation about how and why we saw this absence of critical literacy, as well as some ideas about how this key learning domain can be part of what students start to grapple with in first-year writing. As Mel, Anthony, Lor, and Lance's perspectives illustrate, instructors need to lay groundwork to demonstrate that critical literacy is valuable, that is something to aspire to, and that it can be learned. This is particularly relevant to work in two-year colleges because of the degree to which cultivation of critical literacy is a key distinction between working-class and middle-class educational environments. Likewise, critical literacy skills can function as a gatekeeper for students who are aiming for social and economic mobility, because critical literacy can involve grappling with ways of viewing the world that require giving up or even actively rejecting the stances that characterize their home cultures and communities (see Calarco's "strategies of deference" versus strategies of influence). Tony Scott summarizes this key idea: "To be immersed in culture is to learn to see the world through the ideological lenses it validates and makes available to us. Writing is always ideological because discourses and instances of language use do not exist independently from cultures and their ideologies" ("Writing" 48). In some ways, students at open-access colleges, many of whom come from linguistic, cultural, and ethnic minority groups and socially marginalized discourse communities, are intimately acquainted with the challenges of this DLD and may even have a visceral recognition of this reality, including the relationship between prior writing experiences and identity.

When considering these material realities of two-year-college teachers and students, omitting a pointed emphasis on the relationship between language, culture, and power has potentially deleterious effects. Further, we would argue that it has significantly greater implications for students who have been marginalized by school as an institution. For those of us in the field who are committed to socially just educational practices and liberation pedagogies, this should be deeply troubling. In what ways might a revised WPA outcomes statement, or other professional documents, or other disciplinary documents center the relationship between literacy and power? The current attention to antiracist pedagogies and curricula is one promising direction—but we think here that the stratified and compliance-focused educational system itself dissuades real engagement with questions of literacy and power. Put differently, we invite readers to reflect on how the tracked school structure (from K–12 to college, "college prep" programs that start from middle school and predetermine access and who has it, etc.) functions to sort and track students. And ultimately, how does that system shape who goes to university, who goes to work or the military, who drops out of high school—and maybe comes back to college years or decades later? What literacy needs do those students have that will help them meet their specific academic needs—and also achieve social and structural change by supporting broader civic participation, greater levels of educational attainment, and more engaged critical information literacy across broader swaths of the population? For students whose prior schooling experiences have been oppressive, entering into and accepting this knowledge domain means accepting a stance that has systematically rejected the validity and value of their literacies. For many instructors trained to teach writing in selective institutions, it can be tempting to identify these students' responses as dispositional or attitudinal failings rather than as a pedagogical or curricular need. Here we see another example of how an integrated agenda in writing studies that includes research and best practices in support of pedagogical adaptability could benefit these instructors and these students.

DLD 3: Process Skills and Knowledge: Material and Emotional Writing Classroom Realities

One of our participating students, Jim, wrote in his portfolio, "I am not a strong writer, nor do I enjoy writing, which I believe makes it even more harder to write. Writing will be my top struggle in this class." When reading through student writing like Jim's, it is difficult to avoid the emotional element connected to many students' experiences in learning how to think like college writers. Jim admits that writing—of all kinds—calls up negative feelings and the knowledge that writing will be a significant obstacle for his potential success in college. Jim identifies a lack of enjoyment, and "struggle" (a word we saw over and over again in our analysis of student writing for this project) in ways that signal the many emotional dimensions of writing classrooms. However, much of the work on emotion or affect in writing studies focuses largely on the instructor experience, the work of writing program administration, or the job market (see Micciche, "More than a Feeling"; Sano-Franchini; Ede). An exception is Rebecca Nowacek's *Agents of Integration: Understanding Transfer as a Rhetorical Act*, which observes the importance of accounting for the affective dimensions, for students, of what she calls recontextualization. As one of the four principles that are the foundation of her book, "Transfer understood as recontextualization recognizes that transfer can be both positive and negative and that there is a powerful affective dimension of transfer." Like Nowacek, we agree that when students write—and make connections to prior learning (for Nowacek, this is transfer) it is "not simply an intellectual accomplishment; for many students, it is an emotional experience: Transfer as revelation, as the 'a-ha!' moment" (27). Nowacek's work, however, focuses in large part on the positive affective dimensions of revelation or "getting it." In this section, we explore the flip side of the moment of revelation—how for students who have been alienated by schooling, the act of reflection and accessing prior learning has a powerful negative affective dimension, one that fundamentally shapes their perspective on academics and teachers (see Sternglass for other accounts). We analyze students' writing in relation to DLD 3 that focuses on process knowledge and skills, but also consider the emotional dimensions of this kind of composing and revising work, in particular, for struggling writers.

When assessing student work for DLD 3, process knowledge, we focused on the writing process and the internalization of specific dispositions of and beliefs about the utility of failure or the value of revision. Two conclusions stand out to us: first, this was the set of metaconcepts that our two-year-college students were most likely to have "crossed" in terms of a threshold of writing studies. On the flip side, however, doing this work came with some emotional and affective costs, and those dimensions of the work must be placed at the center of our writing classrooms.[14] As Table 3.8 documents, the vast majority of students in this study demonstrated that they were making progress in this writing studies learning domain. But with that progress came an emotional acknowledgment that was often negative for students. In this section, we use examples from students' reflective writing as well as comments from participating instructors to flesh out the data in Table 3.8 and show more than

Table 3.8. Percentage of Assessed Students' Progress toward DLD 3, Process Knowledge Outcomes, Threshold Concepts, and Domains of Knowledge

All sections aggregated (78=n)	DLD 3: Process Knowledge
Developing	35% (27)
Accomplished	42% (33)
No evidence	18% (14)
NA	5% (4)

just the academic assessment of whether students accomplished a particular learning domain or outcome. We will also show how some of the more common curricular components of process pedagogy can affect two-year-college students differently; for example, the literacy narrative often finds students recalling negative experiences with literacy or reinforcing their mistrust of the classroom and learning.

A common thread that ran through the student writing we reviewed was an emotional undercurrent connected to shared writing. When students were asked to consider their past and present experiences with literacy or discuss their writing with an instructor and/or peers, many of them revealed anxieties that illuminate the emotional costs that come with some of these practices. Students spoke of feeling "nervous," "uneasy," "concerned," and "very [uninterested]," and, as discussed in the previous section, tended to focus on their concerns about their deficiencies with lower-order issues related to grammar and mechanics. Students also use a language of emotion to describe their writing process—the descriptive words illustrate the ways that for at-risk or struggling students, evaluation is a powerful and negative emotional experience, not just an intellectual one. Here, we consider the implications of disciplinary best practices and standards for students and instructors at open-access institutions, particularly how the affective dimensions disproportionately negatively impact such stakeholders in our disciplinary enterprise.

When viewed through the lens of research on emotional labor, it becomes clear that we must examine the costs for students (and instructors) that might come with these practices. Such an examination has taken place in other areas within writing studies, particularly in the context of WPA work. As Laura Micciche argues, an "analysis of disappointment. . . . can be *one* basis for exploring the relationship between work practices and emotional dispositions that contributes both to the larger discourse on administration and to an understanding of those factors that create a culture of disappointment in the academy" (434–35; see also Payne; Schell, "Is It Worth It"). Patrick Sullivan, as well, has spoken movingly of the work of teaching at-risk and sometimes academically underprepared students: "English teachers spend more time—both qualitatively and quantitatively—with underprepared students than any other single group of college staff. And as any English teacher will tell you, this is some of the most challenging work we do as teachers. . . . We become invested in our students' successes and failures in ways that are significantly different than any of our colleagues" ("Essential Question" 8). Our analysis of student writing and instructor materials reveals the striking contrast between the simultaneous benefits and risks that come with integrating many best practices that help students engage in an academic writing community including reflective writing, conferences, and peer review.

Reflective writing is, in our observation, critical to vulnerable students who have had very little experience with structured opportunities to think about their preparation for college writing. They also likely have very little practice conducting self-assessment in relation to course outcomes in part because they often did not attend college immediately after high school, or if they did they had not been planning on going to college for very long (see Sullivan's *College English* discussion of such college writers in "Measuring 'Success' at Open Admissions Institutions: Thinking Carefully about This Complex Question"). As an example, consider Sandra, who only after multiple reflective writing opportunities was able to understand what she saw were weaknesses more accurately:

> At the time of submission, I thought the letter was laid out well and had a good plan as to how I would push myself during the semester. When I received the letter back at the end of the semester and reread it I realized I had been wrong. The letter included spelling errors, wasn't as specific as I had originally thought, and it was very repetitive. I had mentioned that I was worried about the in-class writings which weren't bad at all, but I didn't even mention what I actually struggled with which was paraphrasing.

Yancey notes that with reflection comes a number of risks, including too much focus on the individual process and assigning a disproportionate sense of authority to students (202–03). We see reflections of Yancey's observation threaded throughout the student portfolios we examined.

In our analysis of student writing, we note anxiety as another risk, and it became clear to us that reflection appeared to be distressing for some of these students, even when they ultimately came around to understanding the value of that reflection. Such reflection demonstrates, at least on some level, what Yancey sees as the coming together of "cognitive, affective, and intuitive aspects of ourselves" to understand how past and present work meets a set of criteria (6). One student, Alan, reveals the costs and benefits of reflective work:

> I have never ever done anything like the cover letters in my academic career. At first I was very skeptical on the first one with the way it was structured and seemed slightly off-putting. Going back to read it, it seemed incredibly formal and bland in a way. As the essays went on and I opened up more to this practice, they got better, specifically in essay 2 on how honest I was with my own writing. I believe I even used the word garbage to describe the essay. Granted I was being overall too harsh with myself but I am glad I have revised it. These cover letter helped force me to take a deeper look at my own work and be critical of it.

Alan's story is reflective of themes in "Remembering Reading, Remembering Writing," where Deborah Brandt argues for the importance of literacy narrative, saying that examining these reading and writing experiences is "useful for enriching conceptions of literacy and literacy development and for encouraging more conscious pedagogy in English classrooms" (460). Brandt acknowledges that these narratives are sometimes "painful," and it is this element of recalling one's literacy history that can bring the most anxiety to students at two-year colleges. The process of documenting past and present experiences with literacy can be accompanied by feelings of inadequacy and memories of failure or contempt, sometimes cementing a student's fear that they are unable to succeed in writing classes. Alan's narrative is reflective of just how difficult it is for some students to describe their literacy journeys in purely "academic" ways—those journeys are always connected to the material context of their past and present lives outside the classroom.

The emotional labor and emotional work accompanying assessment in two-year-college writing instruction for instructors is also heavy. Though certainly all writing teachers can struggle with the intellectual effort that teaching and assessing writing brings, the intense focus on helping students bridge what can be a wide gap between their previous educational experiences and the expectations of college literacy can be especially taxing, particularly when layered onto the material challenges open-access students face. "TYCA Working Paper #7: Making the Emotional Labor of Open-Access Teaching Visible" synthesized responses from the workload survey of over a thousand two-year-college faculty. Instructors described the emotional dimensions of their teaching in compelling words: "On top of all of this, because we work with so many students who are some of the most vulnerable students in the population in terms of preparation, social support, and systemic oppression, the emotional labor of being a community college [instructor] is enormous," commented one respondent. Others commented on the challenges associated with helping

> students who fall behind because they are working multiple jobs with shifting schedules, who are one medical or transpor-

> tation bill away from being unable to make ends meet, who simply believe they don't belong in college because so much is new or unfamiliar, who lack support at home because they are the first in their families to go to college, or who don't seek treatment for anxiety, depression, or other mental illness because of the cost, the stigma, or simply not knowing how.

Respondents describe the "emotional work that goes into managing so many students, who are in tenuous life positions. Students lose jobs, become homeless, struggle with addiction, have PTSD, and so much more" (Hassel et al. 3), which results sometimes in a crisis of conscience. "TYCA Working Paper #6: Two-Year College English Faculty Workload: Making the Labor of Assessment Visible," quotes one respondent who captures an assessment dilemma specific to open-access teaching: "The toll it takes on us when our students aren't prepared for a college-level class. They work hard, we root for them, and they still don't succeed. It's heartbreaking. I'm starting to feel complicit in a scheme designed to limit some folks access to education by setting them up to fail" (Hassel and Klausman 5). This is to say that though we know that best practices drawn from disciplinary research are essential to student success, the emotional dimensions of this daily labor can be magnified for faculty working in two-year colleges with multiple sections of developmental, corequisite, or first-year writing, and with structurally disadvantaged and minoritized student populations.

Conferences, like reflective writing, are a recommended best practice in writing instruction (see Ching; Lerner; *Professional Knowledge*) but are also a kind of interaction, as is peer review, that can cause anxiety for students as they fear sharing their work or facing what they assume will be (more) criticism of it. The requirement of these established practices that students "make public" or share their ideas or their writing brings with it both a fear and a sense of powerlessness over what they might see as an inevitable negative judgment by an instructor or a peer, especially based on past experiences.

This is a contrast to the ways, broadly speaking, we see even less-prepared university students approaching their learning. Literacy interventions such as private tutoring or at-home support from educated parents orient some student writers toward the regular experience of talking about their work with educated adults, with an understanding that, yes, "all writers have more to learn," as *Naming What We Know* notes. Our underserved students, whose strategies of deference (rarely making claims on teachers' time or attention, working through struggles independently, accepting the consequences of failures through deference to teacher-authority, as Calarco argues), means that we might see our two-year students interacting with us much differently than do university students. Anecdotally, we know from our combined four decades of two-year-college teaching that students often don't schedule a conference, or don't show up for conferences for a wide range of reasons, and the instructors in our study also noted that several students in their classes missed workshops and peer review. For students whose backgrounds do not put them in contact with college-educated (let alone PhD-credentialed) individuals, the prospect of one-on-one conversation with a professor can be nothing less than anxiety-inducing if not frightening.

The emotional dimensions of these practices can be just as significant a barrier as the logistical ones. For at least some of these students, meeting with an instructor is not just challenging in terms of time but can be difficult or painful. Briana was resistant to peer feedback, according to her instructor, and her reflections indicated that in addition to experiencing some anxiety she was also concerned about trusting her readers: "Once I had an opportunity to have someone trustworthy read my paper, however, I felt much better about the organization, because it seemed like the fluency was fine." English 101 student Alan, as well, expressed his ongoing frustration with sharing his work in his final self-assessment: "Upon completion of this course, I have many mixed feelings about my performance. I feel overtly strongly on improvements as a writer, but I feel slightly more discouraged in a way. . . . My only complaint is peer review. I understand it helps, but it is incredibly nerve racking to me and I wish it was a thing of the past. I hate sharing my work before it is finished and essentially have it criticized in my face." One instructor, Rachel, observed that her English 101 student Shane's shyness may have played a factor in his reluctance to meet with her earlier in the semester for a conference. There is a complex nexus of negotiating past negative experiences with literacy (see Brandt) coinciding with anxiety associated with engaging in a college writing community that can impact these kinds of learning activities. These dynamics are reflected in Cassie's opening vignette to this chapter, where she describes two regular components of the initial conference in a two-year classroom—first, that most students either don't show up or schedule, and second, that when they do attend, the conferences are often about issues unrelated to writing.

The interrelationship between affective dimensions of process pedagogy, and the emotional labor for teachers and students in executing it, is complicated when considering the materiality of the classroom with teaching and learning in two-year colleges. For the diverse populations at two-year colleges, conferences seem like an ideal way to provide individualized feedback that can accommodate a variety of learning styles. Conferences, Neal Lerner states, provide instructors "a way to create meaningful relationships with an increasingly diverse student body or at least one that was increasingly different from the teaching class" (203). However, as Lerner also acknowledges, and as the coauthors' contrasting narratives about midterm conferences in this chapter illustrate, the logistics of conferencing with each student, especially for contingent faculty with heavy teaching loads, is an unreasonable expectation of labor: "Reliance on part-time, contingent instructors, unease about students underprepared for higher education, and a renewed push for higher admission standards at historically open access institutions all threaten the teaching-learning ideal that conferencing represents. We manage our fifteen minutes or so once or twice a semester, wishing we could do more, knowing we are unable" (187). Though we are firmly committed to conferencing as a critical component of effective writing instruction, it is essential to consider the material constraints that distinguish the working conditions of two-year-college teachers in order to make conferences a workable component of writing instruction in such settings.

These time constraints are also true for students—according to the Community College Research Center, 69 percent of community-colleges students work while attending school, and 33 percent of those students work more than thirty-five hours per week. In addition, around 30 percent of community-college students are parents, which is the largest share of student parents across all types of institutions (Noll et al. 3). When analyzing student writing for this chapter, we noted comments from several instructors about the substantial workload and domestic responsibilities many of their students carried. For example, one of our participating instructors, Kristen, noted that Brianna was one of her best students, but struggled finding time to sleep as she worked more than forty hours a week. (Brianna also received a lower grade on an essay because she did not submit the essay on time.) For students like Brianna, finding time to schedule a conference outside of a regularly scheduled class meeting time can be very difficult.

Reading Relationships

In "Prototypical Reading: Volume, Desire, Anxiety," Amy Robillard writes, "we cannot get a mental image of literacy, something that is not reading or writing but something more general. Perhaps this explains the necessity for repeated claims about the indivisibility of reading and writing: because we have basic mental images for each that do not intersect, we need to be reminded, or persuaded, again and again, that the two processes are integral to each other" (205). Robillard's piece speaks to a topic that is substantially underaddressed in writing studies, particularly the DLDs that shape the curriculum, pedagogy, and outcomes of the field—the relationship between reading instruction and writing instruction. The integrated and mutually refreshing role of reading and writing as they relate to each other is not reflected in the 2015 *Naming What We Know* (though the 2019 follow-up book does begin to address this gap) and though it is a component part of the WPA outcomes, it is not a separate area of emphasis. Any DLD that drew from the learning needs of two-year-college students would firmly recognize the role of reading in open-access institutions. In this case, our study illuminated the ways that critical reading, rhetorical reading, and the relationship between writing activities and reading activities were particularly important to writers whose past experiences were not well aligned with the expectations of college literacy tasks. However, it also exposed this DLD as one of the most difficult for instructors to integrate and/or adapt, given its differences in pedagogy and assessment.

The reading-writing relationship has remained of consistent interest to writing-studies scholars and teachers, with recent book-length collections tackling a series of interrelated questions about how reading and writing interact within the context of a writing classroom. Sullivan, Howard Tinberg, and Sheridan Blau's *Deep Reading: Teaching Reading in the Writing Classroom* and *What Is College Reading?* edited by Alice Horning, Deborah-Lee Gollnitz, and Cynthia Haller are two such examples (see also Horning and Kraemer; and D'Angelo et al.), as is a 2021 special issue of *Pedagogy* addressing reading and information literacy. Horning et al. frame their volume as a response to "the need for more consistent attention to reading instruction across the curriculum" (6), drawing from quantitative and qualitative research to anchor the collection's multidisciplinary contributions about reading in college. By contrast, Sullivan et al., like Ellen Carillo (*Securing*), focus their attention on how reading functions in writing classrooms, with Sullivan specifically naming "deep reading" as a threshold concept in composition studies (143). Of course, writing studies' differentiation from English (previously defined by the study of belletristic literature) in the 1980s and 1990s has shaped how we as a field engage in discussion of the interactive processes of writing and reading. Carillo observes that in our professional conversations, and even convention submission categories, "discussions of reading as it relates to composition focus on which texts one should teach in the composition classroom (if any at all) rather than the practice of reading itself. In other words, composition scholars spend time focusing on reading(s) as a noun—rather than on reading as a verb, as a practice or process" (7). We provide this context to emphasize that any DLD that spoke to the pressing literacy issues facing open-access students would recognize that reading—critical reading, deep reading—is a significant barrier for those students in their participation in college learning.

Our first-year writing program outcomes, like the *WPA Outcomes Statement for First-Year Composition*, include "critical thinking, reading, and composing" as a course outcome. Students and instructors in our project regularly identified reading as a challenge—either students themselves spoke to their own struggles to read and understand complex, college-level texts, or participating instructors identified critical reading and reading skills as a barrier for students to progressing through the first-year writing sequence and achieving the learning outcomes. Less directly, many of our student writers struggled to see relationships between the literature-based or reading-based courses they took in high school and the tasks they were currently asked to do in their college writing courses. For example, English 101 student Joe observed, "One problem that I have always had is, I'm not good at comprehending what I'm reading. I know throughout this class I'm going to have to read material over and over again to understand it." Another student, Shane, self-assessing his prior experiences, wrote:

> I have not had fun with my past writing. For that reason I do not enjoy it now, and don't look forward to it. Growing up, I have always enjoyed the thought of reading and writing. I would always try to read books and write poems or other forms of writing. I was never any good at either of them. It would just cause me to get frustrated and give up on it. I was always a slow reader. I would get confused or lost with my writing. I was never any good at connecting my ideas with the topics. It was also hard making things flow in my writings.

More than in university contexts, we observe how significant the barriers—true obstacles—that students' struggles with reading are for their progress toward not just college literacy, not just first-year writing, but a college degree. These student-identified challenges with reading were demonstrated throughout the three writing courses, whether non-degree-credit or degree-fulfilling. An English 098 student, Karl, recalled, "We did different homework assignments that required us to evaluate an article and reflect on it. I would later find out that I knew nothing about the 5-7 page articles that we were assigned to read." A more advanced student completing English 102, Brianna, expresses her difficulty with writing because of reading difficulties in an author's note: "To be entirely honest, I had a really difficult time completing this assignment. Understanding one of the readings was an absolute nightmare, and therefore made compiling information confusing. I spent many all-nighters repeatedly mulling over the texts and considering comparisons in order to bring about this paper. Whether or not I achieved the learning outcomes, I'm not sure." In other words, it was as likely for students in the basic writing class as in the core, degree-fulfilling course to note that reading complex texts and comprehending them, let alone undertaking the kind of analytical writing that our first-year writing curriculum (like many) requires in the form of rhetorical analysis, research reviews, or research-based arguments, was a significant barrier.

We also saw cases where a student did not independently or directly identify reading as a struggle but the instructors believed reading comprehension or critical reading ultimately made the learning process challenging. In English 102, student Dean's reflection, "Since writing is not really a strong suit of mine, most writing assignments are difficult, but the literature review was especially difficult because I had to analyse a lot of articles pertaining to my topic," was confirmed by his instructor Jack, who made connections between the nontraditional teaching and learning site and the way that it made it challenging to address the needs of students like Dean and his classmates: "I think Dean's biggest barrier is his critical reading ability. He would benefit from an academic reading course, which is not currently offered at [the off-campus] military academy, where I teach this class. It would be ideal if we could offer such a course at some point in the future, as there are other students who would benefit from a course such as LEA 101 or 103 [our institution's non-degree reading support course]." This particular observation is useful because it identifies some of the overlapping themes of this chapter. This instructor's graduate study prepared him with pedagogical theory and composition studies coursework. Though he works off the tenure track and had a five-course appointment, he was able to make note of curricular gaps in his teaching appointment at an off-site dual-credit version of the English 102 course that fulfills the degree requirement for most college credentials. At the same time, the intersecting circumstances of Jack's teaching appointment and his assessment of Dean stand out as illustrative of the labor, pedagogy, and scholarship questions we address in this book. As a selective, residential private school, the dual-credit option is attractive to students and parents who want their students to accumulate college credit prior to high school graduation; simultaneously, the relative affluence of the student population in this section doesn't insulate them from challenges with adapting to the demands of college reading. And without the institutional will (or recognition of student needs) from both the two-year-college campus sponsoring the dual-credit program or the private military academy that would likely be unwilling to adopt a non-degree-credit course to address a learning need, the ability of Jack or the writing program administrator of the sponsoring program to effect change that would respond to those needs is limited, and as we have noted and the scholarship has documented, the vast majority of two-year colleges do not have a dedicated WPA.

◈◈◈◈

Midterm, Fall 2019
Holly

Here is what I miss, though: helping students who never expected to go to college believe they can do it; helping students who haven't always planned to be college graduates, for whatever reason, to see themselves at the end of their studies, throwing their caps in the air; my students now are kind, earnest, and conscientious. They are very good at participating in the game of school. They don't turn things in late, and if they do, they are deeply apologetic. But my open-access students needed me more. I could see deep, transformative change happening in a single class period. The act of validating their experiences and perceptions about school had a visible effect on their beliefs about themselves and their ability to be successful college writers.

I also miss being in a context where everyone was committed to and responsible for the same thing—first-year writers and writing. All my department colleagues were in the game, man. That's what we did. It wasn't something you avoided because it's labor intensive, or because the students need more feedback, time, and patience; it was the core work of the place. In this way, universities feel different because they are different. The segmentation of first-year courses being charged primarily to highly inexperienced graduate students and to very-experienced but often departmentally alienated adjunct faculty or full-time lecturers (or contract faculty, as they are sometimes called) is viscerally different. Faculty do this; instructors and graduate students do that. Decisions about the writing program are made largely with attention to what GTAs will experience in delivering the FYW writing curriculum, not what first-year writers will need or experience. This is not a critical assessment so much as a description of how universities with graduate programs seem to operate, which is to sustain themselves and, primarily, their graduate programs. What I miss most is the shared responsibility and commitment to the work of foundational writing instruction.

◈◈◈◈

Much of the research that informs this chapter comes from our belief that university-centric shaping of the field doesn't speak to the needs of the students that we have described in this chapter. Very rarely do university programs have to account for the level of material and cultural differences that are intrinsic to two-year-college writing programs. Even further, when we raise such questions, they have often been minimized—typically with the assertion that universities also have diverse students, and those who fit the demographic profiles of those we describe here. As we conclude this chapter, we want to reinforce just how inaccurate such claims are despite being repeated. In part, it's because the culture and reality of two-year colleges are invisible to our university colleagues. And in being invisible—and also part of a low-status and low-regard environment—the paradigms that govern these different parts of higher education, and the people who teach and learn in them, are not necessarily recognizable to each other. But because status, power, and resources dictate whose perspective is privileged, two-year-college students and faculty not only do not have the authority to shape the scholarly and disciplinary conversations, they are often ignored or minimized, and as a result badly served.

In reality, some of the biggest challenges for two-year-college writing programs are the gaps between the stated values of the different DLDs and the teaching and learning practices that are superimposed on our students, in part because graduate programs by definition train the instructors who subsequently are writing faculty at two-year colleges. This means, for example, that pedagogical attachments to writer compliance—and classrooms that do not actively seek to disrupt writer compliance—are both still common in college writing environments and disparately impactful on marginalized student writers. One thing the 2020 pandemic has done is force many instructors to really rethink how they are going to measure engagement, learning, and proficiency, as some of the proxy measures that have often stood in for those things such as attendance, work submitted on time, and the frequency with which students participate in class discussion have had to be radically rethought.

Further, writer-compliance orientations that are imposed on new college writers, particularly those who already have the most marginalized relationship to higher education, require critical engagement by college writing instructors. This critical engagement means potentially intervening in and navigating competing value systems, including the classed and hegemonic assessment criteria (see Bloom; *Framework for Success*; Poe et al., "Legal"; Poe et al., *Writing Assessment*; Kalish et al.) still embraced by many first-year writing teachers and faculty across the curriculum. This means challenging both the language of standards and classroom practices and policies. If there is any upside to a global pandemic, it's that we see more instructors in more disciplines working to champion flexibility and compassion—recognizing that students are living through and in challenging circumstances (as are instructors themselves). Yet, this pedagogy of compassion and flexibility has always benefited marginalized students—those who are most likely to attend open-access and two-year campuses—and has always been necessary for students who have been underserved by education and who juggle poverty, health issues, paid work, dependents, and other material realities that create barriers to academic engagement and success.

When we look at the enactment of policies and practices that value compliance over engagement and learning, we see how they might negatively impact students like these, who are the majority of two-year-college students:

- Brianna, writing about her selected research argument topic of financial aid for college, admitted the sense of shame she had internalized about receiving financial support in college: "When it comes to grants, it is almost as though they have a stigma about them. As a grant recipient, I am often embarrassed to even admit that I receive them or report what I use the portion that does not go toward tuition for due to the fact that I feel heavily judged." This same student, her instructor Kristen noted, works more than forty hours a week while also being a full-time student.
- Joe, a returning adult student who self-identified as having a learning disability and worked full-time, articulated the challenges of managing his intensive work schedule and navigating the content and tasks of a course that was very difficult for him, as it can be for students who have struggled as writers: "After looking many words up over and over again, it tends to take a lot of time, which is a valuable commodity to a college student that is working full time. . . . Finding time to do my homework is a very difficult task because of how much spare time I don't have."
- Lou, a student working a factory job at night and navigating a gender transition, reported about their academic background: "Essay 1 was my first formal paper ever, and it was the first time I'd ever used a word processor. In it, my margins were too narrow, there were several comma splices, and I didn't use very many transitional word or phrases." The desire to learn and

> progress was not the issue for this student—making time for that learning was. As the student wrote in an author's note for a later paper in the course: "My impression of this essay is that it's not too bad considering it's the first essay I've ever written," and, "In all honesty, I learned so much from this, and there is so much more that ought to be in this paper, that it's disappointing to me that I didn't have more time to work on it. I'll definitely write on privilege, oppression and racism again."

If we have any single takeaway from this chapter, it's asking readers to understand and challenge the misconception that the needs of students and faculty in access institutions are the same as those in university settings. In our experience, they're not often on anyone's mind in four-year contexts, not out of malice, but out of ignorance of an entire student and instructor population coming from different directions in the field.

To our minds, scholarly publication is not really the place to call for changes to professional standards or documents—since scholarship can't do the work itself—but organizational service groups can. We do offer here a few examples of what, for example, a revised WPA OS would emphasize:

- Procedural knowledge—as much doing things as knowing how writers do things
- Metalinguistic knowledge—as much emphasis on using language as knowing how writers use language and how language works
- Knowledge of linguistic diversity (see Kareem; Baker-Bell; and Looker).
- Critical reading and information literacy (which are certainly of concern for all students, but our own research and experience suggests are of particular importance to first-generation and working-class students). See, in particular, the Association of College and Research Libraries' *Framework for Information Literacy for Higher Education*, a 2016 revision that moves information literacy skills into a more complex way of thinking than the previous "checklist" model.

- Organizational work that affects first-year writing and writers—whether by CCCC, TYCA, WPA, or other major groups in the field of composition and rhetoric—would include group membership that included the majority of contingent faculty, graduate students, and two-year-college faculty—the teaching majority who teach nearly all the first-year writing in the country.

It is not easy in a field as expansive as writing studies to establish professional guidelines—but we think it is possible to do more to align labor, teaching, and scholarship with material reality, as we outline more fully in the closing chapter of this book.

4

Toward an Integrated Agenda in Writing Studies

> It would seem to be an easy task: to explain to the academy at large what we two-year college faculty do. After all, we are products of academic (read four-year) institutions. But so often when speaking to colleagues at four-year schools we are put into Janice Albert's situation: "I have tried to get them to say community college,' but it always comes out 'junior'" (1994, 10). We are simply not taken seriously as academics—that is, as scholars or researchers. In their eyes, our work has little to do with the life of the mind. In large part, this book represents an effort to represent community college faculty as deeply reflective and impassioned practitioners.
>
> —Howard Tinberg, *Border Talk: Writing and Knowing in the Two-Year College*

THE REWARDS OF TEACHING IN THE two-year environment are many, and in large part are rooted in the experience of working with an extraordinary diversity of students, and of being a part of the pathway to achieving educational and occupational goals for many students who wouldn't otherwise have a chance to pursue a college education. There's a reason that Nell Ann Pickett referred to the two-year colleges as "democracy in action" in her 1997 CCCC chair's address. Because we know so deeply the rewards of teaching two-year-college English, a key part of what we hope to accomplish in *Materiality and Writing Studies* is to make the case that the representative majority of students and instructors needs to be seen more clearly so as to paint a more richly accurate picture of writing instruction in higher education. Likewise, we wanted to do at least some of that visibility work by focusing on the students and instructors at two-year colleges. And while instructors from many institutions might recognize some of their circumstances, students, and instructors within chapters of this book, we want to emphasize that the picture we have created here is one that doesn't necessarily define the ecology of two-year-college writing, writers, and writing teachers, but rather makes at least some key parts of this work more apparent to our disciplinary colleagues.

This visibility and misalignment problem has moral, economic, and sustainability implications. For example, Marc Bousquet, Eileen Schell, and others have written about the gap between the disciplinary knowledge that we seek to establish and the labor practices that put the most inexperienced and unprepared instructors in the classrooms of our most vulnerable students. We think the important first step of aligning labor, scholarship, and teaching is to come back to the questions we posed at the outset of this book: If we can agree with some professional consensus that writing studies is a discipline, then for whom? Who gets to be part of it and whose needs and interests does it reflect? And in what ways can the disciplinary threads that often operate on separate tracks—teaching, scholarship, labor—find productive ways to intersect for the benefits of students and teachers? In this closing chapter, we demonstrate the exigency for these efforts to integrate the components of our field—our teaching, our scholarship, and our labor practices—showing demographics and educational-attainment data that speak to the needs of the plurality of writing students in the United States. We then describe how inattention to first-year writing at open-access and two-year colleges has consequences for the public and legislative support for higher education. Finally, we identify action items and culture shifts within our disciplinary organizations, journals, graduate programs, home institutions, and classrooms that can support an integrated agenda.

TWO-YEAR COLLEGES, EDUCATIONAL ACCESS, AND SOCIAL MOBILITY

Moving toward an integrated theory of writing studies is exigent because the majority of college students in the future will look like those we profiled in Chapter 3 and like those who appear in landmark studies of composition such as Marilyn Sternglass's *Time to Know Them*, Mina Shaughnessy's *Errors and Expectations*, Mike Rose's *Lives on the Boundary*, and Todd Ruecker's *Transiciones: Pathways of Latinas and Latinos Writing in High School and College*. It is exigent because income level, first-generation status, and race all influence in dramatic ways the likelihood that a student will attend college or graduate college. It is exigent because of social justice; it is to everyone's advantage to learn how to effectively help such students develop the reading, writing, and thinking skills required not just for higher education but also for full participation in democratic society. It is exigent because this is the work we can and should do as educators.

This work is also morally imperative, because these students have the deck stacked against them in so many ways. According to a study by the *Washington Post*, wealthy students who drop out of high school do better than college graduates from poor backgrounds. For example, if you are a poor college grad, you are just as likely to end up at the bottom quintile of earners as a rich high school dropout. Further, if you are a rich high school dropout, you are just as likely to stay among the top earners as poor graduates are likely to stay at the bottom (O'Brien). Moreover, data from the Pell Institute demonstrate that just 11 percent of students in the lowest income quartile can expect to earn a degree; by contrast, for students from families in the third and fourth (highest) quartiles, graduation rates reach 41 and 58 percent, respectively (99). First-generation status also influences a student's likelihood of earning a degree (see Figure 4.1), as the National Center for Educational Statistics notes in a recent study:

- Ten years after they were sophomores in high school, a lower percentage of first-generation college students than continuing-generation students had obtained a bachelor's degree (20 versus 42 percent).
- A higher percentage of first-generation college students (54 percent) than continuing-generation students (45 percent) reported they could not afford to continue going to school as a

> reason for leaving college without a postsecondary credential (Redford and Hoyer 4).

And first-generation college students are already a minority of students attending college. Fewer than a quarter of students in the NCES study were first-generation (see the forthcoming collection edited by Kelly Ritter on first-generation students and postsecondary English studies). These data show the significance of attending to the material and learning conditions for first-generation students, particularly as the function of college as a sorting mechanism and a tool for reproducing race and class privilege will only become more entrenched, especially in light of the COVID-19 pandemic. Eric Hoover's 2020 *Chronicle of Higher Education* article emphasizes the demographics of future college students: "nonwhite students will account for the majority of all [high-school] graduates in 24 states. In 2019, 51 percent of graduates at public high schools were white; in 2036 that figure will be 43 percent." This makes it more important than ever, as Demaree Michelau, the president of the Western Interstate Commission for Higher Education, explains, change in higher ed means "better serving all of our students, in particular students of color, low-income students, and first-generation students" (qtd. in Hoover). We know that the 2020 pandemic has already disproportionately impacted the ability of structurally disadvantaged students to pursue college education, with two-year colleges experiencing "the largest fall undergraduate-enrollment decrease of any higher-education sector by far—9.5 percent," losing nearly 19 percent of first-time, first-year students, also the greatest decrease (Hoover). Though this decrease in college access is, we hope, temporary, it highlights how fragile the relationship is for many students between their aspirations to pursue college and the swiftness with which that goal can be disrupted.

What this means is that for today's—and tomorrow's—college students, academic preparation and alignment with college expectations requires a large-scale examination of college literacies and the academy, including how receptive our institutions are to students who face significant material and academic barriers. First-year writing or developmental support courses can address some but not

Figure 4.1. Students enrolling in college by first- or continuing-generation status.

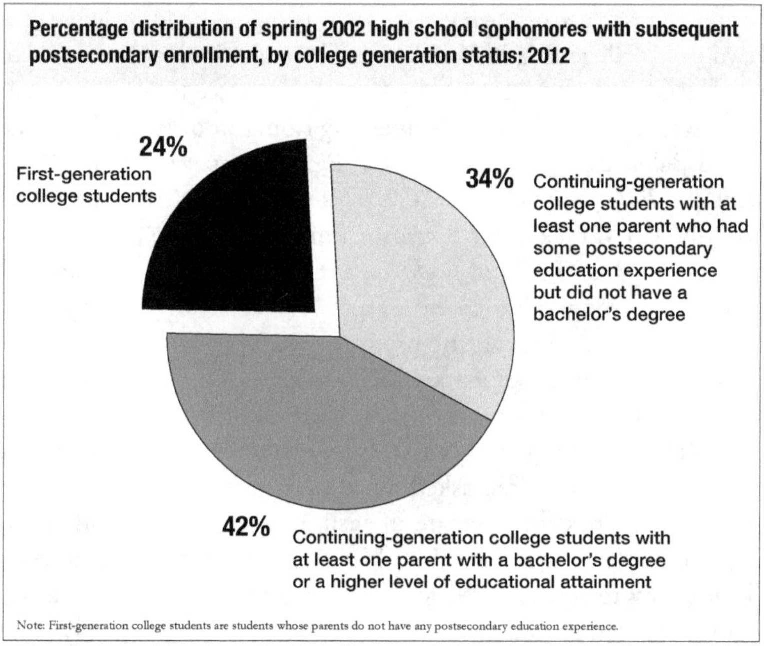

all of this transition to college literacies; however, the teaching and learning research emerging from two-year-college English studies is especially well-poised to help all of the field with supporting this transition. Christie Toth, Patrick Sullivan, and Carolyn Calhoon-Dillahunt, for example, in "Two-Year College Teacher-Scholar-Activism: Reconstructing the Disciplinary Matrix of Writing Studies," seek to "inform colleagues at four-year institutions about the public work two-year college teacher-scholar-activists have been undertaking," highlighting the innovative work of programs like the Accelerated Learning Program that emerged from the Community College of Baltimore County, and productive partnerships developed between the University of Utah and Salt Lake Community College (87). Likewise, ongoing, large-scale big-data studies like those sponsored through the Community College Research Center sometimes ignore and sometimes validate what two-year-college

English faculty on the ground already know: that there are missed opportunities to scale up the programs that work. They are missed opportunities because what they are missing is the knowledge that two-year-college English faculty can share about what the needs of their students are, and what can help them succeed. Likewise, position statements and research emerging from our organizations, like April Baker-Bell's *Linguistic Justice: Black Language, Literacy, Identity, and Pedagogy* and the CCCC *This Ain't Another Statement! This Is a DEMAND for Black Linguistic Justice!,* alongside foundational statements like *Students' Right to Their Own Language,* can and should be productively taken up by two-year-college writing studies. Two-year-college writing programs are where a greater proportion of students of color start their college studies. The editors of the 2020 issue of *Writing Program Administration* focused on two-year-college writing programs report, troublingly, that two-year college faculty are often asked by administrators and colleagues in other disciplines "how we are to ensure the correctness and grammar of students' writing." In addition, because two-year colleges have many technical and vocational programs, "writing situations and tasks [can be] dangerously narrowed—do students only need to know how to write a resume?" (Spiegel et al. 9).

What we want to emphasize here, then, is the importance of multifaceted approaches to inclusive and expansive writing studies. This means two-year colleges have an obligation to take up the research that is especially relevant to their student populations and writing-studies scholarship must account for the different material realities of two-year-college contexts. For example, two studies showing that "remedial fixes" alone are not enough to help students move through college coursework are already well-known to community-college English faculty. *Inside Higher Ed* reports that "a new study found that reforms to remedial education, even a promising one that reaches back into high school, do little to move the needle on students' credit completion or the likelihood of earning a college credential" (Fain); and Florence Xiaotao Ran and Yuxin Lin's research from the Community College Research Center concluded that:

> we did not find any significant effects of corequisite remediation on enrollment persistence, transfer to four-year colleges, or degree completion up to three years after initial enrollment. This suggests that improvements in gateway course outcomes are important but insufficient barometers of academic momentum and college success. (34)

Does this mean that we shouldn't pursue ways of helping students progress through gateway courses? Of course not. Our experiences and our research show that each course completed helps students in direct and perhaps not immediately apparent ways—regardless of whether they earn a credential.

And our direct experience with students who "stop out" of college, and, again, our own research, shows us that we can never predict who will or will not be successful—or when they might return to resume their education. But we also need to be frank, and call bullshit on remarks like those from Bridget Terry Long, dean of the Harvard Graduate School of Education, when she claims during a keynote at the "Reimagining Developmental Education" conference: "Developmental education is really the true gatekeeper" (St. Amour). Such claims illustrate the problematic gap between those who do the work of teaching students from a wide spectrum of educational backgrounds, and those who teach students who have been conditioned from birth to feel entitled to college credentials and professional careers.

An integrated and recentered writing studies matters because in 2013, just 36 percent of whites age twenty-five and older had earned a bachelor's degree, but that attainment rate was even lower for Black (22.5 percent) and Latinx (15.5 percent) populations. We cannot fulfill the promise of democratic access to higher education, of any of the disciplinary calls for social justice, or even of the careerist emphasis on the value of college degrees to provide socioeconomic mobility without attending to the real issues facing working-class students, poor students, first-generation students, and students of color, particularly those who start in two-year colleges and open-access institutions. As we have shown throughout this book, this is the new majority of college students, and it is where most instructors of college writing teach. And to us, this matters, because if we don't reconceive of college as developing smartness rather than rewarding smartness, as Alexander Astin has argued, we overlook how class, race, and other types of privilege are baked into the structures of higher education (see also DiAngelo):

> When SATs and ACTs are used to screen and select, they put poor students, first-generation students, and underrepresented students of color at a competitive disadvantage. If colleges were equivalent in terms of the opportunities they provide, this wouldn't be a problem, but they are far from equivalent. In public higher education, which enrolls 80 percent of all college students, the four-year colleges spend more than twice as much per full-time undergraduate student on instruction as the community colleges do. If we were to compare the community colleges with just the flagship universities, the instructional expenditure ratio would be well over three-to-one. (24)

Ignoring this reality is possible for those instructors and institutions who can screen out and or lavishly invest in the support structures that help students succeed academically. For the majority of institutions of higher education in the United States, however, this is not an option. Our mission is expansive, our doors are open, and our classrooms must be places where learners of all types can flourish.

We see these demographic data intimately connected to the work of writing studies as we outline it in our chapters. Some of the most exciting recent scholarly work in writing studies looks at the social justice functions of writing instruction. Writing assessment has begun to unpack intersections of access, opportunity, and assessment practices, such as Mya Poe, Asao Inoue, and Norbert Elliot's *Writing Assessment, Social Justice, and the Advancement of Opportunity*. And yet, the core values of a rhetorical education continue to be compromised by neoliberalism in the academy. Whether it is literacy instruction encountered by students when they start college, opportunities in the upper division for more advanced study, or academic programs that abandon the curricular breadth that is the signature dimension of liberal education, neoliberal frameworks will inevitably harm the most vulnerable and at-risk student populations—those with the most to gain and the most to lose in their quest for postsecondary learning. Wealthy and upper-class white students will always have access to a liberal education. Harvard will stay open, as will Middlebury and Reed colleges. They will emphasize the liberal arts, and students will study literature, philosophy, art history, classics, history, anthropology, social justice studies, and other subjects.

Meanwhile, dropping public confidence in higher education is accompanied by a disinvestment in and devaluing of the liberal arts.[1] One recent high-profile incident directly affected one of the coauthors—the University of Wisconsin-Stevens Point's call to cut thirteen liberal-arts programs—essentially grossly limiting access to such degree programs for most of the northern half of the state. As MLA President Paula Krebs wrote in the *Washington Post*,

> [T]he message could not be clearer. Working-class and middle-class Wisconsin students should use their college years to focus narrowly on skills that will plug them into existing holes in the state's workforce. The children of the state's upper-middle-class and rich, on the other hand, who have the opportunity to attend elite private colleges or public research universities, can spend four years discovering skills and knowledge that they can use in many different careers.

We see relationships here between the vocationalization of public universities and the critical functions of first-year writing, relationships that are relevant to working toward an integrated agenda. We would resist completely conceptualizing first-year writing as a service course that is the end-all-and-be-all of literacy education in college. We see (as does Patrick Sullivan) the ways that basic writing, or first-semester writing, or second-semester writing, or a writing studio or ALP course that provides more intensive instruction for students, can have the greatest impact on a student's' desire, willingness, and ability to stay in college or drop out. Courses like these that introduce students to college literacies can influence whether they pursue a wide range of studies versus a narrow focus on a technical, vocational, or professional field. What we do in the first-year writing classroom matters. As Sullivan asked in his award-winning *Teaching English in the Two-Year College* article, "'A Lifelong Aversion to Writing': What If Writing Courses Emphasized Motivation?": "Recent research has provided a compelling theoretical argument for this focus on motivation. This work suggests that intrinsic motivation is a prerequisite for any kind of significant learning or achievement" (119). But the consequences of disengaging from or in some cases completely ignoring the work that takes place in these classrooms are significant. We see more and more newspaper stories and scholarly articles with titles like "'Is College Worth It?' Arguing for Composition's Value with the Citizen-Worker" (Bollig) and "Is College Worth It? One Professor Says No" (Pearlstein).

And last, the exigency exists to address and correct disciplinary gaps and misdirected attention. There is a great deal of knowledge missing from the foundational scholarship of our discipline, as John Lovas first noted in his 2002 CCCC Chair's Address, "All Good Writing Develops at the Edge of Risk." He calls the absence of two-year-college writing and writers from the field's discussions a "scholarly and intellectual failing. You cannot represent a field if you ignore half of it. You cannot generalize about composition if you don't know half of the work being done" (276). And, frankly, the work is just more stressful than it needs to be. Jessica Restaino notes how instructors participating in her book-length study taught her that an "analysis of the struggle to survive in our first-year writing classrooms uncovers deep roots in the tensions between theory and practice" (22). Sarah Z. Johnson reports from her work coordinating a national survey of writing instructors that two items achieved consensus: "First, respondents agreed hiring institutions needed robust mentoring and orientation programs; otherwise new faculty, no matter how good their academic preparation to teach, floundered a bit until they learned their new context and student population. Second, many graduate programs weren't providing enough coursework about or practical opportunities to work with diverse learners, as defined by language, age, academic preparation, ethnicity, and disability" (22). Providing throughout graduate education in English the kinds of curriculum and professionalizing experiences that acquaint future writing teachers with the skills and knowledge for adapting to and succeeding in a wide range of teaching and learning environments benefits both those instructors and their students. We need research-based practices to work toward the goal Sullivan sets in his article on motivation: "We cannot continue to present as self-evident the value of reading and writing. We need to work every day to help students discover, experience, and feel the joys of reading and the magic of written communication" ("Lifelong" 125). And this is not what graduate students receive training in, generally. We are in an era where the *Chronicle of Higher Education* leads with headlines like "Columbia Had Little Success Placing English PhDs on the Tenure Track. 'Alarm' Followed, and the University Responded," and the response is to identify "alt-ac" careers rather than identify the actual range of careers available in academia and for which they have earned degrees (Pettit). The system of production of elite PhDs for positions in elite or research-intensive positions is not sustainable—and addressing it will respond to the actual needs of the teaching and learning majority at nonselective and open-admissions campuses, if we are willing to do this difficult work of reimagining.

Jessica Lyn Van Slooten, UWC Manitowoc:
Integration within the context of restructuring is hard. How do you integrate previously separate institutions with their respective people, cultures, programs, values, policies? At its best, we used a collegial process: diverse folks from all four campuses of our soon-to-be-unified institution met in person, listened and talked about areas of overlap and difference, and then decided together how to best integrate. Less satisfying were decisions that were made without the input of folks from the former UWC campuses. At these times, I felt as if our expertise wasn't valued. I learned that this decision-making process defines much of the culture at my new institution. I am adapting to a looser, less

bureaucratic structure on the unit and department level, where decision making happens more sporadically and often—but not always—more administratively, rather than the largely strategic, grassroots approach at my former institution.

My colleagues and I from the former UWC pride ourselves on being scrappy. Ever the underdogs, we worked hard—perhaps too hard, sometimes—to prove ourselves and our students worthy of accolades, resources, support, recognition. We created nationally recognized programs around teaching and learning, curriculum and program development, and assessment. We supported one another and saw the benefit in providing evidence and resources when making change. These were baked into our culture.

Inequity emerges not just for instructors who labor in difficult conditions, or for students whose opportunities to succeed in higher education are diminished through lack of real access, but also in the field when our emphasis on research and research-intensive institutions overshadows the work of teaching and service, particularly teaching first-year students. We have documented in Chapters 1 to 3 the implications of not taking teaching as intellectual work seriously (as have Leonard Cassuto and others). And as Jane Detweiler et al. note in a *College English* special issue focused on leadership, "Often seen as a necessary evil, service is treated as time taken away from the 'real work' of research. Such attitudes fail to acknowledge that the service many of us take up involves translating our disciplinary expertise into action" (451). A truly integrated writing studies agenda will facilitate cohesion across teaching, service, and research, and in doing so recenter value in work that informs each area—with a particular recommitment to first-year writing education.

WHAT WE CAN DO IN THE PROFESSION

> Because it is a pedagogical field, however, the exchange value of composition scholarship has also had a necessary connection to use value in writing education: it is produced with an at least

> implicit assumption that disciplinary and institutional relations exist that will provide the means through which composition scholarship might shape pedagogical practice. Yet it is still not a common methodological expectation in the profession for theories of pedagogy to attend to the political economic factors that constitute the teaching and learning environments of writing education—as if what we do is not affected by how we do it.
>
> —Tony Scott, "Subverting Crisis in the Political Economy of Composition"

The responsibility for an expansive and inclusive theory of writing and discipline of writing studies is held by the structures, people, and places that intersect to create writing studies as it is experienced by the teachers, students, and scholars who circulate within it. Here we offer a blueprint for the kinds of activities that help expand and create inclusiveness within the field by harnessing the power of disciplinary organizations to employ (or in some cases continue to employ) disruptive practices that will contribute to a recentering of the field.

Disciplinary professional organizations and their member groups that work to fulfill the needs of writing teachers have begun to undertake work that responds to the issues we have laid out in this book. For example, the Two-Year College English Association, in partnership with the National Council of Teachers of English and the Conference on College Composition and Communication, have built on the successful professional development work of TYCA's regional membership model and organized the first national TYCA conference in its history, held in conjunction with the CCCC 2019 convention in Pittsburgh.[2] This type of collaboration has the potential to integrate the work of writing teachers in both organizations; to create new and unique opportunities for collaboration and cross-fertilization, and to integrate the professional work of the two organizations, including reaching out to some of the teaching populations who work in nontraditional spaces like credentialed high school teachers offering college-credit-bearing first-year writing courses in high schools. Additional cross-organizational collaboration has been proposed by the Labor

Caucus, a constituent group of CCCC, and resolutions approved at the 2016 convention (see *2016 Resolutions*). These resolutions seek to develop a labor panel that would include membership from the Council of Writing Program Administrators (CWPA), the Modern Language Association (MLA) and others. We see strength in continuing to build such relationships in inclusive ways.

Further, given the hegemonic structure of the field in which research-intensive institutions and research itself hold the greatest sway, organizations can disrupt this hierarchy in several critical ways. They can dedicate components of funding (such as the CCCC Emergent Researcher and Research Initiative funding) to ensure separate consideration for new or early-career applicants, ensuring a level competitive field, with an accompanying mentoring and consultant component. Other efforts include offering more opportunities to participate in organizational activities remotely, through asynchronous or synchronous means (webinars, Zoom or Skype technologies, etc.). Additional thinking can be done about how to make our organizational committee work more transparent, effective, and inclusive—as research-intensive jobs make disciplinary service a requirement, involvement on governance or other issues can be perfunctory and obligatory. We have an opportunity to ask ourselves questions as a profession and a discipline about how we can invite, and even compensate, participation from members at teaching-intensive positions where travel funds and reward systems do not include disciplinary service.

In addition, all professional organizations should annually offer a teaching award or recognition, or multiple awards and recognitions, that would symbolically communicate the value that the field places on that component of our work. No disciplinary awards given for excellence in postsecondary teaching of writing existed until 2020, after two years of work by a task force to develop one (and in the face of some resistance from organizational leaders). Awards like the newly established CCCC Outstanding Teaching Award, which will be first given in 2021, are one part of changing disciplinary values. However, we should also seek participation from and (whenever possible) participation in our representative bodies from contingent faculty and two-year-college faculty, perhaps even allocating funding to support instructors who are working in underresourced material conditions. It is critical as a field that we show that good teaching matters.

In addition, peer-reviewed journals play a critical role in creating knowledge in the field and thus play an important role in aligning the material realities of writing instruction with knowledge creation. Journal editors, editorial boards, and peer reviewers can all work toward creating an inclusive discipline by valuing systematic inquiry into teaching and learning and by demanding that we hear about the challenges and failures as well as the "wins" of particular pedagogical approaches or classrooms. We can all support recursive and in-depth pedagogical research on the concepts that as a field we have agreed are important to developing as writers and to our knowledge about composition—the *Framework for Success in Postsecondary Writing*, the *WPA Outcomes Statement for First-Year Composition*, and the growing body of threshold concepts in writing studies. We can ask that the experimental pedagogy article include an assessment component so that readers who need to justify and address resistance to innovation within their departments can help naysayers overcome skepticism about employing new methods. Editors and peer reviewers can approach the process of reviewing and evaluating manuscripts as a formative and mentoring job: potential writers need to hear about what they can do better and how, as much as journals, by dint of limited space and for the maintenance of academic rigor, necessarily have to reject most of the submissions they receive. Kelly Blewett, Christina LaVecchia, Laura Micciche, and Janine Morris have presented multiple specific strategies for this kind of work in their 2019 *College English* article, "Editing as Inclusion Activism."

Within our home institutions, there are a myriad of ways to create equitable, inclusive, and expansive cultures in our field. Ethical labor practices are the basic material conditions of employment (including compensation, position stability, processes for evaluation, availability of resources, etc.)—but beyond that we miss an understanding of whole swaths of the field of writing studies when our contingent faculty do not have a voice. Whenever possible, contingent faculty should have voting rights and governance representation—ideally proportional to their numbers in the governance unit. As Chapter 1 documented, non-tenure-line faculty positions are the majority in many English departments, but resource-hoarding in which they are not granted support for ongoing professional development will deepen the schism between knowledge production and the work of writing classrooms unless faculty across the institution and departments share the capital—fiscal, human, cultural, and academic—and change policy and practice to integrate NTT faculty into the life of the department. The voices of non-tenure-line faculty are particularly valuable when discussing how teaching and learning are evaluated, including curriculum or program assessment, department or program review, and evaluation of instructors. The whole volume of *Contingency, Exploitation, and Solidarity: Labor and Action in English Composition* (Kahn et al.) offers a range of paths forward in this regard, but Rolf Norgaard's chapter and Chris Blankenship and Justin Jory's contribution in particular speak to the issue of involvement in governance.

To reflect and strengthen in our local sites an expansive and inclusive theory of writing, we must build institutional partnerships. These include building relationships between universities and community colleges for mutually enriching conversations about transfer student success, curricular alignment, and the needs of the respective sites of learning. Anne Ruggles Gere et al. productively documented such research, service, and relationship-building work in their 2017 *College English* article "Mutual Adjustments: Learning from and Responding to Transfer Student Writers." Deploying systematic inquiry into the successes and challenges of the students who begin their studies at the universities and those who transfer in, the authors identify the importance of looking closely at, and listening to, students who experience that transition as a data source for program, curricular, and instructional development. As they describe, such developments were important components to "understanding how transfer student writers adjust to the university environment and considering the kinds of institutional adjustments we might make in turn" (336). Likewise, partnerships that build on the knowledge two-year-college faculty have to inform graduate programs about the rewards and challenges—and required skills—for working in this sector of higher education are critical (see Spiegel and Blaauw-Hara and Jensen and Ely for an overview of some successful models of this sort). Stephen Ruffus and Christie Toth's model of curricular collaboration is one example of a program resulting in a seamless transfer pathway for community-college students into a writing and rhetoric major. As Ruffus and Toth explain: "We have developed an AS degree in writing studies, which we are launching in 2018. Notable components of the AS degree are the creation of two new 2000-level courses—Introduction to Writing Studies and Digital Writing—both of which have a course-to-course articulation with the U's department" (341). Also emerging from this partnership is a summer bridge program called Writing Studies Scholars which is designed to support Salt Lake CC students transferring into the writing and rhetoric studies major at the University of Utah, a program built collaboratively between the community college and university faculty.

WHAT WE CAN DO IN THE CLASSROOM

> If we compositionists—let's let our English colleagues off the hook for a moment—are too busy navel-gazing to get on with our work, what is this work we're not getting on with? The short answer to this question is teaching.
>
> —Chris Gallagher, "We Compositionists: Toward Engaged Professionalism"

A recentered writing studies that encourages instructors to think institutionally is necessary to change the structures that push the teaching of writing—specifically, the teaching of first-year writing and even more specifically the teaching of writing in the two-year college—into marginalized spaces. Recentering the preparation of new instructors and the training of experienced instructors would have the added benefit of more opportunity for distribution of the intellectual work of program and resource development. As it is, many writing programs and WPAs (if they exist at all—see Chapter 1) are othered into marginal positions within departments or schools.

We argue that this means cultivating a broader understanding of what it means to be an instructor in the field. As Micciche notes, "Teaching, learning, and administration are not simply intellectual activities that one masters, but a complex blend of emotional and professional issues that involve the whole person" (454). The intellectual work of teaching—curricular and pedagogical development, administrative tasks, research, assessment, even clerical and emotional labor—are all important elements in the FYW classroom, yet we often theorize them as disparate acts or processes that are specialized to a particular position (a WPA, an instructor, a chair, a tutor). The reality is that on some level all of these skills are needed for effective teaching. Instead of concentrating the responsibility in the hands of an administrator or assuming that there is a position "in charge" of all the writing, we have to better equip future (and current) academic workers to understand the contours of what effective teaching looks like, and better understand the ways that they will need to adapt within a variety of institutional contexts. Thomas Miller, Steve Lamos, Eileen Schell, and others have written persuasively and imaginatively about a new vision for labor conditions, including the credentialing of writing instructors and strategies for changing the status of non-tenure-track writing instructors. We need to seek expansive theories of writing and writers that emphasize the complexity of teaching, dispelling the notion that elements can be outsourced elsewhere. Dual-credit courses sponsored by universities and offered by high school teachers in high schools come to mind here—both in terms of spaces writers learn in and in fair and professional working conditions for all writing teachers.

Earlier in this chapter, and in more detail in Chapter 3, we discussed the importance of pedagogical adaptability—what we see as a critical part of instructor training and professional development. Without a larger picture of how students learn and what instructors experience in all writing classrooms, such adaptability will continue to be difficult to integrate into the discipline. Charles Bazerman similarly refers to this type of knowledge as a kind of "local judgment" that instructors must make at a particular time and within a particular context—these types of judgments are based on a kind of knowledge that can be difficult to make generalizable or empirically proven. These judgments, these decisions, these learning moments, as discussed earlier, are undertheorized and underresearched, especially in the two-year-college environment. Based on the data and research included throughout this book, an expanded theory of writing studies would include more theory and research on inclusive pedagogies in the first-year writing classroom. Such research should assess how students learn, so that instructors working with a wide range of learners know they can ethically adopt those practices in their classrooms. Such instructors need evidence-based practices for creating inclusive learning environments. They need to know how to engage and support the success of writers from diverse backgrounds with varying levels of proficiency as college readers and writers, and they need the capacity to critically reflect on their own professional practices in relation to new student populations and material circumstances. Like Eric Hayot, we agree that the current circumstances warrant these changes immediately:

> The humanities right now simply cannot afford to have faculty members who do not engage or connect with students, no matter how smart or interesting the faculty research is. Does that mean teaching the students at their level? Yes, it does. They are coming to us differently prepared—the Common Core has radically reduced the amount of reading and writing K–12 students in the United States do—and under more financial pressure than any generation before them. There's no point in blaming them for it. Doctors don't complain that all their patients are sick people; their job is to heal them. Our job is to increase capacities and reduce ignorance.

If we are to engage with all students, then we must prioritize the assessment of practices that have the potential to reach a wide range of learners. These practices range from examining the impact of grades and low-stakes writing assignments on student learning (see Elbow; Bain), to exploring how holistic assessment impacts academically at-risk students (see *Standards*; Huot), to supporting struggling readers (Holschuh and Paulson; Sullivan et al.), to assessing placement and student readiness (Hassel and Giordano, "Blurry" and "FYC Placement"). As an MLA task force reported in 2011, "about 50% of the non-tenure-track faculty members in four-year colleges and some 60% of tenured and tenure-track faculty members in two-year institutions hold an MA as their highest degree. In fact, overall in two-year institutions, about 89% of English faculty members do not hold a doctorate," noting that many programs assume their PhD students are pursuing a postsecondary career in teaching and research, and yet, "How many of us can say we know what to expect from the master's degree holder? Does the MA prepare graduates for the academic jobs many will take on?" (*Rethinking*, 3). We know what many of these degree recipients will do: they will teach students in the first year, and be the ones who welcome students to college, or gatekeep. They will be the ones who maintain language standards or cultivate critical engagement with linguistic diversity. They will teach a large number of high school students who are earning college credit while in high school, and such instructors must clearly understand distinctions—whichever we as a discipline are hoping to make—between secondary and postsecondary levels of critical reading, writing, thinking, and research.

REVISING GRADUATE EDUCATION IN ENGLISH

The RhetMap job map (Figure 4.2) tracked by Jim Ridolfo offers a pretty clear picture of the employment reality of English studies, though we grant that the COVID-19 pandemic year is likely to be unusual. At the time of this book's writing, the 2020–2021 rhetoric and composition position advertisements stood at less than half of what they had been in previous years (a third if one goes back to 2012). It is unlikely that hiring in the field will be transformed any time in the near future, as institutions and states deal with large enrollment drops and funding crises.

Figure 4.2. Rhetoric, composition, and technical communication job postings per year, RhetMap.org.

Market comparison by week: Sheet 1

	2012–2013	2013–2014	2014–2015	2015–2016	2016–2017	2017–2018	2018–2019	2019–2020 RC	2020–2021 RC & TBW
Week 1 - 9/12	68	61	51	38	49	41	38	40	14
Week 2 - 9/20	83	77	66	56	62	57	49	56	20
Week 3 - 9/27	95	91	79	71	73	77	62	65	24
Week 4 - 10/4	113	103	98	85	91	95	78	77	29
Week 5 - 10/11	123	127	113	102	102	102	91	89	34
Week 6 - 10/18	134	135	135	125	117	119	99	99	36
Week 7 - 10/24	149	149	154	137	132	130	108	111	38
Week 8 - 11/1	155	160	168	148	141	146	113	115	45
Week 9 - 11/8	167	176	178	161	147	154	118	126	48
Week 10 - 11/15	176	191	189	171	152	161	122	131	51
Week 11 - 11/22	184	201	200	175	155	170	124	134	55
Week 12 - 11/29	193	209	210	183	161	173	129	138	57
Week 13 - 12/6	196	213	216	185	166	179	141	144	59
Week 14 - 12/13	198	223	226	189	170	186	145	150	63
Week 15 - 12/20	201	231	235	193	174	190	149	156	
Week 16 - 12/27	205	232	236	193	176	195	151	157	
Week 17 - 1/3	205	234	238	201	178	198	153	158	
Total for whole season	278	318	325	273	243	280	220	203	
Percentage of season	73.74%	73.58%	73.23%	73.62%	73.25%	70.71%	69.54%	77.83%	

Given this exigency, we strongly agree with Cassuto's *Graduate School Mess* and Elaine Maimon's *Leading Academic Change*, as well as the many other online writers and scholars who argue for a few key ways to reform graduate education: undergraduate, especially first-year, education has to be a primary, if not the main, priority of faculty; graduate education must do better at integrating pedagogical training into the curriculum; and cultivating pedagogical adaptability has to be an outcome of graduate school, since most instructors will work with different kinds of students and in different institutional contexts than the ones they themselves were taught in and are teaching in during their graduate training. Thus, graduate education is an important site of change, with the recognition of the constraints that many programs have in human and fiscal capital.

There are a range of moral and ethical reasons that graduate education should be a focus of our reimagined disciplinary work. First, graduate degrees are expensive, and not only is the opportunity cost for students who continue their schooling after a bachelor's degree high but many also go into significant debt for these credentials. Master of Arts degrees, MFAs, and PhDs take years and can leave degree-seekers in debt to the tune of anywhere from tens to hundreds of thousands of dollars (see Carey). A 2014 *Chronicle of Higher Education* article reported that "[t]hree-quarters of master's-degree recipients graduate with debt, with an average of $40,000, according to Debra W. Stewart, president of the Council of Graduate Schools. About two-thirds of PhD recipients accumulate debt, with an average of $60,000" (Patel). This kind of investment of time and resources requires that graduate education provide students with the skills that are going to allow them to find productive and rewarding careers that align with their educational goals. And, as we show in Chapter 1, most of those careers will not include a tenure-line teaching job within a selective institution (see Pettit).

For most of those students who are leaving with MAs, MFAs, or PhDs in English—whether literature, creative writing, or writing studies—and who plan on an academic career, teaching will be their primary responsibility. Though many programs have required teacher-training courses, few of them extend beyond the first semester or year, and even fewer spend significant time helping students understand pedagogical theory and working with diverse students. We also acknowledge that English departments and independent writing programs likely do more than most academic departments to focus on teaching and learning, in part because of the role of required first-year writing courses.

The importance of engaged, quality, and committed teachers at the lower-division level cannot be overstated, particularly when we consider graduate education alongside data on students' experiences in their first years of college. Some of the data produced by the National Survey of Student Engagement and the Community College Survey of Student Engagement are troubling and invite us all to think about the purpose of college and what we believe about students' capacity to learn and grow. As we have noted, community college students in particular are often marginalized from higher education and at risk of nonretention. However, the majority of those students embraced what has been called the "growth [versus 'fixed'] mindset" (see Dweck). This is good news: "Seventy-one percent of community college students who responded to the CCSSE survey measuring student mind-set and engagement had a productive mind-set, or said they believed they could improve their intelligence in English courses." But what is more distressing are the data that suggest that just 41 percent of faculty are confident that "all of their students can change their basic intelligence," and, perhaps even worse, that "nearly 24 percent of faculty members responded that only some or none of their students could change their basic intelligence" (Smith, "Positive Mind-Set"). In other words, a quarter of faculty admit that they do not believe in learning for this student population. From our perspective, this is often those instructors who are more focused on rewarding what students bring with them to the classroom and less on growth and progress that take place during the course. This is when students are blamed for not knowing the rules of the game or how to follow behavioral expectations that are implied rather than directly stated. However, we also acknowledge that for many instructors, absent the tools to develop pedagogical practices to work with these students, such resignation is a likely outcome.

Thus we emphasize one of our central arguments of this book—it is imperative that instructors who work with the new majority of college students are prepared to do so. We know from published research that graduate programs could more effectively prepare instructors to work in two-year and teaching-intensive four-year college positions. In this area, though, as Darin Jensen and Christie Toth argue in their *College English* article tracing historical and current challenges for two-year-college faculty and effective graduate education, a lack of research and scholarship focused on the two-year environment is a key problem:

> The biggest barrier to integrating two-year college–related content across the English studies curriculum may be that relatively few graduate faculty are knowledgeable about these institutions or well-versed in their scholarship. It will require some listening, some learning, and, perhaps, some new habits of mind to revise our graduate courses to reflect a wider range of institution types. (584)

Working together more effectively across ranks and institutional types to build this knowledge base makes it more possible to respond to material conditions in ways that increase student success and retention, create more ethical working conditions for instructors, and enrich the field's collective understanding of how writers write. The TYCA Guidelines for Preparing Teachers of English in the Two-Year College spell out in depth the strategies that graduate programs can use to do this work, taking as their focus even more directly the role of graduate education in strengthening the preparation of community-college faculty (Calhoon-Dillahunt et al.).

Perhaps the most critical role within our institutions, then, is that of graduate programs and the departments that house them. Graduate training for both masters and doctoral students that incorporates insights from open-access and two-year-college teacher-scholar-activists requires a concerted and intentional effort on the part of writing program administrators and writing studies graduate faculty who prepare the next generation of writing teachers. This is challenging, as Brett Griffiths notes in her study of two-year-college English instructors, because "instructors at two-year colleges are rarely—if ever—provided with clear expectations about how to produce, disseminate, and regulate the special knowledge of teaching—to whom and for what purposes beyond the classroom" (48). Her study of eleven community-college faculty from three different campuses concluded that "many instructors limited their own positioning within their institutions by restricting the articulation of their knowledge to the domain of the classroom" (51). As a result, Griffiths concludes, "instructors in this study unwittingly undermined their own positioning within institutions due to a reluctance to engage and critique conversations in their departments, to use those conversations to develop and reinforce departmental control over scope of service, and to advocate for improved writing instruction at their institutions based on that engagement" (51). Only when new faculty in these sites are equipped with training, knowledge, strategies, skills, and confidence to bring their writing studies knowledge to new sites will such change happen—and of course this requires that the sites that these instructors will teach in are reflected in the body of knowledge in the field. Such human, material, and disciplinary capital is a prerequisite for building the kinds of programs that support student learning and ethical working environments.

As GTAs learn to teach, as well as learn the foundational writing studies knowledge that they then take with them to their new sites of employment, building an expansive theory of writing requires paying specific attention to the kinds of disposition development Griffiths outlines—from the point at which students begin to teach, and when they begin their graduate coursework. We can see this illustrated in a series of important studies of GTA identity development. The existing studies suggest several key themes that we see reflected in our own project. First, Dylan Dryer's research showed that GTAs reviewing student papers for the purposes of the study "imagined the undergraduate writers of the papers I asked them to assess and projected versions of their own academic writing histories onto the students" ("At a Mirror" 425). This lack of what Scholarship of Teaching and Learning (SoTL) researcher Bill Cerbin terms *cognitive empathy* (54), or the ability to accurately see and imagine the learning struggles that students—who are not like you, the teacher—is to our minds a guarantee of failure and misery for instructors who are trained in and then work in teaching environments where students have radically different educational backgrounds and orientations toward college study than instructors bring with them. As Dryer observes: "Put another way, the GTAs simply could not grammatically construct the student writer as agent in the same sentence that invoked an ideal text—the lines of coding never overlap. No construction of a future text, in other words, could also be coded as a construction of a writer making choices about that text, only as a demonstration of what that writer had failed to do" (430).

Thinking back to our Chapter 3 discussion of "writer compliance," we see illustrated how and why new instructors might bring with them an expectation that students who do not successfully complete an assigned task are engaging in some kind of behavioral infraction rather than struggling to adapt to new expectations of college literacy. Dryer writes that when he sketches out how the GTAs "grade" papers provided by him as the investigator the "imagined undergraduates" created by the GTAs' responses "have starkly diminished agency in their composing practices, and most lack personal motives apart from grades. But most curiously, any traces of the ambivalence, the cynicism, or even the complexity of feeling about academic writing to which their teachers freely attest are utterly effaced from the projected undergraduates" (438). This cognitive orientation on the part of new teachers is compounded in a revealing study by Shelley Reid and Heidi Estrem, who note that—when trying to get at the influence that the writing program coursework and training has on new TAs, most new teachers ranked the kinds of activities and reading that take place in their composition seminars, presemester workshops, or practica as low (see also Meaghan Brewer's *Conceptions of Literacy* for an overview of how prior knowledge and understanding of literacies influenced the pedagogical approaches of new GTAs).

All this is to say that at present, the emphasis within graduate programs in English does not match up with the realities of the work there is to do—and if there is anything we want to emphasize in this closing chapter, it's that *this is important and rewarding work*. The voices we cite throughout this book of two-year-college teacher-scholars, we hope, have shown how both of these assertions are true. We think about the *Wall Street Journal* columnist Joseph Epstein, who called upon first lady Dr. Jill Biden to stop using her "doctor" title, because she is not a medical doctor. Epstein's column referred to her dissertation as "unpromising." Her dissertation, entitled "Student Retention at the Community College: Meeting Students' Needs" couldn't speak more directly to the focus of the arguments we make in this book. A cascade of other "hot takes" followed, including a *National Review* article that referred to community-college instructors working with "slow learners" and an extended Twitter thread in which the author claimed to identify two hundred "typos" in Biden's dissertation.

We can't help noticing how the public focus on community colleges often takes place in the abstract—there is a general political and symbolic commitment to their value for communities, but the kerfuffle over Jill Biden's dissertation gets at the nature of the misalignment we describe in this book. We cannot both "abstractly value" the institution of community colleges and simultaneously dismiss the teaching, learning, and research that takes place there.

Preparing for the Work: Revising Graduate Programs and Teacher Training

To more aggressively intervene in the current siloing of labor, writing classrooms, and knowledge production we need to recognize how program development, graduate education, and knowledge production have mutually refreshing opportunities to enhance one another, to course correct, and to integrate the knowing and doing of the field in more practical ways with the work of writing program administrators and writing studies researchers. Graduate preparation can reflect this integration both in the content they teach and in the ways their programs are managed. In doing this work together, we produce knowledge in the field that will then be better poised to prepare instructors for the kind of work that ultimately all of us with graduate degrees in English (save for a small number) will be doing. As *Inside Higher Ed* reported in 2018: "In

2015, there were more than 3,000 four-year colleges and universities in the United States, and 115 of those have been designated as R1 institutions by the Carnegie Classification of Institutions of Higher Education. That means that only 4 percent of colleges and universities have a reward structure (tenure, promotion and so on) in which research is much more highly valued than teaching" (Manzo and Mitchell).

These numbers suggest to us a couple of things. First, we believe that systematic inquiry should not be a luxury, and that teaching-intensive faculty should have the material resources to do such work in ways that help them develop professionally. In that way we echo here our call in Chapter 2 for an expansive concept of professional development that can include scholarly inquiry across ranks and position types. Graduate programs—whether masters, MFA, or PhD—will be producing graduates who, if they work in an academic context, will almost certainly be teaching writing. A course that includes writing studies theory and pedagogy should be a requirement as regularly as is—or should even replace—literary theory, which, as we showed in Chapter 1, is the primary course required for master's degrees. To make it possible for instructors in teaching-intensive positions to participate in the research community, graduate programs should offer coursework in classroom research and writing assessment, both to prepare instructors for these parts of large- and small-scale inquiry and to expose students to scholarship that uses diverse methodologies to create new knowledge about writing.

Second, widespread curricular offerings in composition theory and pedagogy should include writing studies scholarship that integrates two-year-college students, basic writing, writing-studio courses, and developmental reading support so that future writing teachers understand the complete range of student writers and also become aware of emerging trends in adapting curriculum and instruction to working with all writers. It is the reality that nearly 90 percent of faculty in higher education can expect to work in teaching-intensive positions. They need not only support to grow and be responsive educators—but also research and scholarship that shares that emphasis. In this way, faculty in research-intensive jobs can reflect open-access and teaching-intensive institutions in their research and scholarship. The alternative is encountering such writers in the highest-stakes contexts of the first day of classes at a new institution, when the consequences are serious for students who may already have a tentative relationship to their college studies.

Last, we should embrace and work toward a culture change that focuses not on CV building but on professional development, in ways that are quite intentionally rooted in the term—that one's activities and ongoing learning should reflect those things that college writing teachers need to develop as professionals. In this way, we call for a reconceiving of why we write, read, or research: inquiry that emerges directly from the work we need to get better at. Such a focus challenges the value system of academia that centers on adding CV lines or accumulating gold stars. Instead, professional development becomes a set of purposeful activities that focus on improving the work we do, and for most instructors in college English departments in the United States that is the teaching of writing. Our professional agendas should be equally balanced between the exigencies of the work we are doing on a daily basis and our intellectual interests, in case those two things might not be perfectly aligned.

Though we advocate for the role of two-year colleges and open-admissions four-year colleges to offer professionalizing opportunities for new instructors, we believe the transition to these teaching contexts could be improved with greater attention in MA and PhD programs to coursework that acknowledges both the variation in college preparation of students in two-year colleges and how this difference is part of developing a larger pedagogical repertoire. In part this acknowledgment means explicitly recognizing and applying some of the theoretical insights that graduate school can provide. For example, Pierre Bourdieu offers a popular theory of the sociology of education suggesting that the educational system tends to reproduce (in the double sense of the word) the structure of relations between the structure of the distribution of cultural capital and the structure of the destination of economic capital among the sections both in and by the relations and complementarity which define the system of institutions of higher education (94). Selective institutions largely convert social and cultural capital into educational and economic capital. Open-access institutions have to help students build cultural and social capital as well as educational capital, operating without economic capital. How can we create and support disruptive approaches that, through the classroom, support social justice teaching and learning practices?

Graduate programs committed to the social justice function of open-access higher education have many options available to them to do this work:

- Sponsoring or inviting faculty with expertise in inclusive pedagogical practices and in theories of learning
- Taking advantage of and incorporating the growing body of scholarship on socially just assessment practices either as standalone coursework or as part of pedagogical seminars on the teaching of writing (Poe et al., *Writing Assessment*; Inoue; Inoue and Poe)
- Creating internship opportunities for graduate students to learn from two-year-college faculty and work with the students in those sites, which can lay a foundation for (and attract graduates to) the important work of open access higher education
- Valuing (through curricular attention to, inquiry into, and time spent on) general education rather than major programs in part because these are the pathways into the liberal arts majors that accrue and distribute cultural capital but that may be unacknowledged as valuable educational pathways for students without cultural and social capital
- Engaging in ongoing discussion about improving introductory courses to the areas of the field as they may be the only exposure some students have to those areas of study
- In case specific partnerships are not immediately available, preparing students who are future writing teachers by assigning scholarly articles from the *Journal of Basic Writing*, *Teach-*

ing English in the Two-Year College, the *Journal of Developmental Education,* and other publications that include research reflecting a wide range of student populations

Graduate programs can also work to be more cognizant of how different types of course offerings and course delivery methods are reflected within their curricula. For example, two-year and open-access colleges are more likely (even in the pandemic) to offer online-only courses and blended courses, areas of pedagogical development which those campuses that are largely residential or that value seat time may not value. However, instructors (at whatever level of graduate credential) are likely to encounter these learning environments at nonselective and open-access institutions that rely on them to reach commuter and nontraditional students. Coursework in effective online writing instruction that makes use of disciplinary best practices has the advantage of bringing the flexibility of online courses to instructors and students at selective institutions, while also preparing those writing teachers who can expect almost certainly to have teaching responsibilities in online environments as part of their future workloads. This preparation can be especially important to initiate in institutions where online course development and instruction takes place in a separate unit from the academic department sponsoring the courses. Similar cross-campus conversations should take place between other, sometimes siloed areas of study that are particularly relevant at open-access campuses, including ESL and TESOL as well as developmental or basic writing programs that are not part of English departments.

To us, that means putting first-year writing and two-year-college students—42 percent of students—at the center of higher education (Ma and Baum). More specifically, required graduate curricula that prepare future writing teachers to develop skills and a knowledge foundation in several interrelated areas are also essential:

a. *Knowledge of accurate placement of students into college writing courses*: At selective institutions with graduate programs (where of course all college educators do their graduate work and experience their first exposure to teaching) the primary placement distinction is between a research-intensive second-semester writing course or an exemption from such a requirement altogether. Graduate students who enter positions that are teaching-intensive and that have multiple levels of first-year writing (from one, two, or even three non-degree-credit courses, through a two-semester credit sequence, and/or an intermediate or advanced subsequent writing requirement) lack familiarity with such writing programs and the assessment knowledge to help do this work within a program or department (see Nazzal et al.). Students in selective institutions and from well-resourced high schools are more likely to bring with them college credit through AP or IB courses, dual-credit courses, or prior learning assessments. In this way, an issue that may seem to be only about student preparation is also actually about curriculum, assessment, and program development.

b. *Pedagogical content knowledge about the teaching and assessment of writing*: Instructors need specific approaches that recognize and can be adapted to the range of student writers in these institutions: Development of disciplinary habits of mind (such as those outlined in the *Framework for Success in Postsecondary Writing*), learning outcomes (like the *WPA Outcomes Statement for First-Year Composition* and those adapted for institution or program-specific purposes), professional standards such as those outlined in the NCTE and CCCC statements on writing assessment and principles for the postsecondary teaching of writing (*Standards*; *Writing Assessment*; *Principles*), and threshold concepts in writing studies and first-year writing in particular (Adler-Kassner and Wardle, *Naming* and *(Re)Considering*; Brown), are critical foundations for effective teaching and learning that will help develop writers, not just better individual papers.

c. *Pedagogical adaptability*: Cultivation of pedagogical adaptability (similar to Bazerman's "local judgments") equips instructors to respond to a range of barriers to student learning in open-access institutions, including academic, material, and noncognitive issues that can impact student success. This cultivation includes:

- Coursework or training, including coursework in learning theory, working with adult and ESL students, process pedagogy and its relationship to growth in writing, and aligning pedagogical choices with the needs of specific students, specifically how to identify and respond to different barriers to student learning.
- Support and resources to identify and adapt to different student populations and their learning needs that will likely differ from the students taught during their graduate training, and the knowledge foundation to develop such resources if they are not currently available in the institutional site.
- Ability to build learning environments to accommodate a range of learners, including significant portions of students who do not reflect traditional college student profiles. Such curricular and pedagogical work may also include classroom management skills and responding to the student challenges that may manifest themselves as behavioral problems that can appear to be noncompliant or "bad students" but actually reflect these material realities (such as inability to purchase course materials, transportation or childcare needs that interfere with classroom attendance; and full-time or greater work or domestic obligations that make it difficult to complete class assignments). Otherwise, instructors bring with them and then impose schemas on diverse student populations that are drawn from the profile of student populations at selective institutions, who are more likely to be academically well-prepared, traditional age, and affluent. It also means developing innovative ways to teach college-level literacy rather than "re-teaching" high school—and shifting from a "remediation" mentality to a developmental and skill-building mentality that builds capacity.

d. *The ability to contribute to and develop program support* that will respond to the above needs, which includes assessing how effectively a writing program curriculum or structure is fulfilling its goals and mission, and being able to implement and assess those challenges in order to foster student learning and success. Such support might include accelerated learning courses; corequisite and/or studio model support; integrations between writing centers, learning centers, and writing programs; integrated reading and writing programs; academic reading courses for struggling readers, and relationships with institutional programs that support students with disabilities. This support should include developing a program that also empowers instructors—particularly the 80–85 percent of instructors who work off the tenure track without the kinds of support structures and employment stability that is often available at and more common at selective and research-intensive institutions. Most two-year colleges also do not have designated Writing Program Administrator positions (see Taylor; Klausman, "Mapping"; Charlton and Rose). To sustain institutions, the work of maintaining a writing program—including the intellectual and programmatic work—should be distributed among more instructors, if not all instructors. As we discuss in Chapter 3, alienating teachers from the intellectual labor of teaching not only deepens a theory/practice divide, but also is simply impractical in most two-year colleges where there is no WPA to do that work or be the voice of writing instructors.

The cost of this educational and preparation gap for instructors in English is huge for two-year-college students. Dedicated attention to cultivating both cognitive empathy and institutional citizenship as Griffiths describes are required to train faculty at open-admissions campuses. Faculty need to understand the struggles of the student populations that are served by these institutions and fulfill their role in maintaining, advocating for, and continually assessing and revising program work to respond to changing student population needs.

This is especially critical because of the external fiscal, legislative, and political pressures to which two-year colleges are particularly subject. Reid and Estrem acknowledge that "[i]n coming to terms with our data, we have found ourselves pulling back the curtain of the powerful pedagogy seminar and deciding that we may yet be good teachers but just very bad wizards. Like legions of FYC teachers, we do not have the power to fully transform students in a single seminar at the beginning of students' intensive graduate study and practice" (Reid and Estrem 56) and in response, call for multisemester teacher training, something we also support. Since, as we show in Chapter 1, practically all jobs in English in higher education are teaching-intensive, more attention to this part of our work is essential.

Some readers may express concern or reservation about dedicating more time in what is often a limited program to this part of graduate education. However, some recent studies show that rather than taking away from research skills and productivity, a focus on pedagogical training alongside traditional disciplinary work actually has a modestly positive impact on both aspects of those professional magisteria: "In fact, the study found that training in what they call evidence-based teaching not only did not have a negative effect on research productivity, it had a net positive impact on students' 'confidence in communicating their research' and students' sense of 'being well-trained for a research career'" (Shortlidge and Eddy).

Further, many programs should reconsider policies which place underprepared graduate students in the front of classrooms with vulnerable students, under the supervision of an often overworked WPA or sometimes no one at all. Instead, there should be a range of additional research, writing center, editorial, or other options for integrating into writing instruction and understanding how students learn and the consequences of being underprepared to meet their needs. If the policies and practices of a program are designed around protecting graduate students at the expense of first-year students, then an integrated theory of writing studies is even more exigent.

In an ideal world, we would reimagine the value of the different kinds of work we do in higher education. We would recognize that research produces a particular kind of impact but that teaching and service both have more widespread and more durable and tangible impacts on the world. Though we realize it's not a zero-sum game, the dramatic and immediate impact on the lives of the students we worked with and have worked with in our two-year-college writing classrooms is transformative and rewarding. Likewise, the service work—the committees that so many academics see as superfluous to their work, or a distraction from research—are remarkably important in shaping the teaching and learning conditions of our campuses (see Hassel and Cole).[3] Committee and governance work establish the structures and policies that codify what we value—do we retain instructors for their teaching or their research? What values are guiding these decisions? What about our senate policies that determine the consequences for bullying, or for students' failures in courses or programs? Departmental establishment of guidelines for degree requirements at the undergraduate and graduate levels can determine, for example, whether students are able to finish a program in two years or three years or four years, potentially incurring significant debt and delaying entry into the labor market (or delaying other goals they have for relocation, family formation, or work). Our service work shapes our institutions, and those institutional forces persist well beyond the specific decisions or careers of individual faculty.

LEARNING FROM OUR CLASSROOMS

> Where we will end up is a mystery to me. I have worked in the past two years to make all this change as neutral for and invisible to students as possible. My goal is to make sure students do not suffer in the process, but it is inevitable that the loss of control, loss of staffing, and loss of diligent care for the process and content of their instruction will ultimately have an effect.
>
> —Julie Tharp, Professor of English, UW–Marshfield

We want to close this chapter with some clarity that explains, beyond polemics or even data, why a recentered discipline of writing studies is so important to articulate, research, assess, and implement. We learned a lot about the participating students and instructors in the research projects which we have drawn from in this book. We would like to push back a bit on what many perceive as success in the classroom. Rigid ideas of success—"retained to second semester," "A," "completed the requirement"—are just some of the ways we assess classroom quality and instructor effectiveness. What we learned from this project, and, really, from teaching and spending time with these students for over two decades, is that many of the conditions, ways of thinking, and setbacks for students are the very things that, when studied, make us better equipped to help them think like writers. The stories of our students helped us re-see what being successful can mean in the classroom, and they underscore the importance of careful, engaged, and supported attention to the access and learning of students in an open-admissions context.

We did not focus on grades when we began this project, or when we discussed the students in Chapter 3. We learned fairly quickly that the grades a student received were not necessarily a measure of that student's relationship with a threshold concept or even their overall success in college. On the one end, there were students like Kayla (ENG 102), who did well in her writing class, but did not demonstrate an adequate understanding of many of the Disciplinary Learning Domains. Her writing was clear and organized, but she struggled with academic conventions of rhetorical analysis and research. In addition, she was not able to accurately assess her development in these areas ("I believe that I did a better job at writing the research paper than I did writing any other papers for this class"). Though she could adopt certain conventions of academic writing, over the course of the semester she did not demonstrate development—or even an understanding of—key outcomes in writing studies. So, while she made her way through the first-year writing requirement (which is in itself an area for research), we are more concerned with her future success in college courses than we are with that of some of the other students who did not have as high a grade.

What was more common—and what we feel is the most important issue to examine and unpack—are the cases where students struggled in FYW, for a variety of reasons. Sometimes this was part of unknown outside or material conditions of students' lives impacting their work in the classroom. For some students, they were able to demonstrate success earlier in the course or on a particular assignment, only to struggle and/or drop off at some point in the semester. Todd, an English 101 student, was very successful academically throughout all of his classes that term. His opening reflection letter demonstrated strong critical-thinking skills as well as a solid understanding of disciplinary concepts:

> Building new skills is fundamental for my growth as a college writer. The skill that is most interesting to me, from an academic standpoint, is critical reading, and writing. My own personality is very analytical, thus functioning far better in math and science, than in language based skills. As a result, I am generally capable of critical thinking with regards to conversations and ideas I am actively engaged in with other people.

Todd, however, had a sudden and dramatic drop-off in attendance and performance in subsequent courses. While we don't know what caused that drop-off, his performance up until that point indicated that he was making progress in understanding key threshold concepts and most likely would have been successful in completing college. It was clear to us (and to his instructor) that he was making progress in thinking like a college writer, even though ultimately he did not stay in college.

Similarly, Immanuel did very well on his English 102 rhetorical analysis essay (one of the more difficult threshold concepts to master according to our data), but then did not finish the course. His instructor said he only submitted two of the five formal assignments and noted how strong the start to his semester was. The instructor was unaware of the reasons for his drop in performance. Likewise, Allen, an English 098 student, also demonstrated growth but then inexplicably disappeared from college. His essays showed a great deal of development across each threshold concept, so his disappearance was particularly troubling to the instructor. What is key about focusing on students like these (indeed, on encouraging research on students like these), is that dismissing them as unsuccessful also dismisses the ways that they were making progress as well as the pedagogies that supported that progress. Upon initial review, Tanner, an English 101 student, did not appear to be successful by more traditional measures. But when we reviewed his final essay we were impressed by the critical thinking he demonstrated with his argument, not so much about what he felt about steroid use, but the way that his research taught him why the problem exists: "[T]he possibility of being kicked out of sports for having a false positive test to come back and the benefit to loss ratio being extremely favorable to steroid use, shows that steroid use is the right choice under the current guidelines in sports. The incentive to cheat outweighing the incentive not to cheat is the main reason for why steroid use is so predominant in sports." Ultimately, Tanner's research and writing process helped him demonstrate independent thought on a level that many of his classmates were unable to during the course of a single semester.

As discussed in Chapter 3, for some students these drop-offs, incompletes, or failures were directly connected to the material conditions of their lives. Joanna was prepared to change her approach to FYW with her second attempt at English 101. "In this class I am prepared to have a few of my downfalls revised and changes done so I can hand in more complete papers. I am willing to work harder and seek more help by either going to the learning center, classmates, or even OWL. I'm willing to be more open to people looking at my writing so I can at least get higher than C's on all my papers." However, Joanna's instructor relayed to us that at some point in the semester she and her family had to suddenly leave their home. The instructor was aware of this because Joanna lost half of her schoolwork due to the suddenness of the move. While Joanna made something of a comeback later in the semester, the instructor noted that the stress of her living situation made a marked difference in her classwork.

In English 101, Ann's student Joe dealt with many of the issues typically experienced by returning adult/nontraditional students, while also juggling a full-time job, placement into multiple developmental education courses, and a learning disability. Ann commented that he struggled to find time to work because of his schedule, and that she spent a lot of extra time working with him to talk through assignments and develop a calendar because of what she saw as a "severe" learning disability. Another student in Ann's class, Ralph, who was not successful in demonstrating any of the Disciplinary Learning Domains in our analysis, was enrolled prematurely in English 101, and Ann surmised that this enrollment was not his decision (rather, at the urging of a parent) and that he was also home schooled. Finally, Ann also noted that another student in her class, Elsa, who ultimately was able to demonstrate an understanding of each of the threshold concepts, had difficulty throughout the semester because she had a rare disease that caused migraines and concentration issues.

These realities were always the case for two-year-college students. But we have observed in the wake of the COVID-19 pandemic how the kinds of experience that two-year-college students have always had—life traumas, tragedies, demands, and disruptions—are more common now among university students and faculty as well. Our pedagogies have always had to respond to the needs of students whose material circumstances made their relationship to college tentative. There is no better time than now to learn from the strategies and responsive pedagogies that two-year colleagues in writing studies have refined so that all students can both succeed and learn.

There was other evidence of development with the learning domains that would not have been picked up by an examination of grades, for example, multiple students who, as they moved through the sequence, were also more successful in their reading- and writing-intensive classes. Increasingly challenging course work and more complicated skills developed perhaps as a result of their progress with disciplinary concepts. Dakota, an English 101 student, did not pass FYW in his first attempt. But he continued to take classes, and by his fourth semester he had passed English 102 while also earning above-average grades in classes including biology and political science. An architecture major, Dakota wrote in his final reflection, "My improvement as a reader is an improvement as a writer," and he made connections to the reading strategies he was developing in the class with his other classes. Another English 101 student, Matthew, made similar progress to Dakota's. He took increasingly challenging coursework and developed increasingly more complicated skills. Crissy, an English 098 student who placed into additional cocurricular support courses, began FYW with a slower pathway and more sheltered curriculum, and she eventually made her way through the FYW requirement as well as other challenging courses with above-average grades.

These nuances are only what we learn from examining their writing. When coupled with the instructor reflections, we gained enhanced insight into the students whose work we were examining so closely. What these insights taught us was that in some cases, these students greatly benefited from having an instructor who understood how less-prepared students learn—inconsistently, at very different paces, and in the context of personal and academic obstacles. We learned a great deal about Tobin, an English102 student in Jack's class, from his instructor. Jack detailed Tobin's strong motivation and growth over the semester, while also acknowledging that his writing "is a bit difficult to understand in first-draft form, and he needs to take his time with his reading in order to analyze it effectively." Because Jack understood this learning need about his student, Tobin benefited from the opportunity to produce multiple drafts and multiple reflections, and to have instructions targeted toward the areas he needed the most support with. As a result, at the end of the semester, Tobin's work was assessed as above average. We saw a lot of students like Tobin during the course of this research: students who, if they were in a class that overemphasized lower-order concerns and high-stakes assessment, might not have been as successful in terms of growth with these threshold concepts. The students who were a part of this study had the benefit of having instructors who were redesigning their courses with specific attention to the learning needs of two-year students. Rick, another one of Jack's students, details his struggles with reading and writing in his reflections, and Jack wrote about him at the end of the semester:

> Rick has a great deal of difficulty with both reading comprehension and critical reading, and I suspect he may have other cognitive processing issues as well. It has taken him a great deal of effort to get to the point he is at, which I'm proud of. He will still need support going forward, and he'll need to devote more time to academics than the average student, but I'm hopeful he will continue to experience success.

Jack noted that Rick had a lot of struggles in the class but worked very hard and took advantage of all of the available learning resources and was able to pass the class.

In one English 101 class, students were given the opportunity to revise each essay three times. The instructor, Carrie, provided feedback with each revision. Her class was interesting to us because we noticed in several cases that students did not make substantive writing and reading progress until the third revision. Payton, for example, began her essay reflections for the rhetorical analysis assignment focusing on lower-order concerns about her grammar, but by the second and third reflections she was able to articulate her questions or even confusion about the assignment or the next steps in her writing process: "I think I am doing this essay right but this was really difficult for me to describe why," or "I have no idea where I want to go with it but I am unsure if I am doing it correctly. The last position essay I didn't do correctly so I am looking back and using the feedback to better this paper. I think I have good conversations and hope I don't sound bumper sticker-ish." Again, the repeated revisions and feedback process were helpful for Payton's development, but key here to note is that it took several tries for her to demonstrate this growth. We see this, as well, connected to the labor conditions and employment status of her instructor—as a full-time tenure-track faculty member with a secure position, classes located at a single physical site, and accompanying benefits that full-time positions offered. Carrie taught four classes a semester and was able to dedicate much of her time to the teaching work she was doing; by contrast, some non-tenure-track instructors teaching at multiple institutions and without those stable employment conditions may not have been able to prioritize revision, conferences with individual students, and the intensive work of providing individualized feedback to students on their writing.

Finally, there is Shane. We'd like close by returning to something Shane said (which we previously cited in Chapter 3) because in so many ways he embodies what we see working in the two-year environment. Shane took both English 098 and English 101 twice (as he wrote in his reflection), and when he began English 101 for the second time, he wrote about his low confidence in himself and a strong dislike of reading and writing:

> However, people do not always enjoy writing. Some people can't stand the thought of reading and writing. People will do whatever they can to try and avoid doing either of these tasks. Some, think that writing and reading is too much. They don't want to take the time to do either of them. I am most definitely one of those people. My past experiences have not been very pleasant. I have not had fun with my past writing. For that reason I do not enjoy it now, and don't look forward to it. Growing up, I have always enjoyed the thought of reading and writing. I would always try to read books and write poems or other forms of writing. I was never any good at either of them. It would just cause me to get frustrated and give up on it. I was always a slow reader. I would get confused or lost with my writing. I was never any good at connecting my ideas with the topics. It was also hard making things flow in my writings.

Shane eventually made it through English 102, but not entirely without problems. He continued to struggle demonstrating an understanding of rhetorical knowledge, but his instructor reflected that with a lot of hard work, he was able to demonstrate progress with the course learning outcomes more than he was the first time he took the class with her. (Shane wrote in his initial reflection, "The fall semester I tried to take 101 for the first time with you. There were a couple personal problems that affected my attendance and someone just cannot pass a class if they do not show up. I liked your teaching approach so I thought I would stick with it and take you for another semester.") These students we describe in this chapter are, in our experience, not atypical for students in our institution. Almost all of the ones we describe here achieved "success" on some level, if not always through more traditional measures. These are the students who need open-access college options the most. And yet, Gary Rhoades, representing the Center for the Future of Higher Education, queries:

> Nationally, hundreds of thousands of students standing in real and virtual lines wanting classes and a community college education are being turned away. Community colleges, which have historically been Open Door colleges, are now closing their doors, denying access. The problem is insufficient public investment in these colleges, not their failure to reduce spending and increase productivity. And an important question that is raised by their closing doors is, who is getting squeezed or blocked out?

As the landscape of higher education changes, open-access colleges in particular may be the first casualties of a larger-scale public disinvestment in the resources required to have a truly democratic access to higher education.

Writing studies as a field can, we believe, play an important role in intervening in that trend—by resisting the values of academic hierarchies, by truly committing to social justice through partnership, collaboration, and visibility for two-year-college instructors and students, and by focusing on learning rather than compliance. Those interventions require more human capital than fiscal capital, a fact that, we acknowledge, also has a cost—but also immeasurable benefit. Equitable literacy instruction should be the cornerstone of what we, as educators, do. But right now, we're not set up for, or even moving in the right direction toward, a postsecondary literacy landscape that centers access over selectivity. To do so is to fulfill the promise of democratic education, as well as build a sustainable, representative, and ethical field of study.

EPILOGUE

WE CLOSE OUR BOOK WITH THE creative work of our brilliant colleague, Professor Marnie Bullock Dresser, whose sestina captures the complex emotional aftermath of our institutional dissolution.

In Memoriam: UW Colleges—A Sestina

> Welcome to the website for support of academic
> literacy at the University of Wisconsin Colleges,
> a statewide, two-year liberal arts
> transfer institution. This site has links to program information, content,
> curriculum guides, professional development workshops, and example curricular materials
> for first-year writing, developmental writing, and learning resources courses.[1]

This summer for my "summer off," I'm working on my courses
for the upcoming year without the kind of academic
community I had for years and years. Updated materials
posted online, the stunning expertise[2] of my colleagues in the UW Colleges,
a set of pro-student policies that actually worked—all gone. Content
creation is a lonely job done this way. The foundation of liberal arts

is reading and writing. The foundation of liberal arts
should be a full set of well-designed, evidence-based courses
(as we used to—but no longer—have). Never mind me. I'm just a malcontent
longing for curricular oomph and coherence. They say academic

battles are so vicious because the stakes are so low,[3] but colleges
sometimes try to build bridges with materials

that are structurally unsound. Stoke furnaces with waterlogged materials.
Prevent diseases with a mix of random tinctures and anecdotal arcane arts.
And what about the students at our now disconnected Wisconsin colleges?
When they transfer, as they're wont to, will what they learned in their courses
transfer with them? Travel with them like an academic
backpack full of useful content?

Methods, philosophies, outcomes—that's what we mean by content,
not a set of copyrighted, illegally xeroxed materials
for the same essay assignments we were given as students.[4] Academic
sometimes means theoretical. Impractical. But the efforts—the arts—
we put forth in our first-year writing courses
were like recipes at a potluck everyone wants copies of. The UW Colleges

as an institution was never perfect.[5] I often howled about it. The UW Colleges
English Department was also, likewise, and similarly, not perfect. I am content,
nonetheless, our work was solid. Of course,
we can, from what has become again pig iron, forge new materials.
"Teaching might even be the greatest of the arts."[6] The magic we made with the work we did made me proud to be an academic.

Shall we now offer courses on being content?
Is it true to say the death of the UW Colleges broke our hearts?
So many questions which are, and are not, academic.[7]

—Marnie Bullock Dresser, Professor of English
University of Wisconsin–Platteville Richland

APPENDIX A: SAMPLE JOURNAL ANALYSIS

Writing Classrooms (*College Composition and Communication*)

Volume, Issue, Year, Author	Article Title (Author in Parentheses)	Writing Classrooms: Approaches to Helping Students or Instructors with:
63.2/December 2011	Toward a Multilingual Composition Scholarship: From English Only to a Translingual Norm (Horner, NeCamp, Donahue)	None
62.3/February 2011	Being There: (Re)Making the Assessment Scene (Gallagher)	None
62.3/February 2011	Toward Graduate-Level Writing Instruction (Micciche with Carr)	2, 3, and 5
62.3/February 2011	Rhetorical Agency as Emergent and Enacted (Cooper)	None
62.4/June 2011	Resisting Age Bias in Digital Literacy Research (Bowen)	None
62.4/June 2011	Successes, Victims, and Prodigies: "Master" and "Little" Cultural Narratives in the Literacy Narrative Genre (Alexander)	3, 5, and 7
62.4/June 2011	Enacting and Transforming Local Language Policies (Tardy)	5
63.1/September 2011	Indian Ability (*auilidad de Indio*) and Rhetoric's Civilizing Narrative: Guaman Poma's Contact with the Rhetorical Tradition (Romney)	None
63.1/September 2011	The Postindian Rhetoric of Gerald Vizenor (Miles)	None
63.1/September 2011	Literacy Stewardship: Dakelh Women Composing Culture (Frost)	None
63.1/September 2011	Cherokee Practice: Missionary Intentions: Literacy Learning among Early Nineteenth-Century Cherokee Women (Moulder)	None
63.2/December 2011	Ecological, Pedagogical, Public Rhetoric (Rivers and Weber)	4 and 5
63.2/December 2011	Re-envisioning Religious Discourses as Rhetorical Resources in Composition Teaching: A Pragmatic Response to the Challenge of Belief (DePalma)	5
63.2/December 2011	A Textbook Argument: Definitions of Argument in Leading Composition Textbooks (Knoblauch)	5

Research Subject Population Sample (*College Composition and Communication*)

Volume, Issue, Year, Author	Article Title (Author in Parentheses)	Population of Research Subjects
55.3/February 2004	Critical Discourse Analysis and Composition Studies: A Study of Presidential Discourse and Campus Discord (Powell)	NA
55.3/February 2004	Towards an Ethics of Answerability: Reconsidering Dialogism in Sociocultural Literacy Research (Juzwik)	None
55.3/February 2004	A New Visibility: An Argument for Alternative Assistance Writing Programs for Students with Learning Disabilities (Barber-Fendley and Chris Hamel)	None
55.3/February 2004	Reimagining the Functional Side of Computer Literacy (Selber)	None
55.3/February 2004	Facing (Up to) "The Stranger" in Community Service Learning (Himley)	Graduate students at Syracuse
55.4/June 2004	Edwin Hopkins and the Costly Labor of Composition Teaching (Popken)	Edwin Hopkins, an English professor at the University of Kansas
55.4/June 2004	Becoming Literate in the Information Age: Cultural Ecologies and the Literacies of Technology (Hawisher and Selfe with Moraski and Pearson)	2 case studies of a stated 350 interviews
55.4/June 2004	Postmodernism, Palimpsest, and Portfolios: Theoretical Issues in the Representation of Student Work (Yancey)	None
55.4/June 2004	Making a Case for Rhetorical Grammar (Micciche)	Students enrolled in sophomore-level style/grammar classes
55.4/June 2004	Your Average Nigga (Young)	1 student and personal experience
56.1/September 2004	An Essay on the Work of Composition: Composing English against the Order of Fast Capitalism (Lu)	None
56.1/September 2004	"Not Too Late to Take the Sanitation Test": Notes of a Non-Gifted Academic from the Working Class (Borkowski)	Author and personal narratives
56.1/September 2004	Reading Student Writing with Anthropologists: Stance and Judgment in College Writing (Soliday)	CUNY, section of anthropology, 21 students
56.1/September 2004	An "Immensely Simplified Task": Form in Modern Composition-Rhetoric (Goleman)	1 student writer in an unidentified course

Research Site (*College Composition and Communication*)

Volume, Issue, Year, Author	Article Title (Author in Parentheses)	Research Site
51.3/February 2000	"Building a Mystery": Alternative Research Writing and the Academic Act of Seeking (Davis and Shadle)	No one site—but does talk about 200- and 300-level courses at Eastern Oregon University.
51.3/February 2000	Rhetorical Sovereignty: What Do American Indians Want from Writing? (Lyons)	None
51.3/February 2000	Traditions and Professionalization: Reconceiving Work in Composition (Horner)	Amherst College English 1–2 Course (secondary)
51.3/February 2000	More Methodological Matters: Against Negative Argumentation (Barton)	None
51.4 /June 2000	Building a Swan's Nest for Instruction in Rhetoric (Bacon)	San Francisco State University
51.4/June 2000	Becoming a Writerly Self: College Writers Engaging Black Feminist Essays (Comfort)	Graduate seminar on contemporary African American women essayists
51.4/June 2000	Evaluating Writing Programs in Real Time: The Politics of Remediation (Gleason)	37 mainstreamed sections of first-year writing
51.4/June 2000	Institutional Critique: A Rhetorical Methodology for Change (Porter, Sullivan, Blythe, Grabill, and Miles)	None
52.1/September 2000	Meet the New Boss: Same as the Old Boss: Class Consciousness in Composition (Harris)	None
52.1/September 2000	The Erasure of the Sentence (Connors)	None
52.1/September 2000	New Faculty for a New University: Toward a Full-Time Teaching-Intensive Faculty Track in Composition (Murphy)	None
52.1/September 2000	Bi, Butch, and Bar Dyke: Pedagogical Performances of Class, Gender, and Sexuality (Gibson, Marinara, and Meem)	Varying
52.2/December 2000	Interrogating the Monologue: Making Whiteness Visible (Marshall and Ryden)	None, anecdotal
52.2/December 2000	Literacy, Identity, Imagination, Flight (Gilyard)	Conversation with a former FYW student
52.2/December 2000	"Everybody Has Their Own Ideas": Responding to Cliché in Student Writing (Skorczewski)	Developmental writing class, Rutgers University
52.2/December 2000	Composition and the Circulation of Writing (Trimbur)	None

Research Methods and Approaches (*College Composition and Communication*)

Volume, Issue, Year, Author	Article Title (Author in Parentheses)	Research Methods and Approaches
60.4/June 2009	Aurality and Multimodal Composing (Selfe)	History, forensics, oratory scholarship, comparison to print composing, some discussion of ethnic rhetorics
60.4/June 2009	Chaos Is the Poetry: From Outcomes to Inquiry in Service-Learning Pedagogy (Stenberg and Whealy)	Description, narration, not systematic
60.4/June 2009	Hospitality in College Composition Courses (Haswell, Haswell, and Blalock)	Etymology, historical enactments of three different types of hospitality—Homeric, Judeo-Christian, and nomadic
60.4/June 2009	Composition as a Thermostatic Activity (Lynch)	Thermostatics as a metaphor for classrooms employing critical pedagogy
60.4/June 2009	Teaching Propriety (Agnew)	History of rhetoric and discussion of Scottish rhetorician Blair; group of Syracuse students
60.4/June 2009	Theorizing Creative Writing Pedagogy (Kearns)	Theorizing about creative-writing pedagogies
60.4/June 2009	Rhetoric, Literacy, and Social Change in Post-Mao China (Wexler)	Analysis of written and oral texts by Chinese migrants
60.4/June 2009	Writing the Genres of the University (Wardle)	Interviews, focus groups, surveys, reflective writing, student texts
60.4/June 2009	Retention and Writing Instruction (Powell)	Narratives about selected students
61.1/ September 2009	Institutional Dimensions of Academic Computing (Selber)	Theorizing
61.1/ September 2009	Gaming, Student Literacies, and the Composition Classroom: Some Possibilities for Transformation (Alexander)	Interviews with 2 students regarding their playing in World of Warcraft.
61.1/ September 2009	Popular Literacy and the Resources of Print Culture: The South African Committee for Higher Education (Trimbur)	Analysis of various texts including cartoons and a curriculum focused on educating community members
61.1/ September 2009	Lydia J. Roberts's Nutrition Research and the Rhetoric of "Democratic" Science (Jack)	Analysis of rhetoric in texts from twentieth-century women scientists in nutrition
61.1/ September 2009	*Not* Going It Alone: Public Writing, Independent Media, and the Circulation of Homeless Advocacy (Mathieu and George)	Description, quotations from publications of the region and time
61.1/ September 2009	The *BUST*in' and *Bitch*in' *Ethe* of Third-Wave Zines (Helmbrecht and Love)	Description and analysis
61.1/ September 2009	Working Boundaries: From Student Resistance to Student Agency (Gorzelsky)	Ethnographic study of a writing course

Assessment Orientation (*College Composition and Communication*)

Volume, Issue, Year, Author	Article Title (Author in Parentheses)	Research Methods and Approaches	Assessment Orientation
52.4/June 2001	School Sucks (Johnson)	Historical	None
52.4/June 2001	A Pedagogy of Charity: Donald Davidson and the Student-Negotiated Composition Classroom (Porter)	Yes, examines students in unspecified composition classroom, uses Davidson's "principle of charity" to design a "pedagogy of charity" and discusses its implications for classroom.	Codes student responses for (1) types of comments made, (2) critical terms used, and (3) their distribution to see how they change after the "pedagogy of charity" is introduced to them
52.4/June 2001	Resistance Theory and Illegitimate Reproduction (Welsh)	Selected student essays	None
52.4/June 2001	The Way of Sweat (Leonhardy)	Narrative about sweat lodge	None
53.1/September 2001	Understanding Metaphors for Writing: In Defense of the Conduit Metaphor (Eubanks)	None specified	None
53.1/September 2001	John Wesley and the Liberty to Speak: The Rhetorical and Literacy Practices of Early Methodism (Burton)	Historical	None
53.1/September 2001	Ethos and Error: How Business People React to Errors (Beason)	(1) Questionnaire ranking error and (2) interviews about reactions to error	Yes
53.1/September 2001	Finitude's Clamor: Or, Notes toward a Communitarian Literacy (Davis)	None specified	None
53.2/December 2001	Revealing Silence: Rethinking Personal Writing (Gere)	None specified	None
53.2/December 2001	Conversation and Carrying-On: Play, Conflict, and Serio-ludic Discourse in Synchronous Computer Conferencing (Rouzie)	Part of a larger study examining InterChange transcripts, newsgroup postings, and hypertext projects. Also interviews with the section instructor.	None specified
53.2/December 2001	Against the Odds in Composition and Rhetoric (Bishop)	None	None
53.2/December 2001	Online Exclusive: Writing Workplace Cultures (Henry)	Historical description of pedagogical and curriculum approach in classrooms	None
53.2/December 2001	A Rediscovered Tradition: European Pedagogy and Composition in Nineteenth-Century Midwestern Normal Schools (Fitzgerald)	Historical—examines historical documents (including lesson plans, policies, presentations)	None
53.2/December 2001	Moving beyond the Written Comment: Narrowing the Gap between Response Practice and Research (Fife and O'Neill)	Synthesizes research on responding to student writing	None

APPENDIX B: EXAMPLES OF CODING OF STUDENT WRITING

We tagged the students' writing as showing whether the DLD was accomplished, developing, or not yet present, according to the learning outcomes specified for the course students were in (English 098, English 101, English 102). See Appendix B for course outcomes.

Rhetorical and Genre Knowledge

DLD Evidence Category	Examples of Evidence (Accomplished)	Examples of Evidence (Developing)	Not Present
Rhetorical analysis (use of appropriate strategies, recognition of rhetorical situations)	"She brings in her own experiences, researchers, and even an old French poet! This essay proves to be adequate in terms of shaping ideas. Those three combinations create a strong impact on the readers." (Anthony)	Thesis: ". . . two main strategies she uses more frequently, quotations and repeated terms." (Shanna)	"In this essay I will be discussing some rhetorical things such as what Tan repeats throughout her essay, the images, and also how much emotion was involved in this essay." (Octavia)
Interpretation	Student is able to identify source credibility and how the writer uses the sources to appeal to audience, and thinks in a rhetorical way.	The student identifies strategies but does not link them to their context.	Student is not showing the ability to identify (or understand) rhetorical strategies and their purpose.
Genre knowledge (texts show rhetorical choices aligned with conventions of the assigned genre)	"In their respective essays, Stuart Buck and Peggy McIntosh both explore how white privilege subtly affects the social classes and hierarchies of America while also delving into the internalized values that drive these behaviors." (Jamison)	"Both of the articles are written as a personal experience of the author's lives and how they had a rough education, but found out things that they were better at, other than most. The two authors in the articles were depicted of something they both weren't. This would play on, and they would find out who they really are in the long run." (Karl)	"Gilbert brings up the Titanic and how in the midst the tragedy the people still followed their upbringing and saved rich people and forcefully kept the poor from escaping. I would agree that we are satisfied when we have more money. Yet money or things can't buy happiness; only Jesus Christ can bring lasting joy." "This information is important because our intuition says "Yay, more money!" but in reality it just gets us even more greedy. In closing this should be shared because people want so badly to get rich that they forget about the true happiness that waits for them: Jesus." (Ralph)
Interpretation	The student's thesis for a synthesis essay identifies the authors and texts, their common themes and perspectives, and how they interact with each other.	Student is beginning to grasp the language of synthesis but still working toward proficient discussion of common themes in the text. (Karl)	In this position, paper, the student does not write a thesis or include evidence that is derived from the text about which they were assigned to assert a position and support it with textual evidence.

Critical Literacy

DLD Evidence Category	Examples of Evidence (Accomplished)	Examples of Evidence (Developing)	Not Present
Content of writing critically engages language, power, and identity	"'Multiple independent kinds of intelligence implies that anyone can be intelligent . . . (pg. 2).'" This phrase doesn't prove that Gardner's Multiple Intelligence Theory is incorrect or that they favored IQ and EQ, but shows a biased view and also only states a narrow-minded comment about a type of general intelligence." (Lor)	"For me, I have never given much thought as to the '"how"' of a company's grand design of marketing. I do know however, that it works on me. I own nearly every Disney movie there is, I have taken three vacations to Disney world, and I have bought my sister four different princess dresses. As for my view on things, I think that many companies and corporations have the same problems as Disney that these authors are talking about. Disney is just getting a lot of bad publicity for it because they are so large and so known by everyone." (Bethany)	"Although terrorism is considered evil and heinous across the globe, and countries are going to war to try and stop it, in reality nothing can stop terrorism; it is inevitable in human nature, and this has been shown throughout human history." (Mel)
Interpretation	Student engages critically with the texts, unpacking the multiple perspectives in the readings and raising questions about the claims in the text.	Student is starting to unpack her previous assumptions about ideology and rhetorical work, but is not fully able to critically analyze the topic.	Student retains a reductive approach to the topic and uses broad, sweeping generalizations about power and politics.
Reflective writing articulates relationship between prior literacy experiences and current writing context	"During this course I have learned a few things about research. I believe actually researching is my biggest improvement, I use to just google a topic without much thought into it. Now using the research databases I know how to find good articles and spend time researching to find quality articles. One thing that I need to work on is learning how to use the databases better to find the correct results. One thing I will continue to use is the databases themselves, I have found that the	"I have always highly valued the skill of writing. Certainly, I appreciated good writing in itself, but I also had a less rational appreciation for it. I simply couldn't understand how great writing ever happened. To me, the process of writing was somewhat mystical. There was no secret formula to writing; it seemed to be just a spectacular act of pure creation. That was the approach that made writing difficult for me, and this is the approach that I grew out of this semester. Good writing definitely requires a bit of creativity, but it also needs a rational foundation. By learning to apply solid structural elements to my writing, I was able to demystify the creative process."	"I had many different particular strengths and weaknesses when writing my assignments. Certain strengths included good organization of my essays, word choice, and employment of rhetorical knowledge. I was also strong in the use of critical reading and the inclusion of supporting detail. Some of my weaknesses included redundancy, lack of conciseness, the occasional lack of a clear thesis, and the fact that I sometimes used large words and phrases too many times." (Norman)

	databases are the best way to find good peer reviewed articles, unlike the ad and agenda filled articles you find on 'google.'" (Olaf)	"In the period between high school and college, I spent a lot of time deciphering complex works of critical theory and philosophy. I wasn't worried about reading difficult texts and academic journals because complicated content was my forte. I didn't feel that I would have any problems completing the essays either, even though I wasn't quite as confident a writer as I was a reader." (Darrin)	
Interpretation	Students articulate specific areas in which their reading and writing practices have evolved from past to current contexts. They also consider how these practices will impact future writing tasks.	Student shows progress toward understanding his prior literacy experiences and current context but without a level of specificity or clear connection to a developing writing process.	Student identifies areas of strength anc growth but focuses largely on sentence-level issues and does not identify specific prior learning.

Process Skills and Knowledge

DLD Evidence Category	Examples of Evidence (Accomplished)	Examples of Evidence (Developing)	Not Present
Uses multistage writing process, states commitment to multistage writing process	"A perfect example is from my '"Synthesis Essay.'" I gave it to Evan for peer review and he helped me make it better. He explained to me how I did not summarize the two essays before I analyzed them enough for the reader to understand where I'm getting at. This allowed me to go back and insert the summary paragraph which would have been lost if it wasn't for peer review. I believe that it's very crucial for other people to look over your paper in order to receive constructive criticism. This helped me become a better	"There are different steps that can be followed when writing an essay. Those processes are pre-writing, drafting, revising, and editing. The process of pre-writing is the initial stage where you consider what is to be included and the overall purpose. This can be assisted by talking with other people who are working on the same assignment. The following process is drafting when ideas about the topic are written down and help you progress towards the main goal. Revising is the next step which gives the opportunity to focus the writing purpose, establish a thesis statement, and organize ideas. This step lets the writer stabilize the essay structure and also produce another draft for more revision and editing. For the essays I have written for this class, I have	"This is fine and pa of the process but at times I challenged with writing outline because that isn't typically how I write papers. What I like to do is sit down anc just write. Of course have a plan, but whe I came to making ar outline detailed and showing how I plan to use everything, it' just not my style. I find it confusing anc hard. When it come down to how I feel I met the rhetorical situation and demands, I feel I did a great job. If there is one thing didn't like about the

	writer and understand my own mistakes and correct them." (Anthony)	gone through part of these processes. Some of my weaknesses may include revising and editing the essays after they get reviewed by another student or the professor. My strengths include pre-writing and drafting the essays which include the '"Interview Essay'" and the '"Synthesis essay.'" After reading both of those essays, I have seen an improvement in the way that I have composed all of the essays." (Keven)	course, or didn't make sense to me, was the forced upon writing strategies in terms of outlines. I explained in once before, but its really not how I work, so it made things harder than they needed to be, and almost made me not want to do them at all. Im not sure how to change that though; so there's that" (Nina)
Interpretation	Provides a specific explanation of how he worked through stages of drafting and revision.	Discusses multistage process in a general way.	Struggles to find a way to use a multistage writing process.
Self-assessment aligned with formal writing features	"I believe I improved most on is my ability to use constructive feedback to better my writing. From day one of peer review I knew it would be an asset to my writing. Through using peer review I am able to catch many mistakes that I have made. One thing I still need to work on as I move to English 102 is the synthesis of articles in my essays. I have never synthesized articles until this semester and I believe that I still struggle with them. A strategy that I intend to continue to use is the use of the strategies given in '"They Say.'" I especially like to use this when creating a conversation between two authors. I also believe I improved as a reader	"The final learning outcome that I always had problems with and today I still feel that I need to improve on would be "demonstrate a command of multistage and recursive writing process to complete a successful researched based academic text" (learning outcomes, Writing Processes). This is shown in my Researched Academic Argument's author's note that I need to make several edits and corrections." (Rick) "Another type of paper that I have never written previously was the literature review. Since writing is not really a strong suit of mine, most writing assignments are difficult, but the literature review was especially difficult because I had to analyse a lot of article pertaining to my topic. But after the first draft it was apparent that I could quickly adjust to doing it." (Dean) Comments from Jack: "Although the majority of this rubric shows David performing	"The Audience in my research paper is TV watchers, the context of the paper is media and the Purpose of the paper is to raise awareness that medias representation of crime has an impact on our lives through our perception of the world, our behavior, and our decision-making. The conversation that prompted the research paper has much to do with one of the assignments that we got in class. We had to read three chapters from the back of the '"They Say, I say'" then choose one to write about. I chose to write about the chapter "'TV makes you smarter.'" The chapter talked about the ways that TV makes you smarter, but it also touched

	throughout this semester. I improved my reading by learning on how to read the abstract portion of the UW researcher. The abstract has allowed me to know what the article was generally about without wasting a bunch of time." (Olaf) Instructor comments: "This dedication to the writing process throughout the semester has resulted in a portfolio that demonstrates advanced performance in regard to many of the above outcomes. He is particularly good at being a reflective writer and at analyzing the demands of different rhetorical situations. Olaf has performed at an '"advanced"' level in completing the core writing requirement."	at a competent level, the severity of some of his issues (demonstrated by the outcomes assessed as 'developing') cause me to give him an overall assessment of 'developing.' He does not demonstrate adequate critical reading ability, nor does he write satisfactorily cohesive, developed, academic essays."	on the impact of crime in media. That sparked my interest to write about the topic of medias representation of crime. From that I developed my research question to talk about how medias representation of crime affects society. The strategic decision that I used throughout my research paper was breaking the paper into three parts." (Kayla) "I believe that I did a better Job at writing the research paper than I did writing any other papers for this class. I believe I met the demands, as well as showing both sides of the argument." (Kayla)
Interpretation	Student and instructor assessment aligned, also triangulated with our review of the student's work.	Student's work begins to get at areas needed for improvement though the instructors' assessment identified areas the student did not speak to in his work, nor did our own review suggest the student's assessment was aligned with some of the areas of further skill development needed.	Our own review of the students' work showed that her assessment was not aligned with the actual expectations for the assignment provided by the instructor; she struggled to assert a clear thesis and integrate credible sources, and did not include her research-based position until the end of the research essay; the student was also still developing the ability to adhere to the conventions of research citation practices.

Reflective writing that describes writing studies' disciplinary knowledge (iterative nature of writing, use of feedback to inform revision, etc.)	"My improvement as a reader is an improvement as a writer." (Dakota)	"I think I am doing this essay right but this was really difficult for me to describe why" (Bella)—c	"This copy of my essay is my final draft of my essay. I met with Professor ___ and talked about what needs to be fixed in my essay. I realized that my first did not make any sense and I had to restart the entire essay and change topics. I believe I followed all the instructions with the exception of having only four and a quarter pages other than the five to six that was asked" (Sunny)
Interpretation	Student demonstrated an advanced understanding of the integrated nature of the diverse literacy skills cultivated in the course.	Student has an impression of her success at the assignment but demonstrates she is struggling to use the language of writing studies to support her impression.	Student relies heavily on the external validation of the expert reader to form a judgment about the rhetorical effectiveness of the work.

Students

Student Pseudonym	Instructor	Course
Alan	Ann	English 101
Alejandra	Ann	English 101
Angela	Morgan	English 098
Anthony	Erica	English 098
Argenta	Rachel	English 101
Bella	Carrie	English 101
Bethany	Ann	English 101
Brandon	Carrie	English 101
Brianna	Kristen	English 102
Byron	Ann	English 101
Callie	Rachel	English 101

Cameron	Jack	English 102
Camila	Kristen	English 102
Claire	Carrie	English 101
Colton	Erica	English 098
Connie	Morgan	English 098
Connor	Carrie	English 101
Conrad	Rachel	English 101
Crissy	Erica	English 098
Dakota	Ann	English 101
Darrin	Rachel	English 101
Dean	Jack	English 102
Dominic	Carrie	English 101
Drew	Kristen	English 102
Elaine	Rachel	English 101
Elijah	Kristen	English 102
Ellen	Carrie	English 101
Elsa	Ann	English 101
Hailey	Carrie	English 101
Henry	Carrie	English 101
Huck	Rachel	English 101
Immanuel	Kristen	English 102
Jamison	Ann	English 101
Jean	Ann	English 101
Jed	Rachel	English 101
Jemma	Rachel	English 101
Jim	Ann	English 101
Joe	Ann	English 101
Josiah	Rachel	English 101
Julie	Erica	English 098
Karl	Erica	English 098
Kayla	Kristen	English 102

Keven	Erica	English 098
Lance	Morgan	English 098
Landon	Carrie	English 101
Laurel	Carrie	English 101
Layla	Carrie	English 101
Levi	Carrie	English 101
Lily	Carrie	English 101
Lor	Morgan	English 098
Lou	Ann	English 101
Madeline	Erica	English 098
Manny	Morgan	English 098
Marcela	Kristen	English 102
Mel	Jack	English 102
Minnie	Kristen	English 102
Myra	Erica	English 098
Nelson	Ann	English 101
Nina	Kristen	English 102
Noah	Kristen	English 102
Norman	Erica	English 098
Octavia	Carrie	English 101
Olaf	Ann	English 101
Ralph	Ann	English 101
Rick	Jack	English 102
Ronald	Kristen	English 102
Roxie	Kristen	English 102
Roy	Rachel	English 101
Sam	Rachel	English 101
Shane	Rachel	English 101
Shanna	Carrie	English 101
Shannon	Rachel	English 101
Stan	Ann	English 101

Sunny	Carrie	English 101
Tobin	Jack	English 102
Todd	Ann	English 101
Warren	Rachel	English 101
Yael	Morgan	English 098

APPENDIX C: UW COLLEGES' WRITING PROGRAM LEARNING OUTCOMES

Learning Outcomes	098 Learning Outcomes	101 Learning Outcomes	102 Learning Outcomes
Rhetorical Knowledge: **Reading Texts**	Read and understand different kinds of nonfiction academic texts Analyze and evaluate the basic rhetorical features of an academic text	Read and understand different kinds of complex nonfiction academic texts Analyze and evaluate the rhetorical features of a text to understand writing strategies used to communicate ideas	Read and understand scholarly (research-based) texts Analyze and evaluate how disciplinary and generic conventions shape a text
Rhetorical Knowledge: **Writing (Audience, Purpose, and Form)**	Adapt content, form, and style to the audience, purpose, and requirements of a formal academic essay Make choices as a writer that are appropriate for the stated demands of a specific writing task and situation	Adapt content, form, and style to the audience, purpose, and requirements of multiple formal academic essays Write for a variety of rhetorical purposes, including analysis, synthesis, and argument	Produce a variety of research-based texts that adapt content, form, and style with attention to audience and purpose Write for a variety of rhetorical purposes and in genres typical of research-based writing (the research proposal, synthesis of research, annotated bibliography, or rhetorical analysis)
Critical Thinking, Reading, Writing, and Research: **Reading**	Identify and analyze the main point, key supporting points, and supporting evidence in an assigned nonfiction academic text Identify tone in a nonfiction academic text Understand, analyze, and evaluate the effectiveness of a text's thesis, claims, and evidence Synthesize ideas from at least two assigned nonfiction academic texts Engage with others in discussion about key ideas from assigned course readings	Identify and explain both implicit and explicit meaning in a nonfiction academic text Accurately characterize an author's tone in a nonfiction academic text Identify bias in a text Identify multiple issues or topics within a text that warrant further inquiry Understand, analyze, and evaluate complex arguments in academic texts Synthesize ideas from a variety of sources in a formal academic essay Engage with others in discussion about texts and ideas	Identify subjectivity and bias in complex, scholarly (research-based) texts Identify multiple researched perspectives on a narrowly focused issue Understand, analyze, and evaluate arguments in research-based texts Synthesize scholarly sources and other texts that make complex arguments Discuss a scholarly text in dialogue with other readers

Critical Thinking, Reading, Writing, and Research: **Writing**	Narrow a broad topic to a focused issue appropriate for an academic writing situation Organize a cohesive academic essay around a controlling idea Develop and support a thesis with specific, relevant evidence from course readings	Narrow a topic or question to a focused, complex issue appropriate for an academic writing situation Write academic essays with clear, focused theses supported by evidence from texts Develop cohesive, source-based, academic essays for a variety of rhetorical purposes (for example, analysis, synthesis, and argument) Summarize a text's main claims and supporting points to demonstrate comprehension of the text and use the text as a source	Write cohesive academic essays supported by scholarly research for a variety of rhetorical purposes Distinguish an author's position from the writer's own position using evidence from a scholarly text Accurately paraphrase and summarize scholarly source material to use as support in a research-based text
Critical Thinking, Reading, Writing, and Research: **Research and Sources**	Begin to understand the features that characterize particular kinds of published print and electronic sources Begin to understand the textual and linguistic features that demonstrate an academic text's credibility	Navigate library research resources to find relevant support for a topic Identify the key features and analyze the relative credibility of different kinds of sources, such as scholarly journal articles, trade publications, popular magazines, websites, and others	Organize and manage a research process Develop a research question and connect it to a larger process of inquiry and entry into an existing conversation Independently evaluate the credibility of source material and its relevance and appropriateness to the writer's task, purpose, and audience
Writing Processes	Use the recursive writing process to generate multiple drafts Use appropriate language to assess the writer's own writing process and final products in relation to the department learning outcomes for English 098 Develop a basic proficiency in working collaboratively to:	Independently use the recursive writing process to generate multiple drafts Use appropriate discipline-specific language to assess the writer's own writing process and final products in relation to the department learning outcomes for English 101 Develop proficiency in working collaboratively to:	Demonstrate a command of a multistage and recursive writing process to complete a successful research-based academic text Use appropriate discipline-specific language to accurately assess the writer's own writing process and final products in relation to the department

	• Identify and use appropriate resources for feedback • Use reader feedback to shape revision • Learn to provide feedback as a reader to other writers	• Use appropriate resources for feedback • Critically use reader feedback to shape revision • Provide effective feedback as a reader to other writers	learning outcomes for English 102 Demonstrate proficiency in working collaboratively to: • Use appropriate resources for feedback • Critically use reader feedback to shape revision • Provide effective feedback as a reader to other writers
Composing in Electronic Environments	Demonstrate a basic competence with the tools needed for college-level learning and composing an academic text, including composing for/in electronic environments	Demonstrate competence with the tools needed for composing an academic text, including composing for/in electronic environments	Understand and choose appropriate reading, writing, and research tools to meet the demands of writing tasks, including composing and researching in electronic environments Use and adapt to new technologies for writing and research processes
Knowledge of Conventions	Make appropriate usage choices based on the context, purpose, and level of formality of an academic assignment In a revised and edited essay, write structurally sound sentences that adhere to the conventions of standard written English Make progress toward understanding and following academic writing conventions Understand and avoid plagiarism, especially distinguishing between the writer's own thinking and ideas from course texts Use in-text and bibliographic conventions of a recognized documentation system to incorporate material from an assigned course text (including summary, paraphrase, and quotation)	Distinguish between formal and informal academic writing and adapt writing accordingly Understand academic writing conventions, and make appropriate decisions about grammar, language usage, punctuation, and word choice Understand and avoid plagiarism Use in-text and bibliographic conventions of a recognized documentation system to incorporate material from others' texts (including summary, paraphrase, and quotation)	Demonstrate a command of standard written English, recognizing the social and discursive contexts of language usage Ethically incorporate source material to support the writer's ideas Accurately use in-text and bibliographic conventions of a recognized documentation system to incorporate material from others' texts (including summary, paraphrase, and quotation)

NOTES

1. Materiality, Labor, and Disciplinarity

1. The developmental writing (or basic writing, or "remedial" writing) course referred to here is non-credit-bearing and serves students whose placement assessment through multiple measures suggests they need a transition to degree-credit college writing.
2. Particularly around the work of "field-building": examples include articles and outreach efforts like Maxine Hairston's 1985 Chair's Address, "Breaking Our Bonds"; Chris Gallagher's 2005 "We Compositionists: Toward Engaged Professionalism"; Karen Kopelson's 2008 "Sp(l)itting Images"; Louise Wetherbee Phelps and John Ackerman's efforts with the Visibility Project (2010); the 1999 collection emerging from the early Watson conference, *History, Reflection, and Narrative: The Professionalization of Composition, 1963–1983* (Rosner et al.); and *Naming What We Know: Threshold Concepts of Writing Studies* (Adler-Kassner and Wardle); and *Composition, Rhetoric, and Disciplinarity* (Malenczyk et al., 2018).
3. In this book, we use the term *writing studies* because we see it as more inclusive than other used terms; Wardle and Downs observe that "[t]he field still goes by many names," something that works contrary to the project of disciplinarity as they describe (117, 2018). To us, the term offers a broader umbrella than *composition and rhetoric* and captures the disciplinary training and teaching focus of the teaching majority whose work we hope to represent in this text.
4. We make this distinction because it is an accreditor's designation that changes the level of autonomy that a campus has over its budget, hiring, and other core practices. Additional-location status substantially diminishes the level of individual control that faculty, staff, and administrators have over their working conditions and the teaching and learning conditions of their students.
5. We want to note here that we don't oppose extra-academic, or "alt-ac" jobs: instead, we are arguing that if research and graduate in-

stitutions are, by their mission, structured to issue degrees and prepare students for academic careers, it is more ethical and, frankly, efficient to refocus that existing capacity—not to try to invent a new career path for work outside the academy, for which there are already multiple preparatory pathways tied to such occupations.

6. This is a 2008 document, but it is the most recent, English-specific depiction of this breakdown we could find.
7. For the purposes of our research, it is difficult to track the relationship between graduates with English masters and PhDs and advertisements for positions in the two-year-college sector in part because the major source of data on hiring in English is the MLA *Job Information List*. Certainly, other sites and organizations, such as the Council of Writing Program Administrators, host job advertisements, and listservs circulate positions; but there is not a central location for two-year-college English positions beyond the general advertisements that appear in the trade dailies, the *Chronicle of Higher Education* and *Inside Higher Ed*. As a result, at least for now, it is difficult to get a sense of the growth or contraction of the job market in this part of the employment sector for students earning graduate degrees in English outside of the traditional (and as the MLA list shows, shrinking) number of jobs listed in the *JIL*. As Laurence writes, "The long-standing, chronic imbalance of PhD production and career-sustaining academic job opportunities, which has dogged doctoral education since the 1970s, has once again reached a crisis level, with no sign of improvement in the offing" ("Demand"). Though employment prospects may look different for master's-credentialed versus PhD-credentialed instructors, we see some common issues facing job-seekers in both of these categories, particularly as they make choices about what their professional goals are, what values guide those goals, and what they want to spend their time doing to prepare for those goals (issues we discuss later in the chapter).
8. Indeed, the statement itself elaborates on the points we make in this chapter, noting: "*Avoid myths*: Mentors should not invoke or imply damaging and unrealistic myths about what success on the (academic) job market must look like (e.g., that only R1 academic positions are desirable, that a national academic job search is the only way to secure satisfactory employment). Instead, faculty should work with graduate students to imagine myriad post-degree options and follow students' leads on working to meet their goals" (see also Miller et al.). It's difficult to know, given the recency of the state-

ment, how these recommendations will be taken up by graduate programs.

9. See, for example, the summer 2019 announcement that the University of Alaska system would be forced to absorb a 41 percent cut to their state funding, a cut unilaterally imposed by the governor, Mike Dunleavy, and made by veto over the agreed-upon budget approved by the Alaska state legislature. The university system declared a fiscal emergency, which enabled them to close programs and lay off tenured faculty with just sixty days' notice. Though the proposed budget reduction was ultimately reduced, in summer 2020 the Alaska system eliminated over forty academic programs from their program array.
10. The percentages from the Squire Report add up to more than 100 because unlike those in the other two columns they are not percentages of total responses but percentages estimated by respondents themselves for the categories relevant to their own institutions, which varied across institution types. (For example, only four-year respondents would have offered percentages for the category of "other (graduate teaching assistants)," and only institutions with a tenure structure would have offered percentages for "tenure-line faculty.") The question was: "Please estimate the percentage of writing program instructors whose status is best described by each of the following categories."
11. The Squire report notes that, in aggregate, the percentage of writing program instructors estimated by respondents to hold the MA degree averaged 51.6 percent compared with 13 percent holding an MFA and 36 percent a PhD (7).
12. The percentage of two-year-college faculty holding doctorates seems to vary by year and data source.
13. This is not to say that advanced students in English studies do not need to have a foundation in a range of subfields of English or that there is no benefit to having a grasp of the theoretical underpinnings of the study of letters. It is to say that the graduate curricula at many institutions are not aligned with the actual work that most MA (and some PhD) graduates will end up doing.
14. The MFA, as well, is a degree whose conferral has exploded in the last thirty years, with almost half of programs (47.9 percent) offering an MFA in creative writing. As the report notes, quoting Chad Harbach, "there were 79 degree-granting programs in creative writing in 1975; today, there are 854!" and adds, "Most of these programs are not, of course, ones offering the master's degree in

English" (*Rethinking* 7). This is to say, the MFA degree as a credential for teaching college writing is growing, though the curricula of such programs are not designed to prepare students in composition pedagogy.

15. The survey does not specify what this response category encompasses, but our own roles as faculty who have regularly reviewed instructor credentials suggest that this might include degree credentials as various as master of science in English education or masters' degrees in education, a doctorate of arts (briefly offered as a terminal degree), and even JDs (juris doctorates).
16. See Jeff Andelora's contribution to Toth and Jensen's "Symposium" article in the September 2017 special issue of *TETYC* on graduate preparation in two-year-college English. As Andelora puts it, facing an "unanticipated surge in enrollment, I hired twenty-nine new part-time faculty to staff fall classes. Only one of the new faculty I hired had a graduate degree in rhet/comp. The other twenty-eight met the minimum qualifications, but not one held a degree that required coursework in composition studies. This is not to say they weren't hard-working, dedicated teachers—they were—but they lacked the academic preparation and disciplinary knowledge that those of us in the field have come to value" (41).

2. Materiality and Knowledge Production

1. We don't address here in depth the debate around developmental education, accelerating students into degree-credit writing, or the elimination of developmental education, all of which are important conversations in the field that are largely dominated by four-year institutions and research on four-year students. For two-year-college campuses and students (many of whom are inadmissible to four-year campus programs that have admission restrictions), developmental education can be both a barrier (particularly when coupled with inaccurate and ineffective placement measures) *and* an essential pathway to higher education for students, many of whom have gaps in their education, who did not have secondary school coursework that prepared them for college literacy activities, and who need a transitional period to adapt and develop the critical reading and writing skills that most college courses require.
2. It is important to note that with this analysis, we do not mean to suggest that scholarship focused on areas outside of our specific interests—areas such as cultural and rhetorical theory, genres of writing, cultural rhetorics, the profession, or the many other ar-

eas of specialization within the field—does not have value. We are instead interested in exploring research that works to build knowledge about how people write, how they learn to write in different rhetorical contexts, and specifically how students learn to write for academic purposes. In this way, we particularly focused on writing-studies scholarship that addresses curriculum, instruction, and assessment within different teaching contexts. We argue for the need to build a knowledge foundation that professionalizes instruction, and we emphasize how current trends in knowledge production do not meet the needs of teaching-focused institutions.

3. While there are journals that take as their primary focus the lower-division academic writing function (traditionally) of FYW, they are often then specialized to the extent that they capture only part of that work. For example, the *Journal of Developmental Education* and the *Journal of Basic Writing* have editorial missions that touch on first-year writing as a kind of benchmark for entrance into the expectations of college literacy, but not FYW as a central component of their work. Further, basic writing spans a wide range of institutional types with different student populations (for example, even modestly selective institutions where students have fulfilled other admissions requirements differ from open-admissions community colleges with more than one level of non-degree-credit writing, or transition programs from Adult Basic Education). Likewise, journals such as *Teaching English in the Two-Year College* focus on issues of interest to two-year-college educators, but the journal's editorial scope—because of the nature of TYC teaching—includes not just basic writing or FYW but also literature, creative writing, ESL, community literacy, and professional issues in a similar topical range to what characterizes *College English*. In a kind of interstitial place is *Pedagogy: Critical Approaches to Teaching Literature, Language, Composition, and Culture*, which makes pedagogy the center of its editorial vision, and addresses a wide range of subfields of English, as the subtitle suggests. Those journals that are exclusively focused on writing studies include *College Composition and Communication*, *Composition Forum*, *Composition Studies*, and the *Journal of Advanced Composition* (now defunct, but for many years a significant publication), all of which take FYW as just part of what they disseminate to readers. Last, *Writing Program Administration*, as we discuss below, regularly publishes systematic research on writing classrooms and pedagogy—but with an audience that is primarily only those who have administrative and supervisory responsibilities

within their institutions, and often without directly working to address or invite in the average writing teachers in the United States; very few two-year colleges (as Jeffrey Klausman in "Mapping the Terrain" and "The Two-Year College Writing Program," and Jonikka Charlton and Shirley Rose have shown) have dedicated WPA positions. *JAC* and *CCC*, as well, publish work on advanced writing courses and graduate level curriculum—or rhetorical theory research—as much as or more than on writing-classroom research.

4. Including teachers of first-year writing, basic writing, and upper-level writing-intensive courses designated as part of the undergraduate writing curriculum.
5. It's true that at least some of the pieces that did not explicitly address writing pedagogy or writing classrooms took as their topic contingency or contingency studies, but as we note in the introduction these topics are not linked to or reflected within the context of writing classrooms and labor conditions or discussed in the context of pedagogical implications. See Sledd, 1991 and 2000; Murphy; Harris; Strickland; Lamos, "Credentialing" and "Toward Job Security"; Miller; Scott; "Indianapolis Resolution"; Cox, et al.; Scott and Welch).
6. See Krzus-Shaw and Krzus-Shaw et al. for an overview of service-learning in the two-year college.
7. We acknowledge here that classroom research is limited by the number of students who consent to participate or have their work used in such studies (something we have experienced and struggled with in our own research).

3. Materiality, Teaching, and Disciplinary Learning

1. This is true especially at two-year colleges where instructors are increasingly teaching one- or two-credit support/corequisite or writing studio courses in models intended to move students more quickly through the first-year writing sequence. Other departments offer four- or five-credit first-year writing courses such that faculty have fifteen contact hours but three course sections. See TYCA Research Committee, "TYCA White Paper on Developmental Education Reforms," for an overview of this curricular revision work.
2. See Trader et al. for a discussion of that work.
3. Though we considered the CWPA *Framework for Success in Postsecondary Writing* and Anne Beaufort's five knowledge domains to be important resources of composition knowledge, the limited nature of Beaufort's study (focused on one student) and the less-disam-

biguated nature of the framework habits of mind made them less useful for the purposes of our analysis. As a result, we focus here on threshold concepts and the WPA outcomes statement.

4. And the "average" overall whiteness camouflages the fact that some campuses had much greater proportions of students of color than others, such as Waukesha, located near Milwaukee, which has a higher percentage of African American students, or Wausau, in central Wisconsin, which has one of the highest per capita Hmong populations in the United States because of resettlement efforts after the Vietnam War.
5. Participating instructors have been identified by name or by pseudonym, depending on their expressed preferences.
6. The course cap for degree-credit writing courses is twenty-four students; the course cap for non-degree-credit writing courses is twenty-two. These caps were raised amid a series of increasingly punishing budget cuts, despite strong objections and formal appeals from the English Department to the provost and the UW Colleges senate.
7. Of those 223 responses, "about 86% were faculty and/or administrators who self-affiliated with four-year colleges; 48% identified themselves as writing program administrators; 67% as full-time faculty; 10% as part-time faculty; and 15% as graduate students" (Dryer 133) while a later survey inviting feedback on the revision included a more robust representation of two-year-college respondents, 31 percent (134).
8. We initially imagined incorporating, as well, the habits of mind from the *Framework for Success in Postsecondary Writing* and the domains of knowledge of writing spelled out by Anne Beaufort. However, the habits of mind seem largely dispositional—even though they're intended to be another guiding document for FYW instruction—and not really possible for us to assess because we had access to students' writing, not students (and there are problematic "bootstraps" aspects to the framework). Likewise, Beaufort's domains of knowledge address particular kinds of composing, drafting, and revising knowledge. They could likely be integrated into our DLD model as well, but seemed duplicative of the other two documents in a way that made the analysis more complicated without an accompanying benefit.
9. The project received IRB approval and approval for continued data collection for the duration of the data-collection period of the project.

10. We acknowledge here the many, many problems with some of the traditional benchmarks of college readiness, including biases in standardized tests and the limitations of high school grades. Our writing program used a multiple-measures process that assessed students' standardized test scores (two sets), a writing sample, high school English grades, and a self-assessment statement in order to make recommendations about student enrollment in first-year writing, corequisite support, or reading courses.
11. Student work is presented as written.
12. It should be noted that no two-year-college teachers are contributors to this text, though one chapter focuses on community colleges and directed self-placement.
13. See Elaine Richardson's chapter in *Language Diversity in the Classroom: From Intention to Practice* tracing high school and college English teachers' attitudes about language diversity and standard written English, including the gaps between the demographic profiles of respondents who agreed with statements such as "Students should learn grammar rules to improve their ability to understand and communicate concepts and information" and those such as "There are valid reasons for using nonstandard dialects," the latter of which were more likely to be supported by high school teachers than by college instructors (46–48).
14. See Phillips et al. in Adler-Kassner and Wardle's *(Re)Considering What We Know: Learning Thresholds in Writing, Composition, Rhetoric, and Literacy*, in which we propose alternate language for threshold concepts specific to first-year writing.

4. Toward an Integrated Agenda in Writing Studies

1. See, for example, the 2019 Pew Research Center survey showing that "only half of American adults think colleges and universities are having a positive effect on the way things are going in the country these days. About four-in-ten (38 percent) say they are having a negative impact—up from 26 percent in 2012"; among Republican and independents who lean Republican, the rate of agreement with the belief that colleges have a negative effect in the country is 59 percent. Disturbingly, "96 percent of Republicans ages 65 and older who think higher education is headed in the wrong direction say professors bringing their views into the classroom is a major reason for this" (Parker).
2. Though the second national convention was scheduled for Milwaukee in 2020, the COVID-19 pandemic resulted in the cancellation

of both CCCC 2020 and TYCA 2020. The 2021 meetings of both TYCA and CCCC were held virtually.

3. See, for example, books like Jason Brennan's *Good Work If You Can Get It: How to Succeed in Academia*. Brennan argues: "For one, most service work is not worth doing, period, by anyone. Most committees accomplish little to nothing but consume lots of time" (qtd. in Jaschik, "Good Work"). Or a hot-take *Inside Higher Ed* column by Lance Fusarelli in which he advises, "As for service, do the minimal amount necessary to be considered a good citizen but no more. Service is another one of those metrics that has value only in the negative. Doing twice as much service as others and saying yes to every service opportunity will kill you and your career."

Epilogue

1. This is the introductory paragraph for the web page of The UW Colleges First-Year Writing Program, which had vast, detailed web resources in ten separate categories, everything from Best Practices to an Instructor's Handbook to Resources for Students. We often talk about falling down a rabbit hole on the web, but if this site were a rabbit hole, the furry residents had lined their nests with almost unending shelves of wisely curated information.
2. In addition to the writing program's being awarded a Certificate of Excellence from the Conference on College Composition and Communication and earning a grant from the Bill and Melinda Gates Foundation, and the whole department's winning the 2015 Diana Hacker Award for Outstanding Programs in English for Two-Year Colleges and Teachers, numerous members of the UW Colleges English Department conducted research in the scholarship of teaching and learning, with IRB-approved studies, presentations at regional, statewide, national, and international conferences, and publications in peer-reviewed scholarly publications. Repeatedly, the departmental assessment coordinators conducted research so that the process of assessment, treated as busywork by some educational entities, resulted in useful information and productive departmental change in the UW Colleges English Department.
3. A site called the Quote Investigator does a nice job of tracing the origin of that saying: quoteinvestigator.com/2013/08/18/acad-politics/. The point I'm trying to make is that sometimes, especially where student learning is concerned, the stakes are pretty freaking high.

4. Randy Bass's classic essay, "The Scholarship of Teaching: What's the Problem?" is the first place I remember someone articulating this issue: "Ever since graduate school I had taught mostly the way I had been taught, and tended to replicate the pedagogies that worked best—quite frankly—on *me* (or slight variations of me). Now that I was trying to change my teaching radically, those *naturalized* teaching methods and the assumptions behind them were exposed to be without any clear scaffolding or support by the evidence of learning, however sound or useful some of the approaches were" (3). The warrants behind Bass's thinking were shared, in general, by the supportive community of the UW Colleges English department as the department shifted over the years, becoming a place that relied on what Bass was longing for, clear scaffolding *and* evidence.
5. For example, for the 2017–2018 academic year, when the UW Colleges and its stellar English department were still in existence, the UW Colleges Central Office decided that Multiple Measures Placement would no longer have a writing sample or survey. Thus, students were placed in composition courses based on a standardized, multiple-choice test and possibly ACT scores. In contrast, UW–Platteville, now my main campus, has funded multiple-measures placement coordinators and readers for both the branch campuses, UW–Platteville Richland (my work home since 1992) and UW–Platteville Baraboo Sauk County. That work began late in spring semester 2019 and continues, and will be assessed moving forward.
6. The full quotation from John Steinbeck, "I have come to believe that a great teacher is a great artist and that there are as few as there are any other great artists. Teaching might even be the greatest of the arts since the medium is the human mind and spirit," can be found here: www.brainyquote.com/quotes/john_steinbeck_122146.
7. This envoi is short-changed because I left out the word *materials*, with which I had very much hoped to say something about "dark materials," an allusion to Milton and to Philip Pullman, but *materials* resisted being used that way so I just left it out entirely. That is part of contentment, right? Exerting control where one can.

WORKS CITED

2016 NCTE Education Policy Platform. National Council of Teachers of English. www2.ncte.org/statement/2016-policy-platform/.

2016 Resolutions. Conference on College Composition and Communication, cccc.ncte.org/cccc/resolutions/2016.

Accardi, Steven, and Jillian Grauman. "Structural Barriers and Knowledge Production at the Two-Year College." *WPA: Writing Program Administration*, vol. 43, no. 3, Summer 2020, pp. 73–85.

Adams, Peter, et al. "The Accelerated Learning Program: Throwing Open the Gates." *Journal of Basic Writing*, vol. 28, no. 2, Fall 2009, pp. 50–69.

Adler-Kassner, Linda. "Because Writing Is Never Just Writing." 2017 CCCC Chair's Address. *College Composition and Communication*, vol. 69, no. 2, Dec. 2017, pp. 317–40.

Adler-Kassner, Linda, and Elizabeth Wardle, eds. *Naming What We Know: Threshold Concepts of Writing Studies*. UP of Colorado, 2015.

———. *(Re)Considering What We Know: Learning Thresholds in Writing, Composition, Rhetoric, and Literacy*. UP of Colorado, 2020.

Andelora, Jeff. "Systematic Inclusion: The Need for Redesigned Graduate Programs." "Symposium: Responses to the TYCA Guidelines for Preparing Teachers of English in the Two-Year College," edited by Christie Toth and Darin Jensen, *Teaching English in the Two-Year College*, vol. 45, no. 1, Sept. 2017, pp. 29–46.

Anderst, Leah, et al. "Mapping Trajectories of ALP within Developmental Writing Education." *Transformations: Change Work across Writing Programs, Pedagogies, and Practices*. UP of Colorado, 2021, pp. 123–45.

Anson, Chris M. "The Intelligent Design of Writing Programs: Reliance on Belief or a Future of Evidence." *WPA: Writing Program Administration*, vol. 32, nos. 1–2, Fall/Winter 2008, pp. 11–36.

Astin, Alexander W. "Are You Smart Enough? How Colleges' Obsession with Smartness Shortchanges Students." *Liberal Education*, vol. 103, no. 2, Spring 2017, pp. 22–29.

Bahr, Steven, et al. "Why Didn't Students Complete a Free Application for Federal Student Aid (FAFSA)? A Detailed Look." *Stats in Brief*, NCES 2018-061, United States Dept. of Education, National Center for Education Statistics, Dec. 2018, nces.ed.gov/pubsearch/pubsinfo.asp?pubid=2018061.

Bailey, Thomas, et al. *Referral, Enrollment, and Completion in Developmental Education Sequences in Community Colleges*. CCRC Working Paper no. 15, revised Nov. 2009, Community College Research Center, Teachers College, Columbia U, ccrc.tc.columbia.edu/media/k2/attachments/referral-enrollment-completion-developmental_V2.pdf.

Bain, Ken. *What the Best College Teachers Do*. Harvard UP, 2004.

Baker-Bell, April. *Linguistic Justice: Black Language, Literacy, Identity, and Pedagogy*. Routledge/NCTE, 2020.

Bass, Randy. "The Scholarship of Teaching: What's the Problem?" *Inventio: Creative Thinking about Teaching and Learning*, vol. 1, no. 1, Feb. 1999, pp. 1–10, my.vanderbilt.edu/sotl/files/2013/08/Bass-Problem1.pdf.

Bazelon, Emily. "What Will College Be Like in the Fall?" *New York Times Magazine*, 3 June 2020.

Bazerman, Charles. "The Wonder of Writing." 2009 CCCC Chair's Address. *College Composition and Communication*, vol. 61, no. 3, Feb. 2010, pp. 571–80.

Beaufort, Anne. *College Writing and Beyond: A New Framework for University Writing Instruction*. Utah State UP, 2007.

Berlin, James A. *Rhetoric and Reality: Writing Instruction in American Colleges, 1900–1985*. Southern Illinois UP, 1987.

Bickerstaff, Susan, and Julia Raufman. "From 'Additive' to 'Integrative': Experiences of Faculty Teaching Developmental Integrated Reading and Writing Courses." CCRC Working Paper no. 96, Aug. 2017, Community College Research Center, Teachers College, Columbia U, ccrc.tc.columbia.edu/media/k2/attachments/faculty-experiences-teaching-developmental-reading-writing.pdf.

Biswas, Ann E. "'I Second That Emotion': Minding How Plagiarism Feels." *Teaching/Writing: The Journal of Writing Teacher Education*, vol. 4, no. 1, Spring 2015, 127–41.

Blewett, Kelly, et al. "Editing as Inclusion Activism." *College English*, vol. 81, no. 4, Mar. 2019, pp. 273–96.

Bloom, Lynn Z. "Freshman Composition as a Middle-Class Enterprise." *College English*, vol. 58, no. 6, Oct. 1996, pp. 654–75.

Bloom, Lynn, et al., eds. *Composition in the Twenty-First Century: Crisis and Change*. Southern Illinois UP, 1996.

Boettger, Ryan K., and Laura A. Palmer. "Qualitative Content Analysis: Its Use in Technical Communication." *IEEE Transactions on Professional Communication*, vol. 53, no. 4, Dec. 2010, pp. 346–57.

Bollig, Chase. "'Is College Worth It?' Arguing for Composition's Value with the Citizen-Worker." *College Composition and Communication*, vol. 67, no. 2, Dec. 2015, pp. 150–72.

Bourdieu, Pierre. "Cultural Reproduction and Social Reproduction." *Knowledge, Education, and Cultural Change: Papers in the Sociology of Education*, edited by Richard Brown, 1973, Routledge, 2018, pp. 71–112.

Bousquet, Marc. "Composition as Management Science: Toward a University without a WPA." *JAC: Journal of Advanced Composition*, vol. 22, no. 3, 2002, pp. 493–526.

———. "The Rhetoric of 'Job Market' and the Reality of the Academic Labor System." *College English*, vol. 66, no. 2, Nov. 2003, 207–28.

Bousquet, Marc, et al., eds. *Tenured Bosses and Disposable Teachers: Writing Instruction in the Managed University*. Southern Illinois UP, 2004.

Brandt, Deborah. "Remembering Reading, Remembering Writing." *College Composition and Communication*, vol. 45, no. 4, Dec. 1994, pp. 459–79.

Brennan, Jason. *Good Work if You Can Get It: How to Succeed in Academia*. Johns Hopkins UP, 2020.

Brewer, Meaghan. *Conceptions of Literacy: Graduate Instructors and the Teaching of First-Year Composition*. UP of Colorado, 2020.

Brown, Tessa. "What Else Do We Know? Translingualism and the History of SRTOL as Threshold Concepts in Our Field." *College Composition and Communication*, vol. 74, no. 4, June 2020, pp. 591–619.

Calarco, Jessica McCrory. *Negotiating Opportunities: How the Middle Class Secures Advantages in School*. Oxford UP, 2018.

Calhoon-Dillahunt, Carolyn. "Returning to Our Roots: Creating the Conditions and Capacity for Change." 2018 CCCC Chair's Address, *College Composition and Communication*, vol. 70, no. 2, Dec. 2018, pp. 273–93.

Calhoon-Dillahunt, Carolyn, et al. "TYCA Guidelines for Preparing Teachers of English in the Two-Year College." *Teaching English in the Two-Year College*, vol. 45, no. 1, Sept. 2017, pp. 8–18.

Canagarajah, A. Suresh. "The Place of World Englishes in Composition: Pluralization Continued." *College Composition and Communication*, vol. 57, no. 4, June 2006, pp. 586–619.

Carey, Kevin. "Biggest Offender in Outsize Debt: Graduate Schools." *The New York Times*, 3 June 2019.

Carillo, Ellen C. "Beyond the Research Institution: Preparing Graduate Students to Teach in Various Contexts." *Profession*, Spring 2019.

———. *Securing a Place for Reading in Composition: The Importance of Teaching for Transfer*. UP of Colorado, 2015.

Cassuto, Leonard. *The Graduate School Mess: What Caused It and How We Can Fix It*. Harvard UP, 2015.

Cassuto, Leonard, and Robert A. Weisbuch. "The PhD Isn't Working Right Now." *Chronicle of Higher Education*, 9 Dec. 2020.

CCCC and CWPA Joint Statement in Response to the COVD-19 Pandemic. Conference on College Composition and Communication and Council of Writing Program Administrators, June 2020, cccc.ncte.org/cccc/cccc-and-cwpa-joint-statement-in-response-to-the-covid-19-pandemic.

CCCC Statement of Professional Guidance for Mentoring Graduate Students. Conference on College Composition and Communication, Nov. 2019, cccc.ncte.org/cccc/resources/positions/professional-guidance-for-mentoring-graduate-students/.

CCCC Statement on Preparing Teachers of College Writing. Conference on College Composition and Communication, 30 Nov. 2015, www.ncte.org/cccc/resources/positions/statementonprep.

Cerbin, Bill. *Lesson Study: Using Classroom Inquiry to Improve Teaching and Learning in Higher Education*. Stylus, 2011.

Charlton, Jonikka, and Shirley K. Rose. "Twenty More Years in the WPA's Progress." *WPA: Writing Program Administration*, vol. 33, nos. 1–2, Fall/Winter 2009, pp. 114–45.

Ching, Kory Lawson. "Apprenticeship in the Instructor-Led Peer Conference." *Composition Studies*, vol. 39, no. 2, Fall 2011, pp. 101–19.

Community College FAQs. Community College Research Center, Teachers College, Columbia U, ccrc.tc.columbia.edu/Community-College-FAQs.html.

Cox, Anicca, et al. "The Indianapolis Resolution: Responding to Twenty-First-Century Exigencies/Political Economies of Composition Labor." *College Composition and Communication*, vol. 68, no. 1, Sept. 2016, pp. 38–67.

Daniel, James Rushing. "Freshman Composition as a Precariat Enterprise." *College English*, vol. 80, no. 1, Sept. 2017, pp. 63–85.

Data from the MLA Survey of Department Staffing, Fall 2014. Modern Language Association, www.mla.org/Resources/Research/Surveys-Reports-and-Other-Documents/Staffing-Salaries-and-Other-Professional-Issues/Data-from-the-MLA-Survey-of-Departmental-Staffing-Fall-2014.

Delpit, Lisa. *Other People's Children: Cultural Conflict in the Classroom.* New Press, 2006.

Del Principe, Annie. "Cultivating a Sustainable TYC Writing Program: Collaboration, Disciplinarity, and Faculty Governance." *WPA: Writing Program Administration*, vol. 43, no. 3, Summer 2020, pp. 54–72.

Del Principe, Annie, and Rachel Ihara. "A Long Look at Reading in the Community College: A Longitudinal Analysis of Student Reading Experiences." *Teaching English in the Two-Year College*, vol. 45, no. 2, Dec. 2017, pp. 183–206.

Detweiler, Jane, et al. "Academic Leadership and Advocacy: On Not Leaning In." *College English*, vol. 79, no. 5, May 2017, pp. 451–65.

Developmental Education: Challenges and Strategies for Reform. US Department of Education, Office of Planning, Evaluation and Policy Development, Jan. 2017, www2.ed.gov/about/offices/list/opepd/education-strategies.pdf.

DiAngelo, Robin. *White Fragility: Why It's So Hard for White People to Talk about Racism.* Beacon Press, 2018.

Doran, Erin E. "'What's Expected of Us as We Integrate the Two Disciplines?' Two-Year College Faculty Engage with Basic Writing Reform." *Teaching English in the Two-Year College*, vol. 47, no. 2, Dec. 2019, pp. 149–67.

Downs, Douglas, and Elizabeth Wardle. "Teaching about Writing, Righting Misconceptions: (Re)envisioning 'First-Year Composition' as 'Introduction to Writing Studies.'" *College Composition and Communication*, vol. 58, no. 4, June 2007, pp. 552–84.

Dryer, Dylan B. "At a Mirror, Darkly: The Imagined Undergraduate Writers of Ten Novice Composition Instructors." *College Composition and Communication*, vol. 63, no. 3, Feb. 2012, pp. 420–52.

Dryer, Dylan B., et al. "Revising FYC Outcomes for a Multimodal, Digitally Composed World: The WPA Outcomes Statement for First-Year Composition (Version 3.0)." *WPA: Writing Program Administration*, vol. 38, no. 1, Fall 2014, pp. 129–43.

Dunbar, Mitra, and W. Douglas Baker. "Teaching as Emotional Labor: Preparing to Interact with All Students." *Language Arts Journal of Michigan*, vol. 30, no. 1, 2014, pp. 32–40.

Dweck, Carol S. *Mindset: The New Psychology of Success.* Ballantine Books, 2006.

Ede, Lisa. *Situating Composition: Composition Studies and the Politics of Location.* Southern Illinois UP, 2004.

Education in the Balance: A Report on the Academic Workforce in English. Modern Language Association and Association of Departments of

English, 10 Dec. 2008, www.mla.org/content/download/3255/81374/workforce_rpt03.pdf.

Elbow, Peter. "High Stakes and Low Stakes in Assigning and Responding to Writing." *New Directions for Teaching and Learning*, vol. 1997, no. 69, Spring 1997, pp. 5–13.

Ennis, Daniel J. "The Last of the Tenure Track." *Chronicle of Higher Education*, 3 July 2011.

Entwistle, Noel. "Threshold Concepts and Transformative Ways of Thinking within Research into Higher Education." *Threshold Concepts within the Disciplines*, edited by Ray Land et al., Sense Publishers, 2008, pp. 21–35.

Eodice, Michele, et al. *The Meaningful Writing Project: Learning, Teaching, and Writing in Higher Education*. UP of Colorado, 2016.

Fact Book 2014–2015. U of Wisconsin Colleges Office of Institutional Research, www.uwc.edu/sites/uwc.edu/files/imce-uploads/about/overview/_files/2014-2015_uw_colleges_fact_book_final.pdf. Accessed 22 May 2018.

Fact Book 2016–2017. U of Wisconsin Colleges Office of Institutional Research, www.uwc.edu/sites/default/files/imce-uploads/about/administration/academic-affairs/research/_files/2016-2017_uw_colleges_fact_book.pdf. Accessed 22 May 2018.

Fain, Paul. "Remedial Education Fixes Won't Cure Completion Crisis." *Inside Higher Ed*, 5 Aug. 2019.

Fast Facts: Graduation Rates. US Dept. of Education, National Center for Education Statistics, 2019, nces.ed.gov/fastfacts/display.asp?id=40.

Fox, Tom. *Defending Access: A Critique of Standards in Higher Education*. Heinemann, 1999.

Framework for Information Literacy for Higher Education. Association of College and Research Libraries, 11 Jan. 2016, www.ala.org/acrl/standards/ilframework.

Framework for Success in Postsecondary Writing. Council of Writing Program Administrators, et al., 2011, wpacouncil.org/aws/cwpa/pt/sd/news_article/242845/_parent/layout_details/false.

Fulkerson, Richard. "Composition at the Turn of the Twenty-First Century." *College Composition and Communication*, vol. 56, no. 4, June 2005, pp. 654–87.

Fusarelli, Lance D. "If I Only Knew: Reflections for New Faculty Members." *Inside Higher Ed*, 6 Aug. 2020.

Gallagher, Chris. "We Compositionists: Toward Engaged Professionalism." *JAC: Journal of Advanced Composition*, vol. 25, no. 1, 2005, pp. 75–99.

Gardner, Lee. "Want to Kill Tenure? Be Careful What You Wish For." *Chronicle of Higher Education*, 18 June 2018.

Gere, Anne Ruggles. "Initial Report on Survey of CCCC Members." James R. Squire Office of Policy Research in English Language Arts, U of Michigan, 12 Jan. 2009, csal.colostate.edu/docs/cwpa/syllabus/Report-CCCC-Members.pdf.

Gere, Anne Ruggles, et al. "Communal Justicing: Writing Assessment, Disciplinary Infrastructure, and the Case for Critical Language Awareness." *College Composition and Communication*, vol. 72, no. 3, Feb. 2021, pp. 384–412.

———. "Mutual Adjustments: Learning from and Responding to Transfer Student Writers." *College English*, vol. 79, no. 4, Mar. 2017, pp. 333–57.

Giordano, Joanne Baird, and Cassandra Phillips. "Designing an Open-Access Online Writing Program: Negotiating Tensions between Disciplinary Ideals and Institutional Realities." *Transformations: Change Work across Writing Programs, Pedagogies, and Practices*, edited by Holly Hassel and Kirsti Cole, UP of Colorado, 2021, pp. 240–58.

Giordano, Joanne Baird, et al. "TYCA Working Paper #2: Two-Year College English Faculty Teaching Adjustments Related to Workload." Two-Year College English Association, Nov. 2020, ncte.org/wp-content/uploads/2020/12/TYCA_Working_Paper_2.pdf.

Giordano, Joanne Baird, and McKenna Wegner. "TYCA Working Paper #3: Workload Management Strategies for Teaching English at Two-Year Colleges." Two-Year College English Association, Nov. 2020, ncte.org/wp-content/uploads/2020/11/TYCA_Working_Paper_3.pdf.

Giordano, Joanne Baird, and Holly Hassel. "Unpredictable Journeys: Academically At-Risk Students, Developmental Education Reform, and the Two-Year College." *Teaching English in the Two-Year College*, vol. 43, no. 4, May 2016, pp. 371–90.

Grego, Rhonda C., and Nancy S. Thompson. *Teaching/Writing in Thirdspaces: The Studio Approach*. Southern Illinois UP, 2008.

Griffiths, Brett. "Professional Autonomy and Teacher-Scholar-Activists in Two-Year Colleges: Preparing New Faculty to Think Institutionally." *Teaching English in the Two-Year College*, vol. 45, no. 1, Sept. 2017, pp. 47–68.

Hairston, Maxine. "Breaking Our Bonds and Reaffirming Our Connections." *College Composition and Communication*, vol. 36, no. 3, Oct. 1985, pp. 272–82.

Hancock, Nicole, and Casey Reid. "Am I a WPA? Embracing the Multiverse of WPA Labor in Community College Contexts." *WPA: Writing*

Program Administration, vol. 43, no. 3, Summer 2020, pp. 19–37.

Hansen, Kristine, and Christine Farris, eds. *College Credit for Writing in High School: The "Taking-Care-of" Business*. National Council of Teachers of English, 2010.

Harbach, Chad. "MFA vs. NYC: America Now Has Two Distinct Literary Cultures: Which One Will Last?" *Slate*, 26 Nov. 2010.

Harris, Joseph. "Meet the New Boss, Same as the Old Boss: Class Consciousness in Composition." *College Composition and Communication*, vol. 52. no. 1, Sept. 2000, pp. 43–68.

Hassel, Holly. "Postsecondary Writing Course Caps." Nov. 2020, docs.google.com/spreadsheets/d/16anb0URuLuux0ePk5EZ2fRcfQA1TwbsV2RFZW0-aANk/edit#gid=0.

———. "Research Gaps in *Teaching English in the Two-Year College*." *Teaching English in the Two-Year College*, vol. 40, no. 4, May 2013, pp. 343–63.

Hassel, Holly, and Kirsti Cole, eds. *Academic Labor beyond the College Classroom: Working for Our Values.* Routledge, 2020.

Hassel, Holly, and Joanne Baird Giordano. "The Blurry Borders of College Writing: Remediation and the Assessment of Student Readiness." *College English*, vol. 78, no. 1, Sept. 2015, pp. 56–80.

———. "FYC Placement at Open-Admission, Two-Year Campuses: Changing Campus Culture, Institutional Practice, and Student Success." *Open Words: Access and English Studies*, vol. 5, no. 2, Fall 2011, pp. 29–59.

———. "Occupy Writing Studies: Rethinking College Composition for the Needs of the Teaching Majority." *College Composition and Communication*, vol. 65, no. 1, Sept. 2013, pp. 117–39.

Hassel, Holly, and Jeffrey Klausman. "TYCA Working Paper #6: Two-Year College English Faculty Workload: Making the Labor of Assessment Visible." Two-Year College English Association, Nov. 2020, ncte.org/wp-content/uploads/2020/11/TYCA_Working_Paper_6.pdf.

Hassel, Holly, et al. "The Imperative of Pedagogical and Professional Development to Support the Retention of Underprepared Students in Open-Access Institutions." *Retention, Persistence, and Writing Programs*, edited by Todd Ruecker et al., UP of Colorado, 2017, pp. 74–92.

Hassel, Holly, et al. "TYCA Working Paper #7: Making the Emotional Labor of Open-Access Teaching Visible." Two-Year College English Association, Nov. 2020, ncte.org/wp-content/uploads/2020/11/TYCA_Working_Paper_7.pdf.

Haswell, Richard. "Hieroglyphic World: A Review of Five Background Readers for Novice Writing Teachers." *WPA: Writing Program Administration*, vol. 33, no. 3, Spring 2010, pp. 104–10.

———. "Methodologically Adrift." Review of *Academically Adrift: Limited Learning on College Campuses*, by Richard Arum and Josipa Roksa. *College Composition and Communication*, vol. 63, no. 3, Feb. 2012, 487–91.

———. "NCTE/CCCC's Recent War on Scholarship." *Written Communication*, vol. 22, no. 2, Apr. 2005, pp. 198–223.

Hayot, Eric. "The Sky Is Falling." *Profession*, 21 May 2018.

Hesse, Douglas. "Journals in Composition Studies, Thirty-Five Years After." *College English*, vol. 81, no. 4, Mar. 2019, pp. 367–96.

———. "The Nation Dreams of Teacher Proofing: Neglected Expertise and Needed Writing Research." *College Composition and Communication*, vol. 61, no. 1, Sept. 2009, W416–22.

Holschuh, Jodi Patrick, and Eric J. Paulson. "The Terrain of Developmental Reading." College Reading and Learning Association, July 2013, www.crla.net/images/whitepaper/TheTerrainofCollege91913.pdf.

Hoover, Eric. "The Demographic Cliff: Five Findings from New Projections of High-School Graduates." *Chronicle of Higher Education,* 15 Dec. 2020.

Horning, Alice S., et al., eds. *What Is College Reading?* WAC Clearinghouse, 2017.

Horning, Alice S., and Elizabeth W. Kraemer, eds. *Reconnecting Reading and Writing*. Parlor Press, 2013.

Howard, Rebecca Moore, et al. "Writing from Sources, Writing from Sentences." *Writing and Pedagogy*, vol. 2, no. 2, Fall 2010, pp. 177–92.

Huckin, Thomas. "Content Analysis: What Texts Talk About." *What Writing Does and How It Does It: An Introduction to Analyzing Texts and Textual Practices*, edited by Charles Bazerman and Paul A. Prior, Lawrence Erlbaum, 2004, pp. 13–32.

Huot, Brian. "Toward a New Theory of Writing Assessment." *College Composition and Communication*, vol. 47, no. 4, Dec. 1996, pp. 549–66.

"Indianapolis Resolution." *Compositionist.net*, 30 May 2015, www.compositionist.net/indianapolis-resolution.html.

Inoue, Asao. *Antiracist Writing Assessment Ecologies: Teaching and Assessing Writing for a Socially Just Future.* WAC Clearinghouse, 2015.

Inoue, Asao B., and Mya Poe. *Race and Writing Assessment.* Peter Lang, 2012.

Isaacs, Emily J. *Writing at the State U: Instruction and Administration at 106 Comprehensive Universities*. UP of Colorado, 2018.

Jaschik, Scott. "Good Work If You Can Get It: Author Discusses His Book on Graduate School and Academic Careers." *Inside Higher Ed,* 1 May 2020.

———. "Retaliation at Queensborough?" *Inside Higher Ed*, 17 Sept. 2012.

Jensen, Darin. About. *Teacher-Scholar-Activist*, teacher-scholar-activist .org/about/.

Jensen, Darin, and Susan Ely. "A Partnership Teaching Externship Program: A Model That Makes Do." *Teaching English in the Two-Year College*, vol. 44, no. 3, Mar. 2017, pp. 247–63.

Jensen, Darin L., and Christie Toth. "Unknown Knowns: The Past, Present, and Future of Graduate Preparation for Two-Year College English Faculty." *College English*, vol. 79, no. 6, July 2017, pp. 561–92.

Johnson, Sarah Z. "A Tale of Two Statements." *Teaching English in the Two-Year College*, vol. 45, no. 1, Sept. 2017, pp. 20–28.

Kahn, Seth. "We Value Teaching Too Much to Keep Devaluing It." *College English*, vol. 82, no. 6, July 2020, pp. 591–611.

Kahn, Seth, et al. *Contingency, Exploitation, and Solidarity: Labor and Action in English Composition*. WAC Clearinghouse and UP of Colorado. 2017.

Kalish, Katie, et al. "Inequitable Austerity: Pedagogies of Resilience and Resistance in Composition." *Pedagogy: Critical Approaches to Teaching Literature, Language, Composition, and Culture*, vol. 19, no. 2, Apr. 2019, pp. 261–81.

Kareem, Jamila. "A Critical Race Analysis of Transition-Level Writing Curriculum to Support the Racially Diverse Two-Year College." *Teaching English in the Two-Year College*, vol. 46, no. 4, May 2019, pp. 271–96.

Klausman, Jeffrey. "Mapping the Terrain: The Two-Year College Writing Program Administrator." *Teaching English in the Two-Year College*, vol. 35, no. 3, Mar. 2008, pp. 238–51.

———. "The Two-Year College Writing Program and Academic Freedom: Labor, Scholarship, and Compassion." *Teaching English in the Two-Year College*, vol. 45, no. 4, May 2018, pp. 385–405.

Klausman, Jeffrey, et al. "TYCA Working Paper #1: Two-Year College English Faculty Teaching Workload." Two-Year College English Association, Nov. 2020, ncte.org/wp-content/uploads/2020/11/TYCA_Working_Paper_1.pdf.

Kopelson, Karen. "Sp(l)itting Images: Or, Back to the Future of (Rhetoric and?) Composition." *College Composition and Communication*, vol. 59, no. 4, June 2008, pp. 750–80.

Krebs, Paula. "Opinion: Wisconsin Is Trying to Segregate Higher Education into the Haves and Have-Nots." *Washington Post*, 21 Mar. 2018.

Krzus-Shaw, Kassia. "Bridging Gaps and Creating Rich Service-Learning

Experiences for Marginalized Students." *Teaching English in the Two-Year College*, vol. 44, no. 4, May 2017, 351–71.

Krzus-Shaw, Kassia, et al. "Symposium: Service-Learning in the Two-Year College." *Teaching English in the Two-Year College*, vol. 44, no. 4, May 2017, 388–402.

Lamos, Steve. "Credentialing College Writing Teachers: WPAs and Labor Reform." *WPA: Writing Program Administration*, vol. 35, no. 1, Fall/Winter 2011, pp. 45–72.

———. "Toward Job Security for Teaching-Track Composition Faculty: Recognizing and Rewarding Affective-Labor-in-Space." *College English*, vol. 78, no. 4, 2016, pp. 362–86.

Lareau, Annette. *Unequal Childhoods: Class, Race, and Family Life*, 2nd ed. U of California P, 2011.

Larson, Holly. "Epistemic Authority in Composition Studies: Tenuous Relationship between Two-Year English Faculty and Knowlege Production." *Teaching English in the Two-Year College*, vol. 46, no. 2, Dec. 2018, pp. 109–36.

Laurence, David. "Demand for New Faculty Members, 1995–2016." *Profession*, Winter 2019.

———. *Demography of the Faculty: A Statistical Portrait of English and Modern Languages*. Association of Departments of English and Modern Language Association, 10 Dec. 2008, apps.mla.org/pdf/demography_fac2.pdf.

Lerner, Neal. "The Teacher-Student Writing Conference and the Desire for Intimacy." *College English*, vol. 68, no. 2, Nov. 2005, pp. 186–208.

Leverenz, Carrie Shively, and Amy Goodburn. "Professionalizing TA Training: Commitment to Teaching or Rhetorical Response to Market Crisis?" *WPA: Writing Program Administration*, vol. 22, nos. 1–2, Fall/Winter 1998, pp. 9–32.

Liese, Daniela. "Marilyn Sternglass's *Time to Know Them*: A Review Essay." *Journal of Basic Writing*, vol. 18, no. 1, Spring 1999, pp. 21–26.

Looker, Samantha. "Writing about Language: Studying Language Diversity with First-Year Writers." *Teaching English in the Two-Year College*, vol. 44, no. 2, Dec. 2016, pp. 176–98.

Lorde, Audre. *Sister Outsider: Essays and Speeches.* Crossing Press, 1984.

Lovas, John C. "All Good Writing Develops at the Edge of Risk." *College Composition and Communication*, vol. 54, no. 2, Dec. 2002, pp. 264–88.

Lusin, Natalia. *The MLA* Job Information List, *2017–2018: Final Report.* Modern Language Association, Nov. 2019, www.mla.org/content/download/113931/2428489/Report-MLA-JIL-2017-18.pdf.

Ma, Jennifer, and Sandy Baum. *Trends in Community Colleges: Enrollment, Prices, Student Debt, and Completion*. College Board, Apr. 2016, trends.collegeboard.org/sites/default/files/trends-in-community-colleges-research-brief.pdf.

Maimon, Elaine P. *Leading Academic Change: Vision, Strategy, Transformation*. Stylus, 2018.

Malenczyk, Rita, et al., eds. *Composition, Rhetoric, and Disciplinarity*. UP of Colorado, 2018.

Manzo, Whitney Ross, and Kristin M. W. Mitchell. "We Need to Rethink Training for PhDs." *Inside Higher Ed*, 11 Sept. 2018.

Massé, Michelle A., and Katie J. Hogan, eds. *Over Ten Million Served: Gendered Service in Language and Literature Workplaces*. SUNY P, 2010.

McClure, Randall, and Dayna V. Goldstein. "Different Paths to the Same Goal: A Response to Barbara Cambridge." *WPA: Writing Program Administration*, vol. 35, no. 2, Spring 2012, 190–95.

Micciche, Laura R. "More than a Feeling: Disappointment and WPA Work." *College English*, vol. 64, no. 4, Mar. 2002, pp. 432–58.

———. "Staying with Emotion." *Composition Forum*, vol. 34, Summer 2016.

Miller, Thomas P. "Why Don't Our Graduate Programs Do a Better Job of Preparing Students for the Work That We Do?" *WPA: Writing Program Administration*, vol. 24, no. 3, Spring 2001, pp. 41–58.

Miller, Susan, et al. "Myth Busting the Job Search." *ADE Bulletin*, vol. 154, 2015, pp. 77–85.

Mitchell, Michael, et al. "State Higher Education Funding Cuts Have Pushed Costs to Students, Worsened Inequality." Center on Budget and Policy Priorities, 24 Oct. 2019, www.cbpp.org/research/state-budget-and-tax/state-higher-education-funding-cuts-have-pushed-costs-to-students.

Modern Language Association Office of Research. *Report on the MLA* Job Information List, *2013–2014*. Modern Language Association, Fall 2014, www.mla.org/content/download/31163/1321381/rpt_jil_1314web.pdf.

———. *Report on the MLA* Job Information List, *2014–2015*. Modern Language Association, Dec. 2015, www.mla.org/content/download/40038/1744556/Rpt_JIL_14-15.pdf.

———. *Report on the MLA* Job Information List, *2015–2016*. Modern Language Association, Jan. 2017, www.mla.org/content/download/58256/1846498/RptJIL15_16.pdf.

———. *Report on the MLA* Job Information List, *2016–2017.* Modern Language Association, Dec. 2017, www.mla.org/content/download/78816/2172744/Report-MLA-JIL-2016-17.pdf.

Murphy, Michael. "New Faculty for a New University: Toward a Full-Time Teaching-Intensive Faculty Track in Composition." *College Composition and Communication*, vol. 52, no. 1, Sept. 2000, pp.14–42.

National Census of Writing. "First-Year Writing: General Description." *2013 Four-Year Institution Survey*, writingcensus.swarthmore.edu/survey/4.

———. "First-Year Writing: General Description." *2013 Two-Year Institution Survey*, writingcensus.swarthmore.edu/survey/2.

———. "Identifying and Supporting Diversely-Prepared Students: Basic Writing." *2013 Four-Year Institution Survey,* writingcensus.swarthmore.edu/survey/4.

———. "Identifying and Supporting Diversely-Prepared Students: Basic Writing." *2013 Two-Year Institution Survey*, writingcensus.swarthmore.edu/survey/2.

National Science Foundation. *Doctorate Recipients from US Universities: 2017,* Table 13. National Center for Science and Engineering Statistics, ncses.nsf.gov/pubs/nsf19301/data.

———. *Survey of Earned Doctorates [2018]*, Table 16. National Center for Science and Engineering Statistics, ncses.nsf.gov/pubs/nsf20301/data-tables/#group1.

Nazzal, Jane S., et al. "Writing Proficiency and Student Placement in Community College Composition Courses." *Teaching English in the Two-Year College*, vol. 46, no. 4, May 2019, pp. 317–46.

"The New Freshman Class: Fall 2017." U of Wisconsin System Informational Memorandum, www.wisconsin.edu/education-reports-statistics/download/educational_statistics/informational_memoranda/The-New-Freshman-Class,-Fall-2017.pdf.

Noll, Elizabeth, et al. *College Students with Children: National and Regional Profiles.* Institute for Women's Policy Research, 30 Jan. 2017, iwpr.org/iwpr-issues/student-parent-success-initiative/college-students-with-children-national-and-regional-profiles/.

Nowacek, Rebecca S. *Agents of Integration: Understanding Transfer as a Rhetorical Act.* Southern Illinois UP, 2011.

O'Brien, Matt. "Poor Kids Who Do Everything Right Don't Do Better Than Rich Kids Who Do Everything Wrong." *Washington Post,* 18 Oct. 2014, https://www.washingtonpost.com/news/wonk/wp/2014/10/18/poor-kids-who-do-everything-right-dont-do-better-than-rich-kids-who-do-everything-wrong/.

Parker, Kim. "The Growing Partisan Divide in Views of Higher Education." Pew Research Center, 19 Aug. 2019, www.pewsocialtrends.org/essay/the-growing-partisan-divide-in-views-of-higher-education/.

Patel, Vimal. "Graduate School Debt Is Raising Questions about Degrees' Worth." *Chronicle of Higher Education*. 17 Mar. 2014.

Payne, Michelle. "Administration, Emotional Labor, and Gendered Discourses of Power: A Feminist Chair's Mission to Make Service Matter." *Peitho: The Journal of the Coalition of Feminist Scholars in the History of Rhetoric and Composition*, vol. 21, no. 2, Spring 2019, pp. 279–307.

Pearlstein, Steven. "Is College Worth It? One Professor Says No." *Washington Post*, 8 Mar. 2018.

Pell Institute. *Indicators of Higher Education Equity in the United States*. 2018, pellinstitute.org/downloads/publications-Indicators_of_Higher_Education_Equity_in_the_US_2018_Historical_Trend_Report.pdf.

Penrose, Ann M. "Professional Identity in a Contingent-Labor Profession: Expertise, Autonomy, Community in Composition Teaching." *WPA: Writing Program Administration*, vol. 35, no. 2, Spring 2012, pp. 108–26.

Perl, Sondra. "The Composing Processes of Unskilled College Writers." *Research in the Teaching of English*, vol. 13, no. 4, Dec. 1979, pp. 317–36.

Pettit, Emma. "Columbia Had Little Success Placing English PhDs on the Tenure Track. 'Alarm' Followed, and the University Responded." *Chronicle of Higher Education*, 21 Aug. 2019.

Phelps, Louise Wetherbee, and John M. Ackerman. "Making the Case for Disciplinarity in Rhetoric, Composition, and Writing Studies: The Visibility Project." *College Composition and Communication*, vol. 62, no. 1, Sept. 2010, pp. 180–215.

Phillips, Cassandra, et al. "Thinking like a Writer: Threshold Concepts and First-Year Writers in Open-Admissions Classrooms." Adler-Kassner and Wardle, *(Re)Considering*, pp. 56–75.

Phillips, Cassandra, and Greg Ahrenhoerster. "Class Size and First-Year Writing: Exploring the Effects of Pedagogy and Student Perception of the Writing Process." *Teaching English in the Two-Year College*, vol. 46, no.1, Sept. 2018, pp. 9–29.

Phillips, Cassandra, and Joanne Baird Giordano. "Developing a Cohesive Literacy Program for Underprepared Students." *Teaching English in the Two-Year College*, vol. 44, no. 1, Sept. 2016, pp. 79–89.

Pickett, Nell Ann. "The Two-Year College as Democracy in Action." *College Composition and Communication*, vol. 49, no. 1, Feb. 1998, pp. 90–98.

Pine, Nancy. "Deeper and More Personal: The Role of Narrative in Service-Learning Composition." *Teaching English in the Two-Year College*, vol. 44, no. 4, May 2017, pp. 372–87.

Poe, Mya, et al. "Introduction: The End of Isolation." *Writing Assessment, Social Justice, and the Advancement of Opportunity*, edited by Poe et al., WAC Clearinghouse, 2018, pp. 3–38.

Poe, Mya, et al. "The Legal and the Local: Using Disparate Impact Analysis to Understand the Consequences of Writing Assessment." *College Composition and Communication*, vol. 65, no. 4, June 2014, pp. 588–611.

Postsecondary Outcomes for Nontraditional Undergraduate Students. US Dept. of Education, National Center for Education Statistics, May 2019, nces.ed.gov/programs/coe/indicator_tta.asp.

Principles for the Postsecondary Teaching of Writing, CCCC Position Statement, Oct. 1989, revised Nov. 2013, revised Mar. 2015, cccc.ncte.org/cccc/resources/positions/postsecondarywriting.

Professional Knowledge for the Teaching of Writing. National Council of Teachers of English Guideline, Feb. 2016, dpi.wi.gov/sites/default/files/imce/ela/resources/Professional%20Knowledge%20for%20the%20Teaching%20of%20Writing.pdf.

Queen, Bradley. "Class Size for a Multilingual Mainstream: Empirical Explorations." *WPA: Writing Program Administration*, vol. 40, no. 2, Spring 2017, pp. 98–128.

Ran, Florence Xiaotao, and Yuxin Lin. "The Effects of Corequisite Remediation: Evidence from a Statewide Reform in Tennessee." CCRC Working Paper no. 115, Nov. 2019, Community College Research Center, Teachers College, Columbia U, ccrc.tc.columbia.edu/media/k2/attachments/effects-corequisite-remediation-tennessee.pdf.

Raucci, John. "A Replication Agenda for Composition Studies." *College Composition and Communication*, vol. 72, no. 3, Feb. 2021, pp. 440–61.

Redford, Jeremy, and Kathleen Mulvaney Hoyer. "First-Generation and Continuing-Generation College Students: A Comparison of High School and Postsecondary Experiences." NCES 2018-009. United States Dept. of Education, National Center for Education Statistics, Sept. 2017, nces.ed.gov/pubs2018/2018009.pdf.

Reed, Matt. "A Closed Debate about Reopening." *Inside Higher Ed*, 19 June 2020.

Reid, E. Shelley, and Heidi Estrem, with Marcia Belcheir. "The Effects of Writing Pedagogy Education on Graduate Teaching Assistants' Approaches to Teaching Composition." *WPA: Writing Program Administration*, vol. 36, no. 1, Fall 2012, pp. 32–73.

Restaino, Jessica. *First Semester: Graduate Students, Teaching Writing, and the Challenge of Middle Ground.* Southern Illinois UP, 2012.

"Retention and Graduation: 2017–2018." U of Wisconsin System Informational Memorandum, www.wisconsin.edu/education-reports-statistics/download/educational_statistics/informational_memoranda/Retention-and-Graduation,-2017-18.pdf.

Rethinking the Master's Degree in English for a New Century. Modern Language Association of America, June 2011, www.mla.org/content/download/25406/1164106/2011adhocrpt.pdf.

Rhoades, Gary. "Closing the Door, Increasing the Gap: Who's Not Going to (Community) College?" Center for the Future of Higher Education Policy Report #1, Apr. 2012, www.insidehighered.com/sites/default/server_files/files/ClosingTheDoor_Embargoed.pdf.

Richardson, Elaine. "Race, Class(es), Gender, and Age: The Making of Knowledge about Language Diversity." *Language Diversity in the Classroom: From Intention to Practice*, edited by Geneva Smitherman and Victor Villanueva, Southern Illinois UP, 2003, pp. 40–66.

Ridolfo, Jim. "Market Comparison." *RhetMap.org*, Dec. 2020, rhetmap.org/market-comparison/.

Ritter, Kelly, ed. *Beyond Fitting In: Rethinking First-Gen Writing and Literacy Education*. MLA, forthcoming 2022.

Robillard, Amy E. "Prototypical Reading: Volume, Desire, Anxiety." *College Composition and Communication*, vol. 67, no. 2, Dec. 2015, 197–215.

Rose, Mike. "The Language of Exclusion: Writing Instruction at the University." *College English*, vol. 45, no. 4, Apr. 1985, 341–59.

———. *Lives on the Boundary: A Moving Account of the Struggles and Achievements of America's Educationally Underprepared.* 1985. Penguin, 2005.

Rosner, Mary, et al., eds. *History, Reflection, and Narrative: The Professionalization of Composition, 1963–1983.* Ablex Publishing, 1999.

Rouzie, Albert. "Conversation and Carrying-On: Play, Conflict, and Serio-Ludic Discourse in Synchronous Computer Conferencing." *College Composition and Communication,* vol. 53, no. 2, Dec. 2001, pp. 251–99.

Royster, Jacqueline Jones. "When the First Voice You Hear Is Not Your Own." *College Composition and Communication*, vol. 47, no. 1, Feb. 1996, pp. 29–40.

Ruecker, Todd. *Transiciones: Pathways of Latinas and Latinos Writing in High School and College*. UP of Colorado, 2015.

Ruffus, Stephen, and Christie Toth. "Inter-Institutional Partnerships for Academic Freedom: Reversing 'The Great Credit Grab.'" "Symposium: Academic Freedom, Labor, and Teaching Two-Year College English," *Teaching English in the Two-Year College*, vol. 45, no. 4, May 2018, p. 338–42.

Ryan, Camille L., and Kurt Bauman. *Educational Attainment in the United States: 2015*. United States Census Bureau, Mar. 2016, www.census.gov/content/dam/Census/library/publications/2016/demo/p20-578.pdf.

Ryan, Cynthia. "Cultivating at Cs." *Council Chronicle*, vol. 26, no. 2, Nov. 2016, pp. 24–25.

Sano-Franchini, Jennifer. "'It's Like Writing Yourself into a Codependent Relationship with Someone Who Doesn't Even Want You!': Emotional Labor, Intimacy, and the Academic Job Market in Rhetoric and Composition." *College Composition and Communication*, vol. 68, no. 1, Sept. 2016, pp. 98–124.

Schell, Eileen E. "The Costs of Caring: 'Feminism' and Contingent Women Workers in Composition Studies." *Feminism and Composition Studies: In Other Words*, edited by Susan C. Jarratt and Lynn Worsham, MLA, 1998, pp. 74–93.

———. *Gypsy Academics and Mother-Teachers: Gender, Contingent Labor, and Writing Instruction*. Boynton/Cook Publishers, 1998.

———. "Is It Worth It to 'Lean In' and Lead? On Being a Woman Department Chair in Rhetoric and Writing Studies." *Peitho: The Journal of the Coalition of Feminist Scholars in the History of Rhetoric and Composition*, vol. 21, no. 2, Spring 2019, pp. 308–33.

Scott, Tony. "Subverting Crisis in the Political Economy of Composition." *College Composition and Communication*, vol. 68, no. 1, Sept. 2016, pp. 10–37.

———. "Writing Enacts and Creates Identities and Ideologies." Adler-Kassner and Wardle, *Naming*, pp. 48–49.

Scott, Tony, and Nancy Welch, eds. *Composition in the Age of Austerity*. UP of Colorado, 2016.

Shapiro, Doug, et al. *Completing College: A National View of Student Completion Rates—Fall 2011 Cohort*. Signature Report no. 14, National Student Clearinghouse Research Center, Dec. 2017.

Shaughnessy, Mina P. *Errors and Expectations: A Guide for the Teacher of Basic Writing*. Oxford UP, 1977.

Shayne, Julie. "Recognizing Emotional Labor in Academe." *Inside Higher Ed*, 15 Sept. 2017.

Shor, Ira. "What Is Critical Literacy?" *Journal of Pedagogy, Pluralism and Practice*, vol. 1, no. 4, Fall 1999, pp. 2–32, digitalcommons.lesley.edu/cgi/jppp/vol1/iss4/2/.

Shortlidge, Erin E., and Sarah L. Eddy. "The Trade-Off between Graduate Student Research and Teaching: A Myth?" *PLoS ONE*, vol. 13, no. 6, 2018.

Shulman, Steven, et al. "Higher Education at a Crossroads: The Economic Value of Tenure and the Security of the Profession." *Academe*, vol. 102, no. 2, Mar.–Apr. 2016, pp. 9–23.

Sledd, James. "Disciplinarity and Exploitation: Compositionists as Good Professionals." *Workplace: A Journal for Academic Labor*, vol. 4, no. 1, June 2001, pp. 31–39.

———. "Return to Service." *Composition Studies*, vol. 28, no. 2, Fall 2000, pp. 11–32.

———. "Why the Wyoming Resolution Had to Be Emasculated: A History and a Quixotism." *Journal of Advanced Composition*, vol. 11, no. 2, Fall 1991, pp. 269–81.

Smith, Ashley A. "First-Generation College Students More Engaged than Peers." *Inside Higher Ed*, 26 June 2018.

———. "Positive Mind-Set Tied to Engagement, GPA." *Inside Higher Ed*, 9 Apr. 2019.

Snyder, Sarah Elizabeth. "Preparing to Become a Two-Year College Writing Program Administrator." *WPA: Writing Program Administration*, vol. 43, no. 3, Summer 2020, pp. 106–20.

Sommers, Nancy. "Revision Strategies of Student Writers and Experienced Adult Writers." *College Composition and Communication*, vol. 31, no. 4, Dec. 1980, pp. 378–88.

Sommers, Nancy, and Laura Saltz. "The Novice as Expert: Writing the Freshman Year." *College Composition and Communication*, vol. 56, no. 1, 2004, pp. 124–49.

Spiegel, Cheri Lemieux, et al. "Don't Call It a Comeback: Two-Year College WPA, Tactics, Collaboration, Flexibility, Sustainability." *WPA: Writing Program Administration*, vol. 43, no. 3, Summer 2020, pp. 7–18.

Spiegel, Cheri Lemieux, and Mark Blaauw-Hara. "Response 3: Models for Collaborations between Two-Year College Faculty and Graduate Programs." "Symposium: Responses to the TYCA Guidelines for Preparing Teachers of English in the Two-Year College," edited by Christie

Toth and Darin Jensen, *Teaching English in the Two-Year College*, vol. 45, no. 1, Sept. 2017, pp. 29–46.

Standards for the Assessment of Reading and Writing. National Council of Teachers of English, 2007, www2.ncte.org/resources/standards/standards-for-the-assessment-of-reading-and-writing-revised-edition-2009/.

Statement on Dual Credit/Concurrent Enrollment Composition: Policy and Best Practices. National Council of Teachers of English, Nov. 2012, www.ncte.org/cccc/resources/positions/dualcredit.

St. Amour, Madeline. "Measuring Progress on Developmental Education." *Inside Higher Ed*, 25 Nov. 2019.

Sternglass, Marilyn S. *Time to Know Them: A Longitudinal Study of Writing and Learning at the College Level*. Lawrence Erlbaum, 1997.

Strain, Margaret M., and Rebecca C. Potter, eds. *Degree of Change: The MA in English Studies*. National Council of Teachers of English, 2016.

Strickland, Donna. "The Managerial Unconscious of Composition Studies." Bousquet et al., pp. 46–56.

"Student Financial Aid: 2013–2014 Update." U of Wisconsin System Informational Memorandum, www.wisconsin.edu/education-reports-statistics/download/educational_statistics/informational_memoranda/Student-Financial-Aid,-2013-14.pdf.

"Student Financial Aid: 2014–2015 Update." U of Wisconsin System Informational Memorandum, www.wisconsin.edu/education-reports-statistics/download/educational_statistics/informational_memoranda/Student-Financial-Aid,-2014-15.pdf.

"Student Financial Aid: 2015–2016 Update." U of Wisconsin System Informational Memorandum, www.wisconsin.edu/education-reports-statistics/download/educational_statistics/informational_memoranda/Student-Financial-Aid,-2015-16.pdf.

"Student Financial Aid: 2016–2017 Update." U of Wisconsin System Informational Memorandum, www.wisconsin.edu/education-reports-statistics/download/educational_statistics/informational_memoranda/Student-Financial-Aid,-2016-17.pdf.

Sullivan, Patrick. "An Essential Question: What Is 'College-Level' Writing?" *What Is "College-Level" Writing?* edited by Patrick Sullivan and Howard Tinberg, National Council of Teachers of English, 2006, pp. 1–28, wac.colostate.edu/books/collegelevel/.

———. "'A Lifelong Aversion to Writing': What if Writing Courses Emphasized Motivation?" *Teaching English in the Two-Year College*, vol. 39, no. 2, Dec. 2011, pp. 118–40.

———. "Measuring 'Success' at Open Admissions Institutions: Thinking Carefully about This Complex Question." *College English*, vol. 70, no. 6, Mar. 2008, pp. 618–32.

———. "The Two-Year College Teacher-Scholar-Activist." *Teaching English in the Two-Year College*, vol. 42, no. 4, May 2015, pp. 327–50.

Sullivan, Patrick, et al., eds. *Deep Reading: Teaching Reading in the Writing Classroom*. National Council of Teachers of English, 2017.

Sutton, Mark, and Sally Chandler, eds. *The Writing Studio Sampler: Stories about Change*. WAC Clearinghouse, 2019.

Taylor, Matthew. "It's Official: Class Matters." *The Guardian*, 28 Feb. 2006.

Taylor, Tim. "Writing Program Administration at the Two-Year College: Ghosts in the Machine." *WPA: Writing Program Administration*, vol. 32, no. 3, Spring 2009, pp. 120–39.

This Ain't Another Statement! This Is a DEMAND *for Black Linguistic Justice!* Conference on College Composition and Communication, July 2020, cccc.ncte.org/cccc/demand-for-black-linguistic-justice.

Tinberg, Howard B. *Border Talk: Writing and Knowing in the Two-Year College*. National Council of Teachers of English, 1997. https://wac.colostate.edu/books/tinberg/

Tinberg, Howard, and Jean-Paul Nadeau. *The Community College Writer: Exceeding Expectations*. Southern Illinois UP, 2010.

"Today's Student." Lumina Foundation, 12 Feb. 2019, www.luminafoundation.org/campaign/todays-student/.

Toth, Christie, and Patrick Sullivan. "Toward Local Teacher-Scholar Communities of Practice: Findings from a National TYCA Survey." *Teaching English in the Two-Year College*, vol. 43, no. 3, Mar. 2016, 247–73.

Toth, Christie, et al. "Two-Year College Teacher-Scholar-Activism: Reconstructing the Disciplinary Matrix of Writing Studies." *College Composition and Communication*, vol. 71, no. 1, Sept. 2019, pp. 86–116.

Trader, Kristen Seas, et al. "'Flexible' Learning, Disciplinarity, and First-Year Writing: Critically Engaging Competency-Based Education." *WPA: Writing Program Administration*, vol. 40, no. 1, Fall 2016, pp. 10–32.

Trends in College Pricing 2018. College Board, research.collegeboard.org/trends/college-pricing/resource-library.

Trimbur, John. "Writing Instruction and the Politics of Professionalization." Bloom et al., pp. 133–45.

TYCA Research Committee. "TYCA White Paper on Developmental Education Reform." *Teaching English in the Two-Year College*, vol. 42, no. 3, Mar. 2015, pp. 227–43.

———. "TYCA White Paper on Placement Reform." *Teaching English in the Two-Year College*, vol. 44, no. 2, Dec. 2016, pp. 135–57.

TYCA Workload Task Force. "The Profession of Teaching English in the Two-Year College: Findings from the 2019 TYCA Workload Survey," Dec. 2020, ncte.org/wp-content/uploads/2020/12/TYCA_Final_Report_December_2020.pdf.

"UW System Tuition Chart: 2017–2018 UW System Full Time Undergraduate Tuition and Fees." U of Wisconsin, uwhelp.wisconsin.edu/counselors/navigating-financial-aid/uw-system-tuition-chart/. Accessed 28 June 2018.

Vetter, Matthew A. "Teaching Wikipedia: Appalachian Rhetoric and the Encyclopedic Politics of Representation." *College English*, vol. 80, no. 5, May 2018, pp. 397–422.

Wardle, Elizabeth, and Doug Downs. "Understanding the Nature of Disciplinarity in Terms of Composition's Values." Malenczyk et al., pp. 111–33.

Wardle, Elizabeth, and J. Blake Scott. "Defining and Developing Expertise in a Writing and Rhetoric Department." *WPA: Writing Program Administration*, vol. 39, no. 1, Fall 2015, pp. 72–93.

Warner, John. *Why They Can't Write: Killing the Five-Paragraph Essay and Other Necessities*. Johns Hopkins UP, 2018.

"The Wisconsin Idea." U of Wisconsin–Madison, www.wisc.edu/wisconsin-idea/.

Woodworth, James L. "A Letter From the Commissioner of the National Center for Education Statistics." United States Dept. of Education, National Center for Education Statistics, May 2019, nces.ed.gov/programs/coe/commissioner.asp.

WPA Outcomes Statement for First-Year Composition. Council of Writing Program Administrators, Apr. 2000, amended July 2008, www.in.gov/che/files/WPA_Outcomes_Statement_for_First-Year_Composition.pdf.

WPA Outcomes Statement for First-Year Composition (3.0). Council of Writing Program Administrators, 17 July 2014, wpacouncil.org/aws/CWPA/pt/sd/news_article/243055/_PARENT/layout_details/false.

Writing Assessment: A Position Statement. Conference on College Composition and Communication, Nov. 2006, revised Mar. 2009, reaffirmed Nov. 2014, cccc.ncte.org/cccc/resources/positions/writingassessment.

Yancey, Kathleen Blake. *Reflection in the Writing Classroom*. Utah State UP, 1998.

INDEX

The letter *f* following a page locator denotes a figure and the letter *t* denotes a table.

AUTHORS

Holly Hassel is a professor of English at North Dakota State University. For sixteen years, she was a faculty member at the University of Wisconsin–Marathon County, a two-year college campus in Wausau. She earned her PhD from the University of Nebraska–Lincoln in 2002, has served as editor of the journal *Teaching English in the Two-Year College*, and is serving as chair of the Conference on College Composition and Communication in 2022.

Cassandra Phillips is a professor of English at the University of Wisconsin–Milwaukee at Waukesha, where she has taught for over twenty years. She also serves as the first-year writing and developmental English coordinator for the College of General Studies at the University of Wisconsin–Milwaukee.

CONTRIBUTORS

Rachel Barger is a lecturer of English at the University of Wisconsin–Milwaukee at Washington County. She has taught the composition sequence and additional support courses for underprepared students, served as placement coordinator, and contributed to student support through departmental and cross-departmental committees since she began teaching at the Washington County campus in 2005. In 2018, her dedication to her teaching and her students was recognized by the UW Colleges with the Chancellor's Excellence in Teaching Award. Barger extends her work beyond the traditional classroom as a writing specialist and academic coach for TRiO Student Support Services. Through this additional role, she provides supplementary one-on-one support for first-generation students.

Marnie Bullock Dresser earned her MFA at the University of Montana and has been teaching at the Richland campus (usually the smallest of all the University of Wisconsin campuses) since the fall of 1992. Thirty years of teaching composition, literature, creative writing, and creativity and problem-solving courses have taught her a lot, mainly that she has never once regretted being kind. She has published poetry, fiction, and creative nonfiction, and her plays have been performed numerous times. Her work has also appeared on Wisconsin Public Radio's "Wisconsin Life." Her research on the use of rubrics in the teaching of creativity was featured in a presentation at the International Society for the Scholarship of Teaching and Learning. Most recently, she has shifted to more administrative duties and is serving as the director of academic outreach for all three UW–Platteville campuses, including Richland and Baraboo Sauk County.

Jennifer Heinert, professor of English, earned her PhD in American literature from Marquette University, and began her career as an assistant professor at the University of Wisconsin Colleges in 2006. As a professor at a two-year access institution with a transfer mission, she prioritized research and service that focused on writing studies, which aligned with the majority of her teaching responsibilities. In her time with the Colleges, she contributed to department-wide and institution-wide programs and policies related to student learning and effective teaching. A key part of that work was collaboration with colleagues who valued the important role that writing studies played. Her writing studies research and service supported her as she moved into leadership roles as a faculty developer and department chair. Heinert currently teaches writing at the University of Wisconsin–Milwaukee College of General Studies.

Valerie Murrenus Pilmaier is an associate professor of English and Women' and Gender Studies at UW–Green Bay. From 2009 to 2018 she was an assistant professor of English and women's and gender studies at UW–Sheboygan, one of the thirteen campuses of the UW Colleges (Wisconsin's two-year-college system), where she spent most of her time teaching composition. Her research interests include working-class studies, the scholarship of teaching and learning (SOTL), trauma studies, and trauma-informed pedagogy. She currently serves as the assessment coordinator for UW–Green Bay.

Lisa Schreibersdorf is an associate professor of English at the Fond du Lac campus of University of Wisconsin–Oshkosh. After earning her PhD at UW–Madison, she began her position at the UW Colleges, teaching on the Fond du Lac and UW Colleges online campuses for eleven years before the merger with Oshkosh. With UWO, she worked on development of associate degree standards for the three-campus university as well as the UW System's collaborative online associate degree. During her years on the two-year campus, her research focus shifted from literary and cultural studies to the study of teaching and learning. Her most recent research focuses on the teaching of literature and online pedagogy.

Julie Tharp has been a professor of English and women and gender studies for twenty-nine years. She started in the University of Minnesota system as a grad student and spent her entire career in the University of Wisconsin system teaching composition, American literature, film studies, and women and gender studies. She has also been fortunate enough to have two Fulbright Scholar positions, in Singapore and in India, and to teach in the Wisconsin in Scotland and Experience China programs. Her research has largely focused on writing by women of color.

Jessica Lyn Van Slooten is an associate professor of English, writing, and women's and gender studies at the University of Wisconsin–Green Bay; she's also co-chair of the Women and Gender Studies program at UWGB. She teaches courses on women writers, gender and popular culture, romance writing, and more. Jessica has published numerous articles on teaching and assessing gender studies courses, and on popular romance fiction and film. She is currently working on a scholarship of teaching and learning (SoTL) project about collective well-being in online women's and gender studies classes. In October 2019, she gave a TEDx talk titled "Romance Novels Are Feminist."

Gillian Van Treese received her MA in English pedagogy at Northern Michigan University. She is currently a senior lecturer of English in the Arts and Humanities Department of UW–Milwaukee at Waukesha. Her main areas of expertise are in composition and reading studies, and she maintains an interest in the science of learning. She teaches a variety of courses intended to build students' academic writing and reading skills, and she has recently taught a course in helping identify an academic and career plan for students. As an active participant in her discipline, she regularly presents at national and regional academic conferences.

Jack Van Treese is a senior lecturer of English at the Waukesha campus of the University of Wisconsin–Milwaukee, where he has taught since 2012. He has also taught in the University of Wisconsin Flexible Option program since 2015. He teaches developmental English and first-year composition courses, and his research interests focus on teaching and learning, including issues related to student motivation, writing transfer, and writing program development. He has a BA in English from the University of Michigan and an MA in English pedagogy and literature from Northern Michigan University.

BOOKS IN THE CCCC STUDIES IN WRITING & RHETORIC SERIES

Materiality and Writing Studies: Aligning Labor, Scholarship, and Teaching
Holly Hassel and Cassandra Phillips

Salt of the Earth: Rhetoric, Preservation, and White Supremacy
James Chase Sanchez

Rhetorics of Overcoming: Rewriting Narratives of Disability and Accessibility in Writing Studies
Allison Harper Hitt

Writing Accomplices with Student Immigrant Rights Organizers
Glenn Hutchinson

Counterstory: The Rhetoric and Writing of Critical Race Theory
Aja Y. Martinez

Writing Programs, Veterans Studies, and the Post-9/11 University: A Field Guide
D. Alexis Hart and Roger Thompson

Beyond Progress in the Prison Classroom: Options and Opportunities
Anna Plemons

Rhetorics Elsewhere and Otherwise: Contested Modernities, Decolonial Visions
Edited by Romeo García and Damián Baca

Black Perspectives in Writing Program Administration: From the Margins to the Center
Edited by Staci M. Perryman-Clark and Collin Lamont Craig

Translanguaging outside the Academy: Negotiating Rhetoric and Healthcare in the Spanish Caribbean
Rachel Bloom-Pojar

Collaborative Learning as Democratic Practice: A History
Mara Holt

Reframing the Relational: A Pedagogical Ethic for Cross-Curricular Literacy Work
Sandra L. Tarabochia

Inside the Subject: A Theory of Identity for the Study of Writing
Raúl Sánchez

Genre of Power: Police Report Writers and Readers in the Justice System
Leslie Seawright

Assembling Composition
Edited by Kathleen Blake Yancey and Stephen J. McElroy

Public Pedagogy in Composition Studies
Ashley J. Holmes

From Boys to Men: Rhetorics of Emergent American Masculinity
Leigh Ann Jones

Freedom Writing: African American Civil Rights Literacy Activism, 1955–1967
Rhea Estelle Lathan

The Desire for Literacy: Writing in the Lives of Adult Learners
Lauren Rosenberg

On Multimodality: New Media in Composition Studies
Jonathan Alexander and Jacqueline Rhodes

Toward a New Rhetoric of Difference
Stephanie L. Kerschbaum

Rhetoric of Respect: Recognizing Change at a Community Writing Center
Tiffany Rousculp

After Pedagogy: The Experience of Teaching
Paul Lynch

Redesigning Composition for Multilingual Realities
Jay Jordan

Agency in the Age of Peer Production
Quentin D. Vieregge, Kyle D. Stedman, Taylor Joy Mitchell, and Joseph M. Moxley

Remixing Composition: A History of Multimodal Writing Pedagogy
Jason Palmeri

First Semester: Graduate Students, Teaching Writing, and the Challenge of Middle Ground
Jessica Restaino

Agents of Integration: Understanding Transfer as a Rhetorical Act
Rebecca S. Nowacek

Digital Griots: African American Rhetoric in a Multimedia Age
Adam J. Banks

The Managerial Unconscious in the History of Composition Studies
Donna Strickland

Everyday Genres: Writing Assignments across the Disciplines
Mary Soliday

The Community College Writer: Exceeding Expectations
Howard Tinberg and Jean-Paul Nadeau

A Taste for Language: Literacy, Class, and English Studies
James Ray Watkins

Before Shaughnessy: Basic Writing at Yale and Harvard, 1920–1960
Kelly Ritter

Writer's Block: The Cognitive Dimension
Mike Rose

Teaching/Writing in Thirdspaces: The Studio Approach
Rhonda C. Grego and Nancy S. Thompson

Rural Literacies
Kim Donehower, Charlotte Hogg, and Eileen E. Schell

Writing with Authority: Students' Roles as Writers in Cross-National Perspective
David Foster

Whistlin' and Crowin' Women of Appalachia: Literacy Practices since College
Katherine Kelleher Sohn

Sexuality and the Politics of Ethos in the Writing Classroom
Zan Meyer Gonçalves

African American Literacies Unleashed: Vernacular English and the Composition Classroom
Arnetha F. Ball and Ted Lardner

Revisionary Rhetoric, Feminist Pedagogy, and Multigenre Texts
Julie Jung

Archives of Instruction: Nineteenth-Century Rhetorics, Readers, and Composition Books in the United States
Jean Ferguson Carr, Stephen L. Carr, and Lucille M. Schultz

Response to Reform: Composition and the Professionalization of Teaching
Margaret J. Marshall

Multiliteracies for a Digital Age
Stuart A. Selber

Personally Speaking: Experience as Evidence in Academic Discourse
Candace Spigelman

Self-Development and College Writing
Nick Tingle

Minor Re/Visions: Asian American Literacy Narratives as a Rhetoric of Citizenship
Morris Young

A Communion of Friendship: Literacy, Spiritual Practice, and Women in Recovery
Beth Daniell

Embodied Literacies: Imageword and a Poetics of Teaching
Kristie S. Fleckenstein

Language Diversity in the Classroom: From Intention to Practice
Edited by Geneva Smitherman and Victor Villanueva

Rehearsing New Roles: How College Students Develop as Writers
Lee Ann Carroll

Across Property Lines: Textual Ownership in Writing Groups
Candace Spigelman

Mutuality in the Rhetoric and Composition Classroom
David L. Wallace and Helen Rothschild Ewald

The Young Composers: Composition's Beginnings in Nineteenth-Century Schools
Lucille M. Schultz

Technology and Literacy in the Twenty-First Century: The Importance of Paying Attention
Cynthia L. Selfe

Women Writing the Academy: Audience, Authority, and Transformation
Gesa E. Kirsch

Gender Influences: Reading Student Texts
Donnalee Rubin

Something Old, Something New: College Writing Teachers and Classroom Change
Wendy Bishop

Dialogue, Dialectic, and Conversation: A Social Perspective on the Function of Writing
Gregory Clark

Audience Expectations and Teacher Demands
Robert Brooke and John Hendricks

Toward a Grammar of Passages
Richard M. Coe

Rhetoric and Reality: Writing Instruction in American Colleges, 1900–1985
James A. Berlin

Writing Groups: History, Theory, and Implications
Anne Ruggles Gere

Teaching Writing as a Second Language
Alice S. Horning

Invention as a Social Act
Karen Burke LeFevre

The Variables of Composition: Process and Product in a Business Setting
Glenn J. Broadhead and Richard C. Freed

Writing Instruction in Nineteenth-Century American Colleges
James A. Berlin

Computers & Composing: How the New Technologies Are Changing Writing
Jeanne W. Halpern and Sarah Liggett

A New Perspective on Cohesion in Expository Paragraphs
Robin Bell Markels

Evaluating College Writing Programs
Stephen P. Witte and Lester Faigley

This book was typeset in Garamond and Frutiger by Barbara Frazier.
Typefaces used on the cover include Garamond and News Gothic.
The book was printed on 50-lb. White Offset paper
by Seaway Printing Company, Inc.